HOW YOU CAN INFLUENCE CONGRESS

HOW YOU CAN

E. P. DUTTON · NEW YORK

INFLUENCE
CONGRESS

The Complete Handbook
for the Citizen Lobbyist

GEORGE ALDERSON
and EVERETT SENTMAN

For information contact: E. P. Dutton, 2 Park Avenue, New York, N.Y. 10016

Library of Congress Cataloging in Publication Data
Alderson, George.   How you can influence Congress.
Bibliography: p.   Includes index.   1. Lobbying—United States—Handbooks, manuals, etc.   I. Sentman, Everett, joint author.   II. Title.
JK1118.A59 1979   328.73'07'8   78-31207

ISBN: 0-87690-306-5 (cloth)
      0-87690-320-0 (paperback)

Published simultaneously in Canada by Clarke, Irwin & Company Limited, Toronto and Vancouver

Designed by Barbara Huntley

10 9 8 7 6 5 4 3 2 1   First Edition

To Rosa
and to the memory of my parents

Contents

Acknowledgments

This book owes its existence to my mentors, three pioneers of grass-roots citizen lobbying: David R. Brower, Stewart M. Brandborg, and Michael McCloskey.

I am grateful to many congressional staff members and many of my former colleagues in the public-interest movement who freely contributed their ideas, their experience, and their criticism. I am especially indebted to the following, whose good counsel and inspiration sustained me during the book's two-year gestation: Alice Alderman, Walter E. Barquist, Charles M. Clusen, Nora Davenport, Ernest M. Dickerman, Marion Edey, Cheryl Evans, David H. Foerster, Susan Grayson, Dale Halsey, Peter Harnik, Marian Holbrook, Dale R. Jones, Jeffrey Knight, John O'Connor, Carol Parker, Rafe Pomerance, Douglas Scott, Maitland S. Sharpe, Elliot Siegel, Anne Wickham, Lawrence F. Williams, Joyce Wood, Hastings Wyman, Jr., and Prancer, the dog.

A source that yielded many good ideas is *The Population Activist's Handbook*, by the Population Institute (New York: Macmillan, 1974). Chapter 14, "Your Role in Congressional Hearings," adopts some of the concepts developed by Michael McCloskey, executive director of the Sierra Club, and described by him in the book *Action for Wilderness* (Sierra Club, 1972).

I'm grateful to members of my family who got me started in public-interest causes and encouraged me in my work as an environmental lobbyist: my mother; my aunt, Lora Kelts; and my sister and brother-in-law, Elizabeth and James Robinson. Rosa

Feldman was both a thoughtful critic and a constant source of encouragement and love.

Finally I thank three people who always told me to keep writing when my own instincts were telling me I'd never finish the book: my editor at E. P. Dutton, Susan Brody, and my agents at Curtis Brown, Ltd., Perry H. Knowlton and Arthur L. Martin.

G. A.

Influence Without Money

Will Rogers once said, "Congress is the best that money can buy." Whether money takes the lawful form of big campaign contributions and lavish entertainment, or the unlawful form of bribery, it's a pervasive factor in the United States Congress. Many legislators don't even realize how much their decisions are influenced by money because it's always on the scene.

Money, however, is a poor substitute for the approval of the public. The only reason money is so important in the work of the big industrial lobbies and shady operators alike is that they don't have the public on their side. Money buys them attention and respectability and thus, indirectly, buys them votes in the Senate and the House of Representatives.

You, as a citizen and voter, get for free what these lobbies have to buy. You have the attention of your senators and your congressman or congresswoman, and you have respectability because you put those legislators into office in the last election and can throw them out in the next election. Fundamentally, a legislator wants something from you—your vote, your good word to friends and neighbors, your help in the campaign. Or, if you're making a stink about a public issue, the legislator may just want to shut you up. What the legislator wants from you gives you power.

Many Washington lobbyists wish they had the power you have with your own legislators in Congress. This book will tell you how to use your power to influence how your legislators vote in the House and Senate.

This book is about the power an ordinary citizen has. The power of citizens' campaigns doesn't come from money. It comes from conviction—the convictions of people who are concerned about a public issue.

The citizen's power over a congressman's vote may not be obvious. If you've written your legislator often, you've probably received more than one noncommittal letter saying little more than, "Thank you for your views. I will certainly keep them in mind when this matter comes to the floor for a vote." And, if you've tried to get an appointment to see one of your senators, you've probably been shunted off to see a staff member instead. This doesn't make you feel very powerful.

Yet the power is there, if only you'll use it. Your power is a resource, like energy from the sun. If your house has an ordinary roof, most of the solar energy is reflected or radiated into the air—and wasted. If you install solar collectors on the roof, that energy can heat your house all winter. It's just a matter of using the right techniques to convert the resource into a usable product. Learn to use your political power, and you'll find that you can influence decisions in Congress that you used to think were unchallengeable.

"Inevitable? Not if we say no." Garrett Hardin's challenge to the apathetic is a good motto for anyone concerned about legislation in Congress. You have the power to change things, but it won't do you any good unless you learn how to apply it to the issues that concern you.

Washington lobbyists are commonly regarded as powerful figures, but you never hear about the times when the lobbyists couldn't get in to see your congressman. It happens all the time. They end up talking to somebody on the staff. In some congressional offices they don't even get past the receptionist. That's the experience of both environmental and education lobbyists calling at the office of Senator Robert C. Byrd (Democrat of West Virginia), as Senate majority leader one of the most influential members of the Senate. Time after time, the senator's receptionist accepts their fact sheets and sends them on their way. Byrd's constituents don't get that chilly reception when they drop in from West Virginia.

To your own members of Congress, *your* opinions carry more weight than those of nine out of ten Washington lobbyists. The one lobbyist who has that special influence usually got it by relying on your fellow citizens in your community to back up his pitch with pressure from home in the form of letters, telegrams, and phone calls. It doesn't matter whether the lobbyist represents the public interest or business interests; where the former depends on pressure from individual concerned citizens and citizen groups, the latter depends on pressure from businesses and commercial groups. The common denominator is pressure from constituents. Pressure is simply the expression of opinion by a legislator's constituents.

A good lobbyist will avoid going to see a congressman who doesn't react well to lobbyists, and instead will ask citizen groups in the congressman's district to put the heat on. Rafe Pomerance, the lobbyist with Friends of the Earth who led the fight for the Clean Air Bill in 1976, says that in that campaign he didn't send any lobbyists to call on three key congressmen—Norman F. Lent (Republican of New York), John M. Murphy (Democrat of New York), and Matthew J. Rinaldo (Republican of New Jersey). Instead, he got their constituents to do the work, and with good results. "On the crucial votes," Pomerance says, "all three either voted with us or took a walk. It was all pressure from home that did it."

Byron Kennard, a top strategist of the public-interest movement, has written in the magazine *Environmental Action:* "Few members of Congress may be pure idealists, but few are utter scoundrels. Many, if not most, will vote the public interest if they feel enough heat from citizens in their districts. Some will vote the public interest if they get enough citizen pressure to simply *neutralize* pressure from business groups."

Because members of the House and Senate constantly are confronted with an impossible work load of legislation, it's only natural that the squeaking wheel gets the grease. If a congressman is getting phone calls and letters from his district asking him to vote against H.R. 9620, he'll probably find it easier to go along with what they ask than to defend a vote in favor of the bill. Ernest M. Dickerman, an elder statesman of the environmental movement, says: "You usually get legislators' votes not because they believe in your cause, but because they want to get it out of their hair. Our task is to show the legislators that it's easier to support our side than to support the opposition."

Don't think that to influence your congressman you have to

mount a campaign on the scale of the Panama Canal Treaty or the 1978 Energy Bill. Few issues are that big. Most are settled quietly, with little attention from the news media. If your opponents are inactive or nonexistent in your congressional district, your own individual initiative may be enough to win your congressman's vote; a few letters and a couple of phone calls may do the job.

For instance, early in 1978 free-lance musicians around the country were trying to defeat H.R. 9713, a bill that would have allowed members of Armed Forces bands to take over many civilian musical jobs, putting civilian musicians out of work. A hearing had already been held on the bill, but only the proponents had been invited to testify. In Corvallis, Oregon, a relative of one of the civilian musicians wrote to her congressman, Les AuCoin (Democrat), asking him to oppose H.R. 9713 and to request a hearing for the opposition viewpoint. AuCoin immediately replied:

> Thank you for your recent letter discussing H.R. 9713, the bill to allow military band members to seek civilian jobs in addition to their military band work. This appears to be a real injustice to other musicians who must compete with handsomely paid military band members. I have written to Chairman Melvin Price to ask for a hearing on this bill, and have forwarded your letter for his consideration and comment. As soon as I have a response, I'll let you know. With warm regards,
>
> Sincerely,
Les AuCoin
Member of Congress

The Corvallis woman had no special pull with AuCoin, but her letter led him to take a position and take action against the bill.

This happens all the time on issues that don't reach the headlines. Even with one that does get front-page attention in the newspapers, there was a time when that issue was practically unknown and when the first few letters, phone calls, and visits were giving each legislator the first impressions of the subject. Whichever side gets there first with the most pressure and the best information wins a big advantage in the legislator's final decision. A modest effort at the right time can make a big difference.

To exert your true power over your legislators in Congress, get together with friends, neighbors, and people with whom you work, worship, or socialize. As David R. Brower puts it, "Join with others for strength. If you belong only to your own-personal-self club, you limit yourself too much."

It's not hard to find others who share your concern about an issue if you just start talking about it. Whether it's federal aid to schools, new national parks, military spending, abortion, interstate trucking, or cottonseed subsidies—if you're interested, chances are that others nearby are also interested. People who are interested in an issue but have done nothing about it are often frustrated people, angered by the thought that Congress may do the wrong thing, yet immobilized by the notion that one person can't make a difference. All you have to do is convince them that, together, you *can* make a difference, and you'll see them channel their dammed-up anger into a constructive campaign to win your legislators' votes on the issue. A campaign of this kind can start around your own kitchen table. Later chapters in this book tell how to do it.

Congressional influence is a bargain too good to pass up. You have much more power over congressional decisions now than you would have had twenty or thirty years ago. For one thing, people don't hold legislators in awe any more. There has been a great national disillusionment about politicians and, as a result, people are much more willing to get involved in a legislative campaign and help tell a congressman how to vote.

Congress is also catching up with the country. The old senators and congressmen who dominated almost all the decisions in the early 1960s were even then twenty years behind the times and seriously out of touch with reality. Now there is a larger proportion of young members in the House and Senate who have not been in Congress long, who know better what's on people's minds back home, and who are still listening to their constituents. Moreover, under reforms enacted since 1970, the decision-making power in Congress has been taken away from the old elite of committee chairmen, and diffused among many legislators. In the old days a committee chairman could decide what he wanted in a given bill and tacitly use his position to coerce other members into support- ing it. The demise of that autocratic power has meant that the newer members of Congress have a lot more influence with their colleagues, and a lot more impact on legislative decisions.

This diffusion of power has made the industry lobbyist's job more difficult. No longer can he concentrate his attention and his campaign contributions on the old committee chairman, and then work out the details of legislation affecting his industry during a private lunch with the chairman. Now the lobbyist has to win over the subcommittee chairman and members of the committee. The chairman can't promise to deliver the goods anymore. Anything he proposes will be voted down if committee members don't like it.

That's why industry lobbies have begun to organize "grass-roots" campaigns. It's their only way to counteract the real grass-roots campaigns organized by public-interest citizen groups. When Congress was considering the Clean Air Bill in 1976, for example, lobbyists for the auto manufacturers got local auto dealers all over the country to write their local congressman, urging opposition to tough air-pollution standards for new cars. In 1977, industries that opposed new national parks in Alaska tried to soften up Congressman John F. Seiberling (Democrat of Ohio), chairman of the pertinent subcommittee and a strong advocate of the parks, by organizing a modest antipark effort in Ohio, which produced letters and editorials critical of Seiberling's actions.

The same kind of industry-organized grass-roots influence killed the Consumer Protection Agency bill in 1977 and again in 1978. Byron Kennard analyzed the defeat in these words:

> What went wrong is that business groups mobilized their own grass-roots allies in the last few months (before now they could count on a veto from a Republican president) so every grocery manager and shoe store owner in America complained to Congress about the Consumer Protection Agency bill. But little countervailing pressure from consumer organizations has been felt by Congress.

The same changes that have made the industry lobbyist's job harder have made your role, as a citizen, easier. You're sitting in the catbird seat. The power is back at the grass roots, and you are there.

The rest of this book is devoted to the methods by which you can apply that power to influence how your senators and your congressman or congresswoman vote. In essence, these are methods of getting a legislator's attention on your issue, methods of convincing a legislator to support your position, and methods of holding a legislator to that decision. Influencing a legislator is easy if you know how to do it. It can be fun, too. There is great satisfaction to be found in working together with others who share your convictions, helping to shape national policy.

Always be steadfast in your convictions, but flexible in your tactics. Use the suggestions in this book as starting points for your own thinking. What makes your campaign succeed will be your own brilliance, imagination, and persistence. If you think you aren't strong in one of these qualities, you'll find others who are, as you organize support in your community.

You can help to make this book better in future editions by contributing your own ideas and experiences. Send them to George Alderson, in care of E. P. Dutton, 2 Park Avenue, New York, N.Y. 10016.

The underlying theme of this book was stated in the early years of this century by the governor of Pennsylvania and formidable activist, Gifford Pinchot: "There is no reason why the American people should not take into their hands again the full political power which is theirs by right and which they exercised before the special interests began to nullify the will of the majority."

HOW YOU CAN
INFLUENCE CONGRESS

1

How to Use This Book

This book has been written to help you—any concerned citizen—learn how to influence your legislators in Congress. It doesn't matter whether you're all by yourself, or a person who wants to organize an action group, or someone who already leads an organization. Everyone has a role to play in a legislative campaign, and you can play your role better when you know the particular skills for your role.

Several chapters are about a citizen's direct contact with legislators through letters, in-person visits, public hearings, and phone calls. Several other chapters concern how to organize people in your community to put pressure on your legislators. Whatever your role, you may gain a better understanding of how your efforts fit into the big picture to influence your congressman if you read the whole book.

You can decide for yourself how deeply you want to go into your cause—how much time you want to spend on it, and what kinds of things you feel like doing for that cause. This book will suggest what you can do at any level you choose. For example:

- If you just want to write letters to your congressman and your senators, Chapters 3, 4, and 5 will tell you how to do it, and why.

- If you plan to see your congressman in person, Chapter 6 will help you get ready.

• If you're organizing a committee to fight for your congressman's vote on a bill, Chapters 7 and 8 can save you much trial and error.

• If you're in the midst of a legislative fight already, consult Chapters 11 and 12 for ideas on how to prepare persuasive arguments and deliver them in ways that will put pressure on your congressman.

There are two ways to find the information you want in this book. There is an Index at the back of the book. In addition, each chapter is devoted to a particular function or activity in a legislative campaign, and the chapter is further divided into topics, each with its own subheading. The subheadings are also shown in the Table of Contents to help you find major topics easily.

The methods described in this book have one central objective: to win the votes of your congressman and your senators on legislation that has been introduced in Congress. In this situation, your concern is focused on a particular bill, resolution, or amendment and you want your legislators to vote for or against it.

Getting a Bill Introduced

This book does not cover the more complex task of getting a new bill drafted, introduced, and passed. The process of drafting a bill and getting it introduced, as it's described in civics textbooks, seems simple enough. But it's not simple. The bill has to be written a certain way to avoid stirring up opposition and to make sure it will be referred to a friendly committee. It has to be introduced by the right legislators, who have influence with their colleagues and who believe in the bill strongly enough to spend their time working for its passage. The bill has to be cleared with relevant citizen groups before it's introduced, so they'll be ready to endorse it.

And that's only the beginning. Somebody has to influence the Administration to support the bill. Somebody has to pilot the bill through the committee process and through floor debate, constantly coaching the lead sponsors and prompting citizen groups to be active in support of the bill. Then the same thing has to happen in the other house of Congress. There may be a conference committee on the bill, and finally the President must be induced to sign it into law.

Taking a bill through this process, from start to finish, is an art. The best professional lobbyists do it well, and there are volunteer citizen lobbyists who have done it, too. Novices make lots of mistakes, unless they join hands with others who have plenty of experience. **If you want to propose new legislation, try either or both of the following approaches:**

• Persuade a friendly national organization that has a Washington office to support your idea and take the responsibility for the Washington lobbying. If the issue is one of low priority for them, they may ask you to do most of the work, but at least you'll have their experienced staff to consult as you proceed. This cooperative approach has been effective for many local organizations that have proposed new national parks and wilderness areas. The local group has had its own people spend many days in Washington to help the bill along, but they have been able to talk over their tactics and results with professional staffers of organizations such as the Sierra Club.

• Persuade a friendly legislator to take the leadership responsibility. This is a chancy approach, because legislators' attention is so fragmented that they can put little time into any particular issue. What usually happens to a constituent's good idea is that the congressman has a bill drafted by lawyers on the staff of the House legislative counsel who don't know your issue thoroughly, the congressman introduces it, and he then forgets about it. The bill was a nice gesture, but that's all. It won't go anywhere unless the sponsor builds support for it in the House, gets hearings scheduled, and pushes it through to enactment. To get a legislator to introduce and then *work* for a bill, the issue has to be something he's vitally interested in or something that he's convinced will help him get reelected.

Pressuring the Bureaucrats

Members of Congress have the ability to influence decisions of the President and the multifarious agencies in the executive branch of government. If you favor a decision that has just been made, say, by the Veterans Administration (VA) and you know that the decision will be opposed by other people, one of your first actions should be to ask your congressman and your senators to write the administrator of the VA and express their support.

Another book would be needed to cover the techniques of using congressional pressure to influence the executive branch. However, many of the methods in this book can be used in this connection. These methods can influence your congressman's position on a decision, and can influence whether or not he seriously takes action on the matter.

When you write your congressman about an agency's decision, his easiest way of handling the matter is to send your letter straight to the agency, without adding any comment of his own. This doesn't help you much, though if enough people are doing it, it will create some pressure on the agency.

At the next level of seriousness, the congressman writes the agency a letter urging them to stand firm on the decision (or reverse it). If a number of congressmen and senators are writing to an agency, it will be carefully noted by the head of the agency. But it won't necessarily change anything.

To get real results, especially when trying to reverse a decision, members of Congress must pursue the issue by meeting with agency officials, holding congressional hearings on the decision, making investigations, and so forth. When a congressman sees an agency's decision as important to his constituents, and possibly important to his reelection chances, he can get serious and apply many kinds of congressional pressure on the agency.

By using the methods described in this book, you can help your legislators come to see an agency's decision as an important one to your community, and you may obtain their commitment to support (or oppose) the decision. These methods may also help to influence legislators' choice of actions to carry out that commitment.

To apply this book's methods to an issue of this kind is easy if you know what you want the congressman to do. Instead of asking him to cosponsor a bill or vote for a certain bill or amendment, you may be asking him to write and congratulate the Environmental Protection Agency on an antipollution ruling. To persuade him to write such a letter, you may have to use letters, phone calls, in-person visits, petitions, letters from local VIPs, and so forth. Always stress the specific action you want the legislator to take. If you leave it to him, you'll get little or no action.

If you're in doubt as to what you should ask your congressman to do about an agency's decision, call the national citizen organization that covers your subject. An organization's Washington representatives should be able to help you with this question. (Ways of finding such organizations are explained in Appendix B, "Getting in Touch.")

2

How Your Congressman or Congresswoman Works

Many things influence a congressman or congresswoman. All day, every day, a legislator is being influenced by one thing or another. Sometimes it's direct influence, as when you go to see them and ask them to vote for a bill. Much of the time the influence is more indirect, as in a friendly chat with other legislators in the corridor. Your influence will be more effective if you understand how legislators do their job, and take this into account in your efforts.

One Day in the Life of a Congressman

Robert W. Edgar begins his day like many other people, leaving home in the suburbs at 7:30 A.M. for the drive to work. Bob Edgar is different from most of us, though. He's one of the 535 people who make our national laws. A Democratic congressman from Pennsylvania, he represents some 471,000 people in Delaware County, bordering the Delaware River southwest of Philadelphia—an area combining suburban residential communities and a few manufacturing areas.

To get an impression of how a congressman spends his day, let's follow Bob Edgar in his rounds. The day is Tuesday, September 27, 1977, and the sun is shining as Edgar says goodbye to his wife and three children, gets into his bright orange Volvo station wagon, and sets off for Capitol Hill. En route, he listens to a radio news program. Twenty minutes later he walks into his office in the Cannon House Office Building.

None of his staff has come in yet. Edgar opens his briefcase, takes out two manila folders full of papers he worked through at home last night, and goes to staffers' desks in two rooms of his suite, leaving in their in-boxes work he wants them to do. He returns to the third room, his own office, and, sitting down at the conference table he uses in place of a desk, reads the *Washington Post* and *New York Times* to catch up on national and world news.

At age thirty-four, Edgar is in his second term in the House of Representatives. Before coming to Congress he had been a United Methodist minister and had been active in civic affairs, which led to his decision to run for Congress in 1974, his first try for public office.

By 8:30, seven of his staff have arrived, and they assemble in Edgar's office for the weekly staff meeting, sitting in a circle around the room. It's a circle of young faces, mostly under thirty-five. Edgar himself, a relaxed, unassuming man, presides informally from one corner of his conference table. Edgar calls on one of his legislative assistants, Van Sheets: "To start with, Van, why don't you tell us what's on the legislative agenda?" Sheets takes a couple of minutes to explain what issues are scheduled on the House floor this week. Among them are a vote on federal funding of abortions for the poor and a vote on establishing a House Select Committee on Population.

"How are you going to vote on the population committee?" asks Edgar's administrative assistant, Priscilla Skillman. Edgar answers with a question, "What are your feelings on it?"

"I don't think we need another committee," she says. This provokes discussion by all the staff on the pros and cons of the measure. Edgar reminds the staff of his interest and activity on population and food-supply issues. When they discover that the committee would exist only through 1978, the staff opposition subsides.

The congressman goes on to raise briefly several issues that are active. On one of them, a staffer interjects, "We're getting a lot of mail on that."

Next, Edgar turns to Gary Grobman: "All right, Gary, what's up on your issues?" Like the other four legislative assistants in the

Washington office, Grobman has his own assigned subject areas for which he's responsible; his include energy, water pollution, aviation, paratransit, and water-resource projects. Grobman and the congressman tell the staff about Edgar's recent activities on the issue of waterway-user fees.

Bob McMullan and Skillman report briefly on their issues, and Skip Powers, Edgar's press aide, mentions a newsletter she will soon be putting together for mailing to their constituent mailing list, asking the other staffers to think about what should be in the newsletter.

Congressman Edgar then reports on his weekend's activities in the congressional district. One of his foremost concerns is last Friday night's "public forum" in Marple Township, one of a series of monthly public forums scheduled by Edgar in different parts of his district to give constituents a chance to speak their minds. "It seems everybody there was frustrated over something—the Panama Canal, minimum wage, you name it," he says. "We may need a new format for the next public forum, to prevent the specialized interest groups from taking over."

Powers, who also attended the Friday forum, disagrees. She ventures that Edgar may have been unprepared for the barrage of hostile questions. "I do not feel they took over the meeting," she says. "People come there wanting to talk." She suggests that Edgar talk less and let constituents talk more.

When the congressman has finished reporting on his other public appearances over the weekend, he raises a new issue that he wants his staff to get ready for—a comprehensive urban policy involving transportation, housing, and industry that will encourage businesses to stay in the cities, instead of fleeing to rural areas. "How do we begin?" he asks. After discussion by all the legislative staff, Skillman agrees to organize staff work on the subject, with the goal of having a major speech on urban policy for Edgar to give at a conference in Chicago a few weeks later.

Edgar asks Powers about recent problems with newspapers in the congressional district. She reports that the papers' blasts at Edgar over his stance on the controversial Blue Route freeway are being answered by letters to the editor drafted for Edgar's signature by David Williamson, the transportation specialist on Edgar's staff, based in his Chester office—one of two offices he has in his district.

At 9:40 the meeting ends and Edgar picks up the phone to call Williamson, asking him to help prepare the urban policy issue for the November speech. When the phone call is over, ten minutes later, Edgar picks up his portfolio-style briefcase and leaves the office, walking through the Cannon Building's marble-floored, echoing corridors to the Veterans Affairs Committee room, where a hearing is to be held to receive testimony from the American Legion. This is one of two ten-o'clock committee meetings Edgar is supposed to attend simultaneously. He has decided to spend some of his time at each.

Entering the committee room—a high-ceilinged room with gold-tone walls and carpet, lighted by crystal chandeliers—Congressman Edgar is greeted by American Legion officers, conspicuous in their Legion overseas caps. He goes to the mahogany rostrum at which committee members sit, exchanges a word with the committee chairman, Congressman Ray Roberts (Democrat of Texas), and takes his seat behind the rostrum, facing a standing-room-only audience, most of the spectators wearing American Legion caps.

At 10:00 the hearing begins with the Legion's national commander, Robert Charles Smith, who takes a half hour to read his statement. As Smith reads, Edgar goes through a copy of Smith's written statement, underlining a few passages and jotting down on a scratch pad questions he wants to ask Smith.

When the national commander comes to the end of his statement, the questioning begins with statements of support for the Legion's position by the most senior members of the committee. Few real questions are being asked, but the congressmen are applauded by the audience of Legionnaires. With five minutes to each congressman, the questioning works its way down the seniority ladder until, after half an hour of this, the chairman calls on Bob Edgar.

Edgar asks Smith for the Legion's suggestions on how to improve the Veterans Administration (VA) health-care system to put it "on the cutting edge of medical technology." Smith refers the question to another Legion officer, who answers that the VA health-care system is the best in the country. He has no suggestions for major improvements. Edgar challenges this assertion by reporting that an executive of the VA hospital in Philadelphia had told him last Saturday that the care there is not up to standard. The Legion spokesman replies that better monitoring can remedy such problems.

After one more question of Smith, Congressman Edgar is cut off by Chairman Roberts; it's the end of his five minutes. The Legionnaires do not applaud. So, with two more unasked questions on his scratch pad, at 11:15 Edgar leaves the committee room to go to his other committee meeting. In the corridor he is met by Gary Grobman, who hands him a note from Congressman Glenn M. Anderson (Democrat of California) asking Edgar to raise a few questions for him at an afternoon hearing which Anderson will miss. Edgar adds Anderson's material to the pile in his briefcase, thanks Grobman, and strides away down the hall.

A short walk down Independence Avenue brings Edgar to the Rayburn House Office Building, where the Public Works Committee's Subcommittee on Surface Transportation is holding a hearing on legislation to continue highway and mass-transit programs. In a spacious, modernistic, fluorescent-lighted committee room, a handful of congressmen and a sparse audience are listening to the subcommittee chairman, James J. Howard (Democrat of New Jersey), question Boris Pushkarev, vice president of the Regional Plan Association, a citizen group from New York and adjoining states. A subcommittee staffer brings Edgar a copy of Pushkarev's testimony, and he quickly reads through it, writing questions on a scratch pad.

At 11:30 it's Edgar's turn to ask questions. Pursuing the topic he had raised at the staff meeting earlier in the day, he asks Pushkarev to elaborate on the concept of transportation as an integral part of an urban policy. When Pushkarev has done so, Edgar asks him which categories of urban surface transportation need more federal funds. Pushkarev responds, pointing out that an unglamorous and overlooked need is that of the older cities, such as Chicago, New York, and Philadelphia, for money to rebuild their old and deteriorating subway and elevated rail systems.

Other subcommittee members have run out of questions, so Edgar gets more time, and he goes into detailed questions as to what types of federal aid should be emphasized in the new legisla-

tion the subcommittee is preparing. Edgar finishes by asking Pushkarev for a copy of his recent book for the use of the subcommittee
staff. Though he doesn't say so, Edgar hopes the staff will be influenced by it in their subsequent legislative work, and that they in
turn will influence other subcommittee members.

During Edgar's questions the House bells have rung in the
committee room, signaling that the House is about to convene. At
11:50 the hearing ends so the legislators can go to the House floor.
Pushkarev ambles over for a word with Edgar, who apologizes for
being late to the hearing. Then two young men introduce themselves as reporters for the American News Service, part of a gradu-
ate program in journalism; one mentions his connection with
Edgar's district: "I graduated from Swarthmore, and I worked in
your 1974 campaign." Edgar welcomes their questions about the
transportation bills and explains how his own bill and Chairman
Howard's bill will be considered by the subcommittee.

After fifteen minutes with the reporters, Congressman Edgar
joins his staffer, Van Sheets, who has been waiting to hand him a
black looseleaf binder containing briefing material on the bills that
will be considered on the House floor this week, some of the information prepared by Edgar's staff, most of it prepared by the Democratic Study Group and by the House Environmental Study
Conference, two unofficial House organizations that provide issue
analyses to their members.

Sheets also shows Edgar two letters to the editor his staff have
drafted, and Edgar signs them. Sheets tells the congressman,
"We're getting more calls on abortion." Edgar knows this means
antiabortion calls, because he has been deluged with mail and
phone calls from Right-to-Lifers every time an abortion question
has come to a vote.

Sheets leaves to return to the office as Edgar walks off toward
the Capitol building, carrying a briefcase by now laden with a good
five pounds of testimony and miscellaneous papers, plus the black
briefing book. Edgar takes the "Members Only" elevator down and
rides the House subway to the Capitol, where he is greeted by another congressman and a congresswoman as they take an elevator
up to the House floor. At 12:15, Edgar goes into the House chamber
and uses his vote-identification card to register his presence in a
quorum call. While on the floor, he asks other legislators about the

strategy on today's abortion vote; it turns out to be a maneuver by foes of abortion to reaffirm the House's opposition to federal funding of all abortions except to save the mother's life.

At 12:20, Edgar leaves the floor by way of an ornate, frescoed corridor and walks down one flight to attend a luncheon sponsored by the Pennsylvania School Boards Association. He is welcomed by several school board officials, and chats for ten minutes with State Senator Jeanette Reibman about education issues in Pennsylvania. The dining room reserved for this occasion is a long, narrow, windowless one below the House chamber, with a vaulted ceiling, chandeliers, and a long table seating thirty.

Pennsylvania's senior Democrat in the House, Daniel J. Flood, is tied up somewhere else, so Edgar, as the senior Democrat present, is asked to preside. He asks those present to introduce themselves. Of the twenty-seven people sitting around the table, fewer than half are congressmen; some are staff men and women representing absent congressmen, two are staffers representing Pennsylvania's senators, and the rest are part of the School Boards Association contingent.

While eating the lunch of fried chicken and hush puppies, Edgar talks with staffers and with a school official near him at the table. The conversation ranges from school construction needs (he's on a subcommittee that handles this program) to his stance on abortion and how as a result he was targeted for opposition by the Catholic Church in the last election.

As people are polishing off their desserts (baked custard), Edgar calls for attention and turns the program over to the president of the School Boards Association, who in ten minutes outlines the Association's concerns about current national legislation. Several congressmen ask questions, mainly on how existing laws are affecting schools in Pennsylvania. At 1:20 Edgar thanks the School Boards Association for hosting the luncheon, and adjourns the group.

On his way out, he has a final exchange with Senator Reibman about the abortion issue, and she encourages him to stand firm; she has survived the issue in her elections, she says.

In the elevator down to the subway, Edgar runs into Congressman Norman Y. Mineta (Democrat of California), chairman of the Subcommittee on Public Buildings, to whose hearing Edgar is on his way. Mineta, a former mayor of San Jose, is interested as Edgar recommends Pushkarev's book to him. "It fits in with what Henry Reuss was telling us the other day," Edgar tells him, referring to the Wisconsin Democrat who chairs the Committee on Banking, Finance and Urban Affairs. Mineta agrees that there's a need for an urban policy and points out, by way of example, that the nation puts more money into housing through the tax deduction on mortgages than into all other housing programs put together—a policy that fosters urban sprawl and transportation problems.

At 1:27 the two arrive at the Public Works Committee room, and Mineta calls the hearing to order. The topic is a proposal by the General Services Administration (GSA) to improve an office building in Orange County, California, at a cost of $3.3 million, for occupancy by a Defense Department administrative agency. Congressman Jack Brooks (Democrat of Texas) is the first witness, and he strongly opposes the GSA plan. As Brooks speaks, Edgar leafs through the prepared testimony and looks at photographs of the building, which have been handed out by a subcommittee staff woman. He holds whispered consultations with two subcommittee staffers, who come over and crouch next to Edgar's chair.

On this subcommittee—one of the less-desired assignments in Congress—Edgar is third-ranking Democrat, so he doesn't have to wait long to ask his questions. After questioning Brooks on a few points, Edgar leaves the room through a door into the committee offices, phones his own office to check with the staff on several issues, and reenters the committee room at 2:20.

By this time the GSA spokesmen have made their statement and are being questioned. Edgar looks over the questions Congressman Anderson wanted him to ask, but decides to ask his own first. When his turn comes, he asks the GSA witnesses, "What security do we have that sufficient homes will be provided for the employees moving to this location?" He is concerned that, because many employees in this Defense agency are in the low- to moderate-income brackets, they may not be able to find housing they can afford in the more affluent Orange County. He listens intently as GSA spokesmen respond by showing charts ostensibly proving that no housing problem is involved.

After several brief questions, Edgar raises a basic policy question as to whether it's wise to be moving agencies from city locations out into the distant suburbs. "Perhaps the time has come," he says, "with our energy problem and our transportation problem, to take a look at what our federal policies are doing. Maybe we're encouraging urban sprawl." The GSA witness misses the point at first; when he finally gets it, the House bells ring for a recorded vote on the floor, and the dialogue is interrupted. At 2:50 Mineta recesses the hearing for fifteen minutes so the legislators can go and vote.

Mineta and Edgar are joined by Congressman Bo Ginn (Democrat of Georgia) on the way over to the Capitol, but Ginn loses interest as the two continue talking about urban policy and whether laws concerning public buildings could help to foster revitalization of central business districts. As they go in to the House chamber, Edgar tells Mineta he won't be back to the subcommittee meeting. "I've got a meeting with a mayor from Israel after this vote," he says.

Again Edgar casts his vote by vote-identification card. This vote is on a procedural motion involving an Indian claims bill. He leaves the House chamber by another door and walks through the Capitol grounds to his office in the Cannon Building. When he walks into the office, at 3:05, his office manager, Kathy Keel, quips, "Do we know you?" It was over five hours ago that he left for the first hearing in the morning.

The mayor is going to be late, so Edgar sits down at his conference table, looks through a half-dozen messages on his desk, and picks up the phone to call his office in Upper Darby. He glances at an article published by the American Veterans Committee, praising his work on legislation concerning the military discharge review program. Another item left on his desk by Keel is a wirephoto copy of this morning's story on the front page of the *Delaware County Daily Times*, headlined "Edgar Put Name on Line," critical of his stance on the Blue Route freeway.

After the call to Upper Darby, he phones David Williamson in his Chester office and spends ten minutes talking strategy about the surface-transportation bill.

At 3:30 the Israeli mayor is still not there, so Edgar decides to see two spokesmen for United Parcel Service (UPS), who are early for their 4:00 appointment. Seated in his office, the principal UPS spokesman, Tom Hardeman, an executive from the company's Philadelphia branch office, asks Edgar's support for legislation introduced by Congressman James M. Hanley (Democrat of New York) that aims to prohibit the U.S. Postal Service from using first-class mail to subsidize parcel post. The UPS man produces graphs showing that the Postal Service has not raised parcel post rates in the same proportion as first-class rates, evidently trying to recapture the parcel business that has moved to the private-enterprise UPS.

Edgar is doubtful about the statistics and asks Hardeman for some examples of how the rates affect real people mailing real packages. "What does it cost to mail that package?" he asks. Hardeman has no examples at hand, but promises to get back with some. Edgar tells the UPS men, "I don't know enough about the Hanley legislation to be able to tell you whether I'll be for it or against it, but as far as the thrust is to keep your employees working and keep you in business, I tend to favor that."

The UPS men leave after ten minutes with the congressman, and Edgar strolls into the staff room, glances at the latest news clippings from Pennsylvania newspapers about his activities, and has brief conversations with Skip Powers and Bob McMullan about their work.

At 3:50 Mayor Dov Barzilai and Mrs. Barzilai, of Hadera, Israel, arrive, and Congressman Edgar joins them in his office. Edgar and his wife had met the Barzilais briefly during a trip to Israel and Egypt last spring (at Edgar's own expense). Now Mayor Barzilai is here to ask Edgar's advice on water pollution problems in Hadera. He describes the situation, one of pollution from a paper mill, and he says, "The problem is that we have not a pollution law." Barzilai's story is a familiar one to Edgar, because the Public Works Committee handles water-pollution legislation. Edgar explains different pollution-control approaches the United States has tried, and some of the problems of each. He urges Barzilai to see two paper-company executives in Pennsylvania who can tell about their accomplishments in pollution-control technology—ammunition Barzilai may be able to use in challenging the paper-mill operators in Hadera.

At 4:20 a photographer arrives, as arranged by Powers, and takes pictures of Edgar with Mr. and Mrs. Barzilai. Before the Israeli couple leave, Edgar gives them copies of a few pertinent hearing records of Public Works Committee hearings on water pollution.

When Edgar shows the Barzilais out, at 4:40, a staff man from the Select Committee on Assassinations is waiting. Congressman Edgar is a member of the committee and has asked for weekly briefings on the committee staff's investigative work in progress. Edgar and Bob McMullan sit down with the committee staffer in Edgar's office. After fifteen minutes the House bells ring in the corridor for a quorum call, and Edgar has to interrupt the briefing. He walks over to the Capitol through the tunnel under Independence Avenue, since it's raining out.

At 5:10, back in his office, Edgar resumes the briefing with the Assassinations Committee man. Ten minutes later the bells ring again, signaling the first of what Edgar knows will be several recorded votes on bills debated earlier in the afternoon—measures that are being considered under the Suspension of the Rules procedure. So he leaves again for the walk over to the House floor.

This time the votes will follow at five-minute intervals, so Edgar stays on the House floor, seeking out other House members he wants to see about his surface-transportation bill. He also joins others in congratulating Congressman Edward I. Koch on his nomination as Democratic candidate for Mayor of New York. He sees Congressman Peter H. Kostmayer (Democrat of Pennsylvania), with whom he has cosponsored a bill on commuter rail service; he promises to get Kostmayer some information about the Carter Administration's position on their bill.

At 6:10 Edgar leaves the House floor after voting on the last bill and heads back through the tunnel, joking with two other congressmen on the way. Back at the office all is quiet; the staff have all gone home. Edgar makes Xerox copies to give to Kostmayer, pockets them, and leaves for the first of three evening engagements on Capitol Hill.

First is a reception featuring ballad singer Harry Chapin, sponsored by the World Hunger Year organization to draw attention to world food and nutrition issues, and particularly to a bill that would create a presidential commission on world hunger. Edgar has cosponsored this bill, and he wants to at least put in an appearance to show his support. The reception is in the cavernous Caucus Room of the Cannon Building. A large crowd—mostly young staffers—is munching whole-wheat bread and sipping white jug wine. There's no music, but a small bandstand awaits the arrival of Chapin, one of the celebrities who have been contributing their time to support the World Hunger Year program. Few House members are in the room, and after greeting Congressman James M. Jeffords (Republican of Vermont), who is a leader on the issue, Edgar leaves and walks a block down Independence Avenue to the Rayburn Building.

At 6:40 Edgar arrives at a very different reception, held in the Government Operations Committee hearing room. A three-man combo is playing subdued background music, and the crowd is mostly congressmen and congresswomen. This one is a reception to honor Congressman Koch in his New York City mayoral race, hosted by the Democrats of New York's delegation in the House.

Vice President Walter F. Mondale and his Secret Service entourage have arrived just ahead of Edgar, and Mondale is greeting Koch, surrounded by a knot of House leaders. Soon Mondale beckons Edgar over, says he saw him walking down the street on the way over, and the two go on to discuss the economic problems of Edgar's district, which involve the recent loss of a big military-equipment contract. Mondale, when he was a senator and presidential hopeful, had campaigned for Edgar in his first congressional race in 1974 and has been one of Edgar's best contacts in the Carter Administration.

Another legislator pulls Mondale away, and Edgar repairs to one of two bars in the room, asking the bartender for a straight Coca-Cola. Then he stands around, chatting with other legislators. Soon the band stops playing and the crowd listens to four House leaders and Mondale hail Koch's election victory in short, witty speeches—all variations on the theme, "Congressional boy makes good." During the speeches, Edgar spots Congressman Kostmayer across the room and crosses through the crowd to hand him the memos he had promised earlier. The two stand listening as Koch responds to the accolades with the wittiest speech of all.

Edgar leaves for the walk across the Capitol grounds to the Dirksen Senate Office Building. He arrives there at 7:20 for a reception and dinner of Members of Congress for Peace Through Law (MCPL), a group of senators and House members concerned about international affairs, with a staff to provide issue analyses to members. This evening's dinner is an event to raise funds to pay for MCPL's staff work, and potential donors have been invited to sit in with the legislators. The dinner is held in a large hearing room of the Dirksen Building, at MCPL's expense. After dinner Congressman Morris K. Udall (Democrat of Arizona) addresses the group, hailing MCPL's effective role on international issues, pointing to the Panama Canal Treaty, now pending in the Senate, as an example of how the group can make an impact. When Udall has finished, the legislators discuss current issues briefly—the breeder-reactor program, nuclear disarmament, the B-1 bomber, and again the Panama Canal Treaty. As the dinner is winding down, at 9:00 Edgar returns to his office. He picks up the folder containing his night's work and, at 9:15, he leaves for home.

Handling the Work Load

The average member of the House puts in an eleven-hour working day when Congress is in session, according to a survey done in 1977 by the House Commission on Administrative Review (dubbed the Obey Commission after its chairman, Congressman David R. Obey, Democrat of Wisconsin). Out of that eleven-hour day the average member had only eleven minutes of time free for reading about public issues, and only twelve minutes to work on legislative matters in his office.

The average congressman's day goes something like this, according to the Obey Commission's survey:

Time spent on House floor and in committee:	Total 4 hrs. 25 min.
House floor debate and voting	2 hrs. 53 min.
Committee and conference meetings	1 hr. 32 min.
Time spent in the office:	Total 3 hrs. 19 min.
Meeting with constituents	17 min.
Meeting with organized groups (lobbyists, etc.)	9 min.
Meeting with others (news media, government officials, etc.)	20 min.
Conferring with personal and committee staff	53 min.
Meeting with other House members	5 min.
Answering mail and signing letters	46 min.
Preparing legislation and speeches	12 min.
Reading	11 min.
On the telephone	26 min.

Time spent elsewhere in Washington, D.C.:	Total 2 hrs. 2 min.
With constituents in Capitol Building	9 min.
Meeting with House leadership	3 min.
At events (receptions, conventions, etc.)	33 min.
Meeting with other House members	11 min.
With informal groups of House members	8 min.
Party caucuses and committees	5 min.
Personal business	28 min.
Travel time around town	25 min.
Time spent outside of Washington, D.C., en route to congressional district, etc.	1 hr. 40 min.

The averaging process makes some activities look absurdly short in duration because they are not daily events; their infrequent occurrence reduces a reasonable time span to an unreasonable one. Such is the case with, for instance, "Meeting with other House members" and "Party caucuses and committees."

The congressional work load also involves legislators' keeping up to date on what's happening back home. Most legislators at least skim several newspapers from home, including both dailies and weeklies. According to a 1966 study, House members average about six days a month in their congressional districts, meeting with constituents and speaking to groups. The small staff in legislators' district offices keep them posted when they are in Washington.

Ranging to both extremes from this average, you'll find congressmen who go home to their districts every Friday and return to Washington every Monday, and you'll find others who seldom go home except in the House's scheduled "district work periods" of several days' duration. Distance is a factor, because the time and cost of going to a West Coast district every week is prohibitive for most legislators.

Some who are not activists in pushing or opposing legislation, and just go along with the crowd, have more free time than the average. The activists in the House, on the other hand, use all their time and have to stretch the workdays out to fourteen or sixteen hours. Other differences in work load come from a legislator's leadership role, or lack of one. A legislator who has been in the House for ten or twelve years usually spends more of his time on conference committees and in party leadership work than a more junior member does. Some well-entrenched senior legislators devote less time to meeting constituents and traveling in their congressional districts, in the belief that their seats are secure, while a first- or second-term legislator tends to plow his time heavily into establishing good contacts with his constituents.

Because of the multifarious demands on their time, members of the House function under a big handicap when it comes to their basic work of making laws. As the Obey Commission's draft report observed, "Rarely do members have sufficient blocks of time when they are free from the frenetic pace of the Washington 'treadmill' to think about the implications of various public policies. As a result, legislators are often compelled by circumstance to rely on the judgment of others—agency officials, staff aides, lobbyists, or colleagues—for evaluations of the content and import of various legislation."

The legislator's staff is the first line of defense against the overload of work. According to the Obey Commission survey, the average staff comprises sixteen people, divided between the Washington office and congressional-district offices. Members of the House are allotted $255,144 per year (as of 1977) for staff salaries, and this can be split up in many ways, with these restrictions: no more than one-twelfth of it may be spent in a single month; and no more than eighteen staffers may be on the payroll at one time. Yet even with a staff this large, members of the House find their days long and their time and attention spread thin.

The Senate presents much the same picture. But because senators are more in the limelight than members of the House, the demands on their time are greater and they have even less time available for personal reading and study on legislative issues. Their decisions are therefore more dependent on recommendations and follow-up work by their staff. Being elected to six-year terms, senators devote less time in the first half of a term to meeting and cultivating the electorate, but they usually get serious about it during the two years before the election. Senate committees have fewer members than House committees, so a freshman senator can have more influence on a committee's decisions. A senator gets more time to ask questions in hearings, and can more easily buttonhole the other committee members outside of committee meetings to talk them into supporting his viewpoint.

Senators also have larger staffs, averaging about thirty employees between Washington and home-state offices. Where a legislative assistant on a congressman's staff may have to cover half a dozen major issue areas, ranging from military weapons to environmental laws, a legislative assistant in a Senate office frequently handles only one issue area and can therefore know the subject better and help the senator to be knowledgeable and influential on that subject. It's largely because of the greater staff complement that senators are seen by the public as statesmen capable of acting intelligently in many fields, while House members are more often seen as people of limited scope, interested in only one or two issues.

Getting Information

With decisions on national policy confronting senators and congressmen every day, reliable information is at a premium. Questions must be answered about any proposed bill or amendment, among them:

How will it benefit the country?
How will it benefit my constituents?
What will it cost, and who will pay?
Why is it necessary? What's wrong with the present situation?
Who is for it? Who's against it?

On any bill, these questions can be answered in very different ways, depending on a person's viewpoint. One who is opposed to the measure will see slight benefit, but great harm, in a bill. His estimates of cost will be higher than the proponents' estimates. He will cite convincing evidence that the bill is not even needed. Someone who favors the bill, by contrast, will see everything differently.

Legislators' decisions are strongly influenced by their sources of information. When the oil-depletion allowance is being considered, a senator who trusts information given him by the oil companies will tend to see things as the oil companies want him to. He'll see a short supply of American oil and think this results (as the oil companies say) from repeal of the depletion allowance. On the other hand, a senator who trusts information given him by Ralph Nader's public-interest research groups will see the depletion allowance as a windfall for the oil companies that has no significant impact on oil exploration and production.

Few legislators have time to take information from all interested sources and analyze it. For this, they rely primarily on their personal staff and on the staffs of relevant congressional committees. Yet even the staff must make decisions as to whose information to trust, often reflecting the same bias as their boss because they know what he wants to hear.

Members of the House frankly admit that they need better information in their legislative work. One of the biggest information gaps concerns information on how proposed legislation would affect a congressman's own district. The Obey Commission's survey found that 34 to 40 percent of House members said they had difficulty getting this kind of information. Legislative assistants were polled on the same question, and 40 to 58 percent of them made the same complaint. **Citizens and citizen groups can fill this gap by providing reliable information on how legislation would affect your community and state.**

The information sources that members of Congress rely on most, according to the Obey Commission survey, are:

- Their personal staff
- Committee staffs and committee hearings and documents

To a lesser extent, House members rely on the following sources, according to the survey:

- **Unofficial congressional support groups.** Twenty such groups (Democratic Study Group, Republican Study Committee, Black Caucus, Women's Caucus, etc.) prepare analyses of legislation for their members, who pay dues for the service. Some are nonpartisan, organized around an issue (such as the environment, rural affairs, black or Hispanic affairs), while others are organized primarily on party lines (Democratic Study Group, Republican Study Committee). These groups never tell a legislator how to vote. They prepare issue papers that summarize the pros and cons, provide historical background on the issue, and tell what organizations are for and against the bill. The issue-based groups also look at all legislation actively being considered to find out whether it affects their issue, as, for instance, a transportation bill covering highways and subways may affect not only transportation but also the environment and black, Hispanic, and rural affairs.

• **Congressional-district sources.** These may include individual constituents, businesses and industrial organizations, local politicians and government agencies, colleges and research institutions.

• **Lobbyists and interest groups.** Washington lobbyists and national organizations know that the information they give legislators must be accurate, because if a congressman who relies on their information is made to look foolish as a result, he won't help them again. An effective lobbyist will give legislators solid information in support of his cause and will also furnish the arguments and information the congressman needs to refute his opponents' arguments. Most lobbyists and interest groups stay in close touch with committee staffs and legislators' personal staffs, recognizing that legislators rely more heavily on these staff sources for reliable information than they do on lobbyists. Getting the information to a senator by way of staff makes it more credible because it has been screened by a person the senator trusts.

• **Other members of the House.** When a congressman is about to vote on legislation handled by a committee of which he's not a member, he'll often consult members of that committee whom he knows. It's usually just a brief chat on the House floor or in the corridors.

• **The media.** Newspapers, magazines, radio, and television are heavily relied on by members of the House, especially concerning matters that are not yet the subject of legislation—decisions of the executive branch, state and local policy issues, and so forth.

The information sources least relied on for information by members of the House, according to the Obey Commission survey, were:

• **The Administration and federal agencies.** It's surprising to find this source so little relied upon. Government-agency representatives are ever-present when committees are considering legislation and when legislation is up for floor action in the House. However, the government's lobbying efforts have come to be held in low repute in Congress because, especially during the Nixon and Ford administrations, the information supplied by federal agencies was so often shown to have been badly distorted to fit the Administration's policy line. Actually, the Administration and federal agencies are probably relied on more than the survey shows, but personal staff and committee staff screen the information before a congressman gets it, so this would show up in the survey as information obtained from staff sources.

- **Personal reading and study.** Lack of time precludes this for most legislators, unless they slack off on some other activity. Time to read and study tends to be regarded as "free time" and is easily encroached upon by other things a legislator's staff and constituents want him to do. Legislators who want badly enough to study often do so at home in the evening, at the expense of their families, who get to see them little enough as it is.

- **Floor debate.** In the Obey Commission survey, few members of the House claimed to rely on House floor debate for information on the issues. Indeed, few of them ever stick around during the debate, because they have obtained their best information in advance from staff and other more reliable sources. Information brought up during a floor debate is not always accurate, and there is not much that can be done to winnow the truth from falsehood in a debate among 435 congressmen. There are few legislators who have not made up their minds before entering the House chamber. The main exception occurs when last-minute amendments are being voted on, in which case the most influential information is not substantive at all, but rather who is voting which way; in these votes a legislator will vote with others he respects.

- **The House leadership.** In this category are the notices and issue papers sent out by the Democratic and Republican whips' offices. The House leadership on both sides of the aisle exerts influence not so much through information as through the signals it gives on major issues, indicating that the call is out for party unity on a particular vote. On most issues the leadership does not even take a position.

Several other governmental sources of information are used by Congress which were not raised in the Obey Commission survey. First are the House computer systems, notably the bill-status system, which any House member may use to find out the current status of a bill, and the summary of floor debate systems, which keeps its subscribers (at present some 100 legislators) informed almost instantaneously of what is happening on the House floor, so they can keep working in their offices during much of the routine speechifying.

The Congressional Research Service (CRS), a division of the Library of Congress, has 300 subject-area specialists and thirty senior specialists on its staff to handle the many inquiries received every week from members of the House and Senate. CRS has been especially valuable to Congress in researching the background of legislative issues. If a congressman wants to know what consideration Congress has given during the past fifty years to repealing the income tax, CRS could do the job. It is supposedly nonpartisan and impartial, but in some issues its specialists have been outrageously biased.

The General Accounting Office (GAO), with 5,300 on its staff, does analytical and evaluation work, particularly on numerical data. Its major responsibilities include year-round auditing of federal agencies' expenditures and income. GAO is not an agency of the executive branch, but a congressional one. It can be asked by legislators to check the data used by proponents of a project or a bill. For instance, GAO analyses of the benefit-cost ratios used to justify proposed dams have shown that in some cases the Corps of Engineers had overestimated the benefits; these analyses have brought about a whole new look at such projects, and indirectly contributed to President Jimmy Carter's moves in 1977 and 1978 to curtail these construction projects.

The Office of Technology Assessment, with 130 on its staff, has the job of marshaling scientific evidence and predictions representing diverse scientific viewpoints on subjects that are coming up for action in Congress. It undertakes specific studies at the request of House and Senate committees.

The Congressional Budget Office, with a staff of 208, is Congress's counterpart to the President's Office of Management and Budget. It analyzes the President's budget and economic policies and lays out alternatives to them for consideration by the House and Senate.

While Congress has many different sources of information to draw upon, every voting decision is one person's own individual re-action to the information he has, and that reaction involves a host of personal factors.

What Makes a Congressman Tick

A member of the United States Congress is a person like you or me, but the name Senator Smith or Congressman Black also stands for an institution, of which the senator or congressman is the chief executive. The senator has the ultimate responsibility for every-thing the Senator Smith institution does, but he does not make all the decisions himself. The senator's staff have many decisions to make without consulting the senator—among them what answer to give to a run-of-the-mill constituent letter and what information will be shown to the senator about your issue.

Like any institution, such as a government agency or a busi-ness corporation, the Senator Smith institution is not monolithic. There are conflicting forces at work within it. Different staff mem-bers may be vying for control over your issue; the senator's Wash-ington staff may be at war with the home-state office staff as to how the senator should vote on it; and the legislative assistant may be urging the senator to spend more time getting involved in your issue when the senator really would rather be working on foreign-relations issues instead.

The Senator Smith institution also reacts to outside influ-ences—constituents' letters, visits, and phone calls; senators urging Smith to vote a certain way; lobbyists' advocacy; hearings and re-ports of Senate committees; and so forth. By the time the real per-son Senator Smith casts his vote on your bill, the Senator Smith institution will have gone through a big decision-making process.

You have to treat Senator Smith partly as a person, and think of how he will react to your letter or your tactics in support of your cause. You also have to treat him as an institution, and take advan-tage of that institution's internal diversity in planning your campaign.

Take a random sample of a dozen senators or congressmen,

and you'll find that they react very differently to the same piece of legislation. The positions they take on a bill are determined not so much by their powers of reason as by their attitudes, backgrounds, political philosophies, and political and personal relationships. Just as some people seem to see the world through rose-colored glasses, a senator may look at all legislation through rural-conservative glasses—except it's not so simple. The glasses through which each legislator views legislation are made to order, depending on where he grew up, who influenced him early in life, what jobs he had, how he got into politics, and who his friends are.

Most legislators in Congress have one thing in common—a big ego. You don't get to be a congressman by being shy and modest. The seed of the congressional ego no doubt exists before a man or woman runs for election, but once he or she arrives in Congress, that seed is nurtured by the constant deference and flattery of those who want a legislator's favor—lobbyists, staff, other legislators, and everybody else in Washington and back home who wants to be close to political power. Quite aside from those who have issue objectives in mind, there are many people who simply want to rub shoulders with someone who has power.

In Washington a new senator or congressman is made to feel that he really is somebody. His decision-making role might be much smaller than in his previous job, but a legislator associates with nationally known senators and congressmen, is courted by lobbyists for his vote in committee and on the floor, and is invited to be impressed by the richesse of the industrial lobbies. This last deserves further examination, because it reveals one of the greatest differences between the influence of industrial, private-interest groups on the one hand, and public-interest citizens' groups on the other.

The big-time industrial lobbies use money not only to buy goodwill through campaign contributions and lecture fees. They use it in ways designed to show their respectability. Business lobbyists dress in well-tailored suits, and thus try to make themselves seem believable, as though somebody who spent $400 on a suit were more believable than a public-interest lobbyist who bought his off the rack for $150. Industrial lobbies also stage lavish receptions where the hard liquor flows freely and there's a never-ending supply of shrimp, quiche, and chicken legs. Public-interest groups rarely put on congressional receptions, and when they do, it's a jug-wine-and-cheese affair.

You don't believe that legislators can be influenced by things like this? To be sure, to a congressman the round of receptions is a dull fact of life, but let's face it, senators and congressmen like to be aggrandized, and a lavish reception carries that implication. The average legislator in Congress was not born to high status, but worked for it. Most emerged from jobs back home that were of no great stature. Few were rich, but many admired the rich and aspired to similar status by running for public office. Almost half the Senate and House members held another public office before running for Congress. Again almost half were lawyers, and almost a third were businesspeople. Others were farmers, ranchers, college teachers, and so forth.

The money thrown around by industrial lobbies is influential because it flatters a legislator to find that people and institutions that obviously have money want to associate with him. It's his entry into the high-status world. And there's a tacit inference that those who have money also have respectability. Therefore, when the oil companies come to call—after showing off their money on receptions, television and newspaper advertising, and well-dressed lobbyists—a legislator respects their facts and arguments more than those of the sport-coated public-interest lobbyists, who never make any display of wealth or status. This kind of influence is not rational, but it's a major factor in the decisions of many legislators.

Some legislators who came from wealthy families are also likely to succumb to lobbies that represent big money because they identify with them. However, other such legislators have been noted for their independence of moneyed interests, such as congressmen John F. Seiberling (Democrat of Ohio) and Richard L. Ottinger (Democrat of New York), Senator Claiborne Pell (Democrat of Rhode Island), and former senator James L. Buckley (Republican of New York). They aren't impressed by lobbies that throw around money because they themselves have seen far more money than any of the lobbyists ever will.

Reacting to the Issues

As a rule, members of the House stick closer to what they think are the views of their constituents than senators do, simply because the need to be reelected every other year overcomes any desire to stray far from the beaten path. Senators often show more independence of the electorate early in their six-year terms, and their greater prominence in the state gives them a little more room for independence, too. This difference was intended by the Constitutional Convention in 1787 that drew up the plan for the federal government. Indeed, the 1787 Constitution made this difference even greater in that senators were to be elected by the state legislatures rather than by direct popular vote as they are now, and thus insulated further from the public.

A pervasive factor that can counteract constituents' pressure is legislators' desire for "political capital," as political scientist Lewis Anthony Dexter has observed. This capital, Dexter says, consists of such things as publicity value, the ability to get political contributions or speaking dates, the respect of other legislators, or influence with the executive branch or with other politicians back home or in Washington. Senators and congressmen like to do things that will increase their political capital. This can influence not only their votes but their decisions to take the lead on various issues. Leadership on some issues can be seen to build up a congressman's political capital, while leadership on others, such as an unpopular cause that's clearly destined to lose, can represent an expenditure of one's political capital.

The easiest issues for senators and congressmen to react to are the local "bread and butter" issues that directly affect their states and districts and on which local citizens generally agree. (Traditionally these have included dams, irrigation projects, highways, federal buildings, and research centers. However, the rise of local citizen groups against pork-barrel projects has made these harder to handle.) They are easy to react to because they are seen as issues that will be good for the district, will make local people indebted to the legislator, will get him publicity, and thus will help him get reelected.

It is harder to get a legislator to react to national policy issues. The impact of these issues on his district is not known; it is not clear whether they can help or hurt him with his constituents and local politicians; and his position on them won't get him any big publicity back home. A legislator just can't see much political capital in taking stands on national issues, and he would rather avoid getting involved except when it's necessary to vote on the issue in committee or on the floor. Even at that, the House long resisted the move to have recorded votes on the most crucial decisions—those on amendments to bills—until 1971, when the record-teller vote was instituted, replaced two years later by electronic voting equipment. Legislators usually take a stand on national issues only when they've been convinced that there is political capital to be gained. Many of the tactics suggested in this book are designed to help you convince legislators of that with respect to your own issue.

Senators and congressmen are becoming more responsive to constituents' views because they are venturing outside the old circle of businesspeople and city-hall politicians. The decline of machine politics and straight-ticket voting (voting for all of one party's candidates on the ballot) and the more skeptical attitude of the public toward incumbents have forced legislators to relate more directly to their constituents. This has given individual citizens a far greater influence over their legislators' votes.

The competition for these votes is also increasing. Big business, which used to rely on the crony relationships between congressmen and top businesspeople in their districts, has mounted grass-roots campaigns on major issues to offset the grass-roots campaigns of citizen groups.

Real estate interests and land developers, for instance, mounted a highly successful grass-roots campaign that killed the National Land-Use Planning Act in 1974. Their campaign used farmers' organizations to spread the charge that the bill would place the federal government in the position of telling landowners what they could and could not do with their land. The campaign also got conservative groups to activate their members by telling them the bill was a communist-style move by the government to stifle private enterprise. Many House members had planned to support the bill as a means of giving farmers and landowners *more* control over their land against economic pressures that favored unwanted development. However, the outpouring of opposition letters stimulated by the grass-roots campaign tipped the balance, resulting in a 211–204 defeat on the House floor.

Some House members had been willing to try to correct the misinformation spread by the bill's opponents back home, but too many who favored the bill were afraid of the opposition or didn't want to make the effort required to counteract the misinformation. This campaign succeeded because it was a grass-roots campaign, in which individual citizens and local businesses wrote to their own congressmen and congresswomen, expressing their feelings on how the bill would affect them. The real estate lobby could never have killed the bill without that influence.

Some of the Old Guard senators and congressmen who were elected to Congress before the rise of the citizen-action movement may not know how to respond to citizens' pressure, because it's so new to them. An example was former congressman Sherman P. Lloyd (Republican of Utah), heir to an old tradition of dam building and road building in Utah. In 1972, Lloyd was pushing a controversial road plan drawn up by the state highway department that would cut a highway through a proposed wilderness area near Lake Powell in Utah, and he was encountering stiff opposition to the project from constituents in the urban parts of his district, which encompassed half the state. These protesting constituents wanted the area to be left wild. At one crucial juncture, when Lloyd was feeling the pressure as the November elections drew near, he was visited in his Washington office by David Raskin, one of the Utah citizen leaders against the road project. Raskin was prepared to discuss the issue once more to see if Lloyd would moderate his stance. But before Raskin could get a word in, Lloyd burst into an angry tirade against environmentalists in Utah—who did they think they were, why did they think they could argue with the state's project, and so on. As Raskin recalls, Lloyd couldn't seem to see any legitimate role for citizen-action groups; he obviously felt helpless and frustrated that they were making the issue (to him, so obviously an old-fashioned bread-and-butter issue) so difficult, and he was unable to respond to them. He made no move to compromise with Utah conservationists and instead got the House to mandate the road as part of the law establishing Glen Canyon National Recreation Area. Only two weeks later, Lloyd was defeated at the polls.

There are still many legislators like this in Congress—the last of the dinosaurs, who haven't adapted to the times. Most of them don't have to adapt because their names are so well known by voters that they'll be reelected until they retire or die. While they may not be able to respond to citizens' pressure or citizens' arguments, they may respond to the more traditional pressures that come from local politicians, businesses, campaign contributors, and old friends.

You can't tell how a congressman is going to vote on a given issue just by knowing that he's, say, a conservative Democrat or a moderate Republican. General ideology is not a good basis for prediction, because the congressman doesn't always vote his personal convictions; he has too many other influences at work on him.

Even if your congressman has usually opposed your views on the big issues reported in the news media, you still can't assume that he will oppose your present cause unless you've asked him to support your objective, applied a reasonable amount of pressure, and been rejected in spite of it all. Let's suppose you're working for an increase in the public housing program. You know that Congressman Williams is opposed to federal spending. But he may actually believe in expanding the housing program, or he may be influenceable by housing contractors in your community, by local antipoverty organizations, or by local politicians who represent the poor. Another possibility is that Congressman Williams may have become more receptive to your cause as a result of a close election, or because public housing is an issue that is now in vogue.

A legislator's general ideology may take an unexpected twist, too. Conservative Republicans were divided on the supersonic transport (SST) subsidy in 1971. Some of them were driven by their fiscal conservatism to oppose further federal spending on the SST, while other conservative Republicans were driven by their identity with big business to support the SST subsidy. You can't afford to write a legislator off because of his ideology. Even a rigid ideology may bend when enough citizen pressure is being felt.

Senators and congressmen are often influenced by favor trading. A legislator owes favors to many people back home who helped him get elected—campaign contributors, campaign workers, editorial writers, local politicians who endorsed him, and so on. Each one of these people has a pretty small claim on the legislator, but any significant number of them acting in concert can make themselves heard.

Within Congress, too, favors are traded. Several congressmen may vote with a friend just so he won't look silly voting all alone against a whopping majority. And often a legislator will approach another whose mind isn't quite made up and tip the scales by doing a favor or offering to do one—often involving a vote on another issue.

Respect for other legislators can also influence a congressman's vote. On legislation that is outside a congressman's area of expertise, he may look to certain members of the relevant committee for guidance. Senator Henry M. Jackson (Democrat of Washington) is looked to by many senators as a leader on energy policy; he is chairman of the Committee on Energy and Natural Resources. In the House, legislators interested in more aid to schools follow the lead of Congressman John Brademas (Democrat of Indiana) on education matters; he is the fourth-ranking Democrat on the Education and Labor Committee. This kind of influence becomes pertinent particularly when a last-minute amendment or compromise is being debated and few legislators have taken positions on it in advance. It can also be a problem when your congressman is making up his mind on your issue and is being approached by congressmen who oppose your cause, wooing his support. He can turn them down easily if he has had plenty of letters, phone calls, and visits from your cobelievers; and if he has learned from you how the issue affects his constituents. Then he can tell the other congressmen, "Sorry, but this is a hot issue in my district." In the absence of strongly expressed local support for your cause, it's all too easy for another, respected legislator to talk him into something.

Some senators and congressmen take a position for reasons other than personal conviction or the will of the voters. There are those who have backed legislation from which they would make a profit through their own business arrangements. It's called conflict of interest. Brent Blackwelder, lobbyist for the Environmental Policy Center, recalls the example of Congressman John T. Myers (Republican of Indiana), who owned land involved in one dam project he advocated in Indiana; he stood to gain from selling it at an inflated value after the project was built. Congressman J. J. Pickle (Democrat of Texas) was so embarrassed by news stories revealing his land interests in a similar water project that he did an about-face and got the project killed, according to Blackwelder.

There are legislators who are part-owners of radio and television stations, yet vote on legislation governing the broadcast industry. Outside business interests are commonplace, but they don't necessarily interfere with a legislator's lawmaking activities. The disclosure rules adopted by both houses in 1977 should curtail their influence, because all major financial interests must be disclosed annually by all members of the House and Senate.

As Pickle's case suggests, a legislator's position is not engraved in stone. At most, it's only on paper, with the impermanence that implies. A change in the pressures, a change in the credibility of the legislator's information sources, the emergence of new facts—many things can reverse a legislator's position.

Constant encouragement is always needed to sustain a legislator's commitment to a cause. Letters, personal visits, favorable publicity, and new facts can be a hedge against opponents' attempts to convert him. These can also be a way of keeping a legislator's attention from being attracted by other issues. He usually has ten or twenty issues in the air at the same time, and if you want some of his attention on your issue you'll have to work for it. This reinforcement also counteracts a congressman's tendency to pull his punches, to go easy in pushing your issue in order to keep the goodwill of opponents in Congress. This can be a problem because a congressman knows that his opponents on your issue may be his supporters on the next issue. He may unwittingly be catering to them by conceding too many points in a debate, or by compromising too soon.

Whatever the influence, a legislator likes to think he's voting his convictions. Even when he has a stack of letters on his desk urging him to vote against a given bill, the legislator will prefer to think he's voting against it because the facts led him to that conclusion. And this is only natural. His self-esteem would take a beating if he admitted to himself, "I don't really have any convictions on this. I'm just doing what people pressured me into." So, while congressional staff and lobbyists alike recognize pressure as an important factor in voting decisions, legislators themselves deny that it's significant.

How Laws Are Enacted

Enactment of a law is a long and tortuous process with many steps en route. Opponents of a bill try to stop it at each step or, failing that, try to weaken it every chance they get. Proponents therefore have to be active at each step, guarding against the opposition. With so many threats of compromise, a bill must be a strong expression of the proponents' desires when it is first introduced, because its opponents will whittle away at it throughout the legislative process.

To active citizens around the country, the most important steps—those that most influence whether a bill is going to be strong or weak, and whether it is going to be approved or rejected—in both House and Senate are: (1) its introduction by impressive sponsors and cosponsors; (2) its consideration by committee and subcommittee through hearings and markup sessions; and (3) the floor action. A detailed explanation of the legislative process appears in *How Our Laws Are Made*, by Charles J. Zinn, a booklet available free of charge from your senators or congressman. What follows is a summary of the process, emphasizing the steps most important to you in your efforts to win your legislators' support on a particular bill, resolution, or nomination. Other, more obscure, but crucial steps—especially in committee action and floor action—can only be handled by the legislators who are taking the lead for your viewpoint and by lobbyists on the scene in Washington. However, your efforts in connection with the major steps in the process will also influence these less obvious decisions.

Legislation can take the form of a bill or a resolution. Most issues are handled as bills, designated "H.R." followed by a number if it was first introduced in the House of Representatives, or "S." followed by a number if it was introduced in the Senate. Tax bills and appropriations bills can only originate in the House, but all others can start in either house of Congress.

Of three types of resolutions, the only one that is used to make laws is the joint resolution, designated "H.J.Res." with a number if it originated in the House, or "S.J. Res." if in the Senate. Joint resolutions follow the same process as bills.

To explore the legislative process, let's follow an imaginary bill as it is considered and finally enacted into law:

1. Introduction. The bill has been drafted by a congressman, by a citizen group, or by lobbyists, and it is introduced by the congressman when he places it in the "hopper" on the clerk's desk in the House chamber. The bill is assigned a number—let's call it H.R. 532—and copies are printed and made available a day or two later in the Document Room.

2. Consideration by committee. The bill is referred by the parliamentarian to the one of the House's twenty-two standing committees which has jurisdiction over the bill's subject—in this case, we'll suppose it goes to the Education and Labor Committee. The chairman of this committee may assign H.R. 532 to a subcommittee specializing in the issues raised by the bill. It is in committee or subcommittee that most of the decisions will be made—whether the bill is worth considering at all, what provisions to leave out, what to add, what to modify. Congressmen on the committee are familiar with the general subject, and some of the committee's professional staff spend full time working on education issues.

The referral of H.R. 532 to the committee and subcommittee is routine; all bills get this far, but few get any farther. If the committee and subcommittee chairmen find that the bill is supported by many congressmen and especially by members of the committee, and these supporters are asking for action on the bill, chances are it will be taken up. There are always more bills awaiting action than the committee can possibly handle, so there is usually a delay at this stage. A bill's opponents will take advantage of this, and try to make the delay permanent.

The first stage in a committee's work on H.R. 532 is analysis of the issue by committee staff to identify what the bill would do and what questions should be asked about it. Then hearings are scheduled by the subcommittee chairman. At hearings, the proponents and opponents present their arguments and their facts and subcommittee members ask them questions—many of them often prepared by the staff. If the hearings show strong support for the bill and reasonable arguments for it, and if the subcommittee members generally favor it, the subcommittee will hold "markup" sessions during which the subcommittee members go through the bill, making changes (amendments) to strengthen, weaken, or clarify it. Formal recorded votes may be taken on controversial amendments. These markup sessions are a crucial step in the legislative process. Neither the full committee nor the House will tinker with many of the decisions made by the subcommittee. At most, they will take up a few prominent issues, leaving the subcommittee's product largely intact.

The subcommittee then reports H.R. 532 to the full committee with amendments. Opponents may try to weaken the bill (or proponents may try to strengthen it) through amendments in full committee, or they may try to kill it altogether if they have more supporters here than they did in subcommittee. Votes taken in full committee can be among the most important in the life of a bill.

3. Reporting the bill to the floor. When the full Education and Labor Committee approves the bill, it is reported back to the House for floor consideration with the amendments written in by the committee. A committee report is drafted by the committee staff and scrutinized by the principal legislators involved. The report explains the purposes of the bill, presents the arguments and background information on it, and lists the cosponsors of the bill. If some committee members oppose H.R. 532 or want further amendments, they may submit "minority views" or "separate views," which will be included in the back of the report. The whole report is printed and distributed to each House member, and it is one of the most important sources of information to other House members who will be voting on the bill for the first time when it is considered on the House floor.

4. Bringing the bill up on the House floor. Most bills involving national policy issues must be brought up with a rule from the Rules Committee, specifying the time available for general debate and whether the bill is open to amendment (an open rule) or not (a closed rule, often used for complex tax bills). Some of the less controversial bills do not require a rule and are passed by unanimous consent or are considered under Suspension of the Rules, a procedure allowing only forty-five minutes of debate, permitting no floor amendments, and requiring a two-thirds majority to pass. Opponents may try to get the Rules Committee to delay the bill on grounds that it concerns more than one committee's jurisdiction. With our imaginary H.R. 532, they might claim that the bill should be referred to the Committee on Banking, Finance and Urban Affairs because it involves new programs with major impact on cities. Once the Rules Committee has granted the bill a rule, it is up to the speaker and majority leader to schedule the bill. Further delay can occur here if the House calendar is jammed and H.R. 532 is a highly controversial or complicated bill. Opponents will try to get the House leadership to delay it.

5. Floor action. H.R. 532 is now before the full House with the committee amendments incorporated. First comes a vote on adoption of the Rules Committee's proposed rule for consideration of the bill; some bills are killed by a negative vote at this point. Next comes general debate on the bill, with time divided equally between proponents and opponents. Then the bill is open for amendment, and each amendment may be debated. Amendments are usually decided by voice vote ("As many as are in favor say 'Aye'" and so forth)—in which case there is no record of who voted which way—or by recorded vote using the electronic system—in which case each legislator's vote is shown on a screen above the House gallery and a record of the vote is available the following day in the *Congressional Record.*

6. Passage. A motion to recommit the bill to committee may be made by its opponents; on the rare occasions when this motion passes, it kills the bill. Usually the bill goes right ahead to a vote on final passage. By this time most of the controversies have been resolved by amendment, and the vote on final passage therefore is not one of the most revealing votes as to a legislator's general stance on the bill. Frequently a congressman who fought for weakening amendments, even if he lost them, will turn around and vote for the bill on final passage, knowing that he can't stop the bill, so he might as well get some of the credit for passing it. This is why rating groups such as the Consumer Federation of America and League of Conservation Voters use few final-passage votes in their analyses of legislators' voting records.

7. Transmittal to the Senate. The House-passed version of H.R. 532 is delivered to the Senate by messenger.

8. Consideration by Senate committee. The Senate parliamentarian refers the bill to the appropriate one of the Senate's fifteen standing committees—in this case the Committee on Human Resources. The bill is assigned to a subcommittee and may be considered through hearings, markup sessions, and full committee sessions as we saw in the House.

9. Reporting the bill to the Senate floor. The bill is reported to the full Senate, and a committee report is printed, as in the House.

10. Bringing the bill up on the Senate floor. The Senate has no committee with the House Rules Committee's function of setting ground rules for debate on each bill, because the Senate has unlimited debate. The Senate majority leader decides when bills will be scheduled, and he can delay them if he's sympathetic to the opponents' viewpoint.

11. Senate floor action. H.R. 532 is debated by senators, and amendments are considered and voted upon. The Senate has no electronic voting system, so most decisions are made by voice vote or by roll call. Roll-call votes are printed in the *Congressional Record.*

12. Senate passage. The recommittal motion and the vote on final passage happen the same as in the House.

13. Return to the House. The bill is returned by messenger to the House, with any amendments the Senate has made. Let's say that H.R. 532 has had three major amendments adopted in the Senate.

14. Consideration of Senate version. The House votes to accept or reject the Senate amendments, usually following the recommendation of the House committee leaders who handled the original bill. This is seldom a crucial vote, and it is usually done by unanimous consent. In the case of H.R. 532, we'll imagine that the committee and subcommittee chairmen feel the Senate amendments are not acceptable. So the House by unanimous consent rejects the Senate amendments and requests a conference. The speaker appoints several House conferees from the membership of the committee that handled the bill, usually those suggested by the committee chairman.

15. Conference committee. Upon receiving the House's request for a conference, the Senate's presiding officer appoints Senate conferees, on the recommendation of the relevant committee chairman. The conferees from the two houses form the conference committee, and this committee meets to settle the differences between the two versions of the bill. We'll suppose that with H.R. 532

the conferees agree to accept two of the Senate amendments and they rewrite the third amendment to weaken it. These recommendations and an explanation of them are written up and printed as the conference report.

16. Approval of the conference report. The compromise version recommended by the conference committee is put to a vote by the House and Senate. Only in rare, highly controversial cases are conference reports rejected.

17. Transmittal to the President of the United States. The final approved text of the bill is signed by the speaker and the president of the Senate, and delivered by messenger to the President of the United States.

18. Approval or veto by the President. The bill is referred by White House staff to the affected departments for recommendations, and then the President may sign it into law or, within ten days after he received the bill, veto it. A vetoed bill can be enacted over the President's objection if two-thirds of each house vote to approve it; such veto-override votes must be by roll call.

19. Publication of the new law. The newly approved law is sent to the General Services Administration for publication. It is assigned a public law number beginning with the number of the present Congress—in the case of our imaginary bill, let's say Public Law 96–122. It is first printed as a "slip law," and copies are made available through the House and Senate document rooms. You may request copies from your own senators or congressman. Eventually the new law will be published in the Statutes at Large and in the United States Code, available in law libraries and large public libraries.

3

Correspondence with a Congressman

"Many people believe congressmen pay little or no attention to their mail. Wrong!" says former congressman Jerome R. Waldie of California. "There is no function more vital to a congressman than reading and replying to mail from back home. A congressman's constituents are literally his lifeblood. If they are pleased with him, they will support him in his next election. If he ignores them, he will lose their vote. It really is that simple."

Running for reelection every other year, a member of the House never stops campaigning. The leash is only a little longer for a senator, who has a six-year term. Both need and urgently seek the goodwill of the voters in preparation for the next election. "In most cases," says Waldie, "the only contact a legislator has with his constituents is by letter. These letters are the most important thing a congressional office deals with."

Surprisingly, many issues are decided by legislators who have received no mail on the subject or no more than a handful of letters. Your letter can be one of these few that give the congressman a push in the right direction. Although many legislators receive hundreds of pieces of mail every week, few are letters from individual citizens expressing their opinions and telling how the people at home would be affected.

"We get not much mail on the issues from our district, but lots of letters from corporations outside the district," says Nancy Mathews, legislative assistant to Congressman Richard L. Ottinger (Democrat of New York). "We don't always answer the corporate letters, but we try to answer all personal letters, even those from people outside our district." Even printed form letters are answered with a letter stating Ottinger's views on the issue raised.

Ottinger's administrative assistant, Oren Teicher, points out that Ottinger always must fight hard for reelection. "Coming from a heavily Republican district, we want as much contact as we can have with people," he says.

The feeling is universal on Capitol Hill that the mail provides the best link with the voters, and it's the mail from people who want the congressman to do something that has the greatest potential impact. If a letter is answered promptly and forthrightly, the voter is going to remember the congressman favorably. If the voter likes the congressman's response, he may tell friends about it and show the letter around. Senators and congressmen believe that a good word-of-mouth reputation gained from such contacts has more impact in the election than a spate of television spots or billboards.

The mail is so important that when a congressman's incoming mail from constituents drops off, he gets nervous and directs his staff to do something to stimulate more. This is a prime reason for the questionnaires periodically mailed to voters by many legislators. Hundreds of people not only check off their preferences to the prepared questions; they also send in opinion letters. Even a congressman's newsletter—usually a collection of his most inoffensive views—stimulates opinion mail. Says Oren Teicher, "Every time we send out our newsletter, we get 600 to 700 extra letters."

In the Congress of the United States, few seats are so safe that a senator or congressman can ignore what his constituents are telling him. Dozens of supposedly secure old legislators have been ousted in "upset" elections during the last ten years. This has given the survivors a healthy respect for public opinion. Newcomers also know they have to work to keep their seats.

As a result, the mail is being read and taken seriously. Many legislators read the letters themselves. Senator Gaylord Nelson (Democrat of Wisconsin) every day receives from his staff a folder full of letters from people in Wisconsin. The senator usually finds time during the day to look through the stack, reading some of the letters and skimming through others, before he passes the letters on to his issues staff to draft replies. Many another legislator receives far too much for him to read, but all opinion mail is read by the staff and reported to him.

While legislators' offices use many different methods of handling congressional mail, they have one thing in common: opinion mail is read, considered, and answered. Who reads it, how seriously it is considered, and how it is answered are variables that you can do something about.

How Legislators React to Letters

If you have an opinion on an issue, write immediately to your senators and your congressman. Remember that those who oppose your viewpoint undoubtedly are already making their views known.

Letters can have several different kinds of impact on a legislator's decisions. They can lead a congressman to take a position on a new issue, they can compel him to reverse a position he has already taken, or they can encourage him to renew his efforts in a position he has taken. They have a long-range impact in shaping his attitude toward related issues that come up months or years after you have written to him.

If a congressman is undecided on an issue, or has never had the issue brought to his attention, your letter may influence his thinking toward your viewpoint. If the mail is lopsidedly on your side, he'll probably adopt your position. For every letter he gets on an issue, he will assume that there are many other voters who agree with you but did not take the trouble to write.

"Even on the biggest issues, a single letter can stand out when it shows really thoughtful consideration of the subject," says the administrative assistant to a Midwestern congresswoman. "I would pull that letter out of the pile and give it right to the congresswoman."

On big national issues, such as gun control, the supersonic transport, or abortion, when the mail is heavy an individual letter will rarely get special attention unless it contains a new angle. But volume still has enormous impact.

If 90 percent of the letters are against gun control, a legislator will not lightly disregard the message. But if the legislator wanted to support gun control against those odds, he would get much-needed encouragement from every one of the letters in that 10 percent favoring gun control. No matter which side you might be on, your letter has impact. On the big issues your letter puts you in harness with many other people of similar beliefs. On the lesser issues, your letter will stand out and will influence the legislator's decision.

If a congressman receives letters opposing his position, he will be likely to reexamine his thinking and make sure he has some good answers to the questions raised. These opposition letters may at least persuade the congressman to soften his efforts on the issue or to be less obvious about it. Finally, such letters counteract support mail he is receiving from those who favor his stance.

Above all, a congressman tries to avoid a position that gets him in trouble with the voters. If he receives a short burst of letters opposing his position, he may glance at them and shrug them off. But if they keep coming, a few every day from different people back home, he can't keep ignoring them. This is how Congress was finally turned around on the war in Vietnam. When the letters and phone calls kept coming, week after week, the support for the war faded away.

Even if the opposition letters don't turn the legislator around on the issue that provoked your interest, they will make him and his staff think twice when the issue or related issues come up again. Most issues are never resolved for good. Many federal programs are authorized for a brief fixed term, often two to five years. Appropriations bills are enacted every year to provide money for all federal programs. The congressman's attitude on each of these recurrences of the issue will be affected by your earlier letters. If the congressman got a stack of letters from constituents opposing his position, he will want to avoid displeasing those voters the next time. Be sure to write again, when you know that action on the issue is coming up.

If letters support a position the congressman has already taken, they will strengthen him against opposition letters that your opponents will be writing to him. Support letters can encourage the legislator to be more active and outspoken on the issue. These letters can also give him new information on how the issue affects his congressional district, which he can use to gain the support of other legislators on the matter. If you write that bus service is so bad that it takes you two hours to get to work, he can use this fact to argue for more mass transportation funds in the next Department of Transportation appropriations bill.

If the letters raise an issue that has not yet been addressed by Congress, they may induce the congressman to take a position and, if necessary, possibly even introduce a bill on the subject. Early in 1976, Congressman Ottinger received several dozen letters from constituents taking strong exception to a petition that was rumored to be under consideration by the Federal Communications Commission (FCC) to ban religious programing on television. After having an aide look into the matter, Ottinger wrote back, saying that he would oppose such a ban and informing the writers that according to the FCC no such petition was under consideration. If the rumored petition should materialize as a serious issue in Congress, Ottinger could presumably be counted on for opposition to it because of this earlier commitment.

What Happens to Your Letters

A letter you write to your legislator most likely arrives at his office in the first mail delivery of the morning, at about eight o'clock, as part of a bundle a foot or so thick. The first staff member to arrive at the office finds this orphan bundle outside the door and brings it in. Subsequent deliveries at nine, eleven, and two o'clock bring smaller bundles.

The bundle is opened and the mail is sorted by a receptionist or mail clerk. In some offices the receptionist prepares a tally of the mail, identifying the number of letters pro and con each issue; in other offices this is left to the aides who handle the individual issues.

The amount of mail varies from office to office, ranging from about 150 pieces a week for some rural congressmen to as high as 12,000 pieces a week for senators from the most populous states. Opinion letters on issues or on legislation usually make up less than one-third of the total.

Senators' mail counts vary according to the population of the states and the tendency of people there to send in their opinions. In some regions, especially rural areas, people just are not yet in the habit of writing their senators about issues.

In the House of Representatives, the congressional districts are roughly equal in population, somewhere around 500,000. But there is still a great variation in the mail. "Suburban districts have the highest volume," says Jerome Waldie. "The urban districts have a low volume because where you have several congressmen from the same city, people often don't know who their congressman is. In the suburbs you have community newspapers that give the local congressman more coverage, so people know his name and write to him when they have a notion."

The volume of mail received by most congressional offices makes good staff work essential to get the mail read, answered, and reported to the legislator. The senator or congressman could not possibly handle it all himself and have time to perform his legislative duties.

Though in many offices the mail clerk refers incoming opinion letters directly to the issues staff, in others the top staffer—the congressman's right-hand man or woman—reads these letters first to gain an immediate impression of what political winds are blowing back home. Some letters are pulled out and routed to the congressman, but most go to the staff first.

In Congressman Ottinger's office the administrative assistant, Oren Teicher, gets the eight and nine o'clock mail dumped on his desk shortly after nine, in a foot-high stack of opened letters, Mailgrams, postcards, printed reports, newsletters, and magazines. He glances at each piece to see what it says—first looking at the return address to see if it is from Ottinger's congressional district—and then puts it in a pile for the staffer who handles the issue. Half an hour later Teicher has thirteen small piles of letters on his desk, one pile for the boss and piles for twelve staff members, some in the Washington office and others in Ottinger's three district offices.

The legislator's reply to most letters is drafted by the staff member who specializes in the field involved. This is easy enough when the congressman has already taken a position on the issue. When he has not taken a position, the staffer will recommend one and draft the letter accordingly, usually after researching the subject with a couple of quick phone calls to officials in the relevant federal agency or to the professional staff of a congressional committee. The drafts are typed up in final form, ready for the congressman's signature.

In a few House offices, particularly those of new legislators, the congressman reads all the mail and scribbles a note to the staff indicating the gist of the reply he wants drafted. This is educational for a new legislator, but it can't last as legislative responsibilities mushroom.

However, even the busiest legislators see some few letters and dictate replies. These come from persons the legislator knows well, people who use the legislator's first name, VIPs in the congressional district or state, and local politicians. Since most of us don't fall into these categories, we have developed other ways of getting the congressman's attention.

When a congressman is not particularly interested in the subject of your letter and has no position on it, the staffer handling your letter may refer it to the federal agency that covers the subject. The agency may reply by letter to the legislator, enclosing an extra copy which the legislator will send to you.

In many House offices the completed reply, along with the incoming letter, go straight to the congressman, who reads both and signs the reply or, if the staff draft is not up to snuff, writes in changes and sends it back for retyping. In many House offices the congressman sees all the mail.

There are also many House offices in which the legislator delegates more of the responsibility to his staff and does not insist on seeing the replies before they go out. In the Senate, the large volume of mail makes it impossible for all but a few senators to read all outgoing mail. In these cases the legislator's signature is signed by a top staffer or by an automatic pen, dubbed "Mr. Siggie" by irreverent staffers.

Congressman Ottinger, for instance, signs about one in ten letters, and his administrative assistant signs the others—many of them duplicates of ones Ottinger signed before. When a letter involves a new policy position, Ottinger signs it himself. Even when he doesn't do the signing, he sees a copy of every letter that is mailed, and he often scribbles instructions on the copy for follow-up by the staff.

When a reply has been mailed, a copy is generally filed in the subject file along with your letter. In many offices, a copy of the reply is filed in a master correspondence file under your name, so that when you write again the staff can check to see what subject you previously wrote about and where to find that earlier correspondence.

Automatic Answering Machines

Automation has greatly improved the handling of congressional correspondence. Before automatic typewriters came into widespread use, it was often hard to get a real answer from a legislator. Nowadays you may not get a personal answer, but you do more often receive a reply that tells you the legislator's position on the matter. Automatic typewriters and computers have made it far easier for legislators to keep in touch with their constituents.

Legislators use the automatic typewriter on issues that involve a large volume of correspondence. An aide to one Midwestern congresswoman says, "We may do three hundred letters on issues like abortion or the Land Use Bill. The congresswoman determines what the response will say."

The procedure is pretty much the same in other offices. When a volume of letters starts coming in on an issue, the staffer handling the subject drafts a "roboletter" (so named after one brand of automatic typewriter, the Robotype), which is read and if necessary rewritten by the legislator, then given to the machine operator. The operator puts the text of the letter on punched paper tape or magnetic tape cassette, depending on the type of equipment.

Thenceforth whenever letters come in on the same subject that can be answered by this roboletter, the operator puts the writers' names and addresses on a second tape, the two tapes are put on the machine, and the machine types up the letters in jig time, error-free. Some legislators sign the roboletters themselves, but many have them signed by staff or by "Mr. Siggie."

Different roboletters are often used to answer pro and con letters on the same subject. A writer who agrees with the congressman's position gets one that says, in effect, "I couldn't agree with you more." The person who opposed his position receives one that says, "Apparently we disagree on this issue" or a vaguely worded letter intended to duck the issue. A frequent gaffe on Capitol Hill occurs when the "pro" roboletter is sent to a list of "con" citizens, or vice versa. If you wrote your congressman to urge enactment of a gun-control law and you got an answer that said, "It is greatly encouraging to know that you join me in opposition to the insidious move to confiscate our firearms in the guise of gun control," you can bet that somebody put the wrong tape on the machine.

Roboletters are also used to let constituents know of progress on a bill they wrote in about. Since the passage of most bills is not covered in the newspapers, you'll probably read about it first in a letter from your senator or congressman.

A more sophisticated method of handling correspondence is being used in several Senate offices—a computer-based "office correspondence system." Senator Mark O. Hatfield (Republican of Oregon) uses this system. To answer a constituent's letter, Hatfield's staff aides refer to a handbook of standard Hatfield paragraphs on many subjects and fill out a form with the code numbers of the paragraphs desired, possibly adding a sentence or two to refer specifically to the incoming letter. The computer operator processes the form, and the computer and its automatic typewriter spew out the letter, which is signed by automatic pen and dispatched to the recipient. (Many of Hatfield's replies are sent as Mailgrams.)

It's not like mingling with the mighty, but it certainly beats getting a noncommittal answer or no answer at all—unless, of course, the paragraphs selected by the staff are noncommittal paragraphs.

The mail is reported to legislators in several different ways. Some offices keep a weekly tally by subject. In most offices, the mail is summarized by the staff member who handles the issue.

Aides to one Eastern senator report the mail in their staff memos to the senator or in oral briefings, telling him the content and the character as well as the raw numbers pro and con. One aide says, "On the toxic substances bill, for instance, I'd tell him, 'We got four hundred letters in favor of the bill, all but twenty-five of them obviously stimulated by membership in environmental groups.'"

Even the last-minute letters and Mailgrams may be reported. The aide says, "On the way over for the vote I'd tell him, 'We got fourteen phone calls in the last hour in favor of the bill,' or whatever."

Before a major vote, Congressman Robert B. Duncan (Democrat of Oregon) has his staff give him a report on how the mail stacks up, how local organizations line up on the issue, and whom he knows back home who has taken an interest in the matter.

Most reports on the mail contain at least a concise statement of how many letters were in favor, how many opposed. Beyond that, what is reported depends on the nature of the mail. If many of the letters show a hostile, abusive attitude, the staff will be sure to report that, and it quickly undermines the influence of these letters. If most of the letters repeat the same text or the same stereotyped list of arguments, the staff will report that, too. The greatest influence comes about when the staff can tell their legislator that the mail is from individual citizens who are serious about the subject and are putting real thought into their letters.

Organized Letter Writing

Members of Congress often deplore letter-writing campaigns that have been directed at them, or against a bill they favor. They call the resulting letters "pressure mail" and claim not to be influenced by it. Yet when the shoe is on the other foot, and legislators need mail to win other legislators' support for their own bills, they come to citizen leaders, imploring them to turn on the letters.

Former congressman Waldie says, "I've seen issues turned around by the mail, and some of that was what I'd call ineffective mail." Waldie recalls the postcard campaign waged by a group called Americans Against Union Control in 1975 against the Job Security Bill. The organization, part of an effort to break the influence of labor unions' union-shop rules, distributed postcards already printed with the opposition message, which were signed and mailed by citizens to their own congressmen. Many congressional offices received 200 to 300 of these cards, signed by their own constituents. The result: the bill was killed.

"When you get three hundred messages from your district, even if it's postcards, you pay attention!" says Waldie.

No doubt many legislators would like to see an end to organized letter writing, but all are vitally aware of it and are concerned about the voters who send it. A congressman knows that behind a letter campaign is an organization with strong views on an issue and with members or adherents who are likely to remember his position on this issue in the next election. If they disagree with his position they may vote against him and bad-mouth him among their friends. If they are on his side they may vote for him, talk him up, and even help with volunteer work in the campaign.

If there were no letter-writing campaigns, the average citizen's voice would not be heard in Congress. The only elements of society that don't make much use of letter campaigns are those that can afford to make fat campaign contributions—primarily big business interests and the wealthy.

Letter-writing campaigns vary in effectiveness. In a well-planned letter campaign, the organization will tell its members what is the best time to write to congressmen on a given issue. Then it's up to you to write your letter effectively.

Congressman Ottinger's aide, Oren Teicher, points to an inch-thick stack of telegrams that have just arrived from constituents, 100 of them with the same message, word for word, urging Ottinger to support full funding of foreign aid for Israel. These will be answered with a roboletter to each person, Teicher explains, with an enclosed copy of Ottinger's floor speech on the subject. Since Ottinger agrees with their position, the telegrams will buttress his stance and give him an opportunity to keep in touch with 100 potential voters. But the fact that all were identical shows that none of the 100 signers was putting much thought into the issue, merely signing a text written by somebody else.

Teicher relates a contrasting incident. Ottinger received some 250 identically worded letters opposing the Child and Family Services Bill, which he supported. In looking through them, Teicher realized that all were from only two out of the fourteen communities in Ottinger's district—Ossining and Mamaroneck. "It was clearly organized, because no letters came from the rest of the district," Teicher notes. "It didn't represent a groundswell of opposition, but probably no more than a couple of dedicated opponents who talked their friends and neighbors into sending these letters. If we had gotten *different* letters from two hundred fifty people all over our district opposing the bill, it would have been a whole new ball game."

Industries have often tried to use the form-letter approach, with a different twist. They send out a standard text and ask their member companies to type it on their own letterhead and send it to their own congressman.

Printed postcards have been used extensively by opponents of gun-control legislation as part of their many-faceted campaign. Printed up by the thousands, these cards contain a brief message urging the legislator to oppose gun control, with space for the sender to fill in his signature and address. Distributed by antigun-control activists, especially in states where hunting and guns are part of the prevalent life-style, the cards are made available in places like dentists' waiting rooms or barber shops. In 1975 and 1976, these cards dribbled into congressional offices, a few each day, over a six-month period. While the cards did not show any individual thought on the subject, their persistence and cumulative volume made an impact on legislators and staff over a long period of time in a way that a short burst of printed postcards could never equal. This is only one of many tactics used in the campaign against gun control, and could never do the job alone.

Coupons printed in an advertisement, to be clipped and mailed to a congressman, have about the same impact as printed letters or postcards.

Congressional offices also receive many petitions. According to the conventional wisdom on Capitol Hill, a petition conveys the opinion only of the person who first wrote its text, since it is supposedly easy to get people to sign something they even vaguely agree with. Petition signatures are rarely acknowledged by legislators. Yet when a petition drive is well organized and persistent, it can have an impact, too, as part of a larger effort.

Organized mail is hardest for the senator or congressman to ignore if it consists of individual letters, telling the legislator what the issue means to you or your community. A legislator knows that people who have put their own thoughts into a letter are serious about the issue and won't be likely to forget it at election time.

4

Writing Your Letters

Ten Ways to Write Your Congressman

Every letter to a congressman counts. It takes only a minute or two to write one. Yet you can be much more influential by following these simple and time-tested rules for your letter:

1. Make it a page or less, covering only one subject, written in your own words and including thoughts of your own. It takes more time to condense your ideas into a single page, but it's worth it if you want to be read. Handwritten letters on dime-store stationery are just as influential as letters handsomely typed on expensive stationery.

2. When your letter concerns a bill already being considered in Congress, refer to the bill by its number and name, if you know them.

3. Tell the legislator exactly what you want him or her to do, and give your reasons for adopting this position. Stress how the issue can affect people in your congressional district or state, and cite your own experiences and observations.

4. Ask the legislator to tell you his position on the matter: "Will you support this legislation?" or "Will you oppose this legislation?"

5. Show your awareness of the legislator's past actions. If possible, cite an instance of his recent voting on related issues.

6. Don't mention your membership in a citizens' organization. Legislators usually know the organization's position already. The individual citizen's letter is more influential than the letter obviously inspired by an organization.

7. Don't send in a form letter or preprinted postcard unless you absolutely can't take the time to write your own letter, because a form letter has less than one-tenth the impact of the one you write.

8. Don't repeat slogans or phrases from a newsletter or form letter. *Your own words* will make the crucial difference.

9. Write to your legislators at these addresses. (If you don't know the names of your senators and your congressman, call the information desk of your local public library.)

Senator Samuel Smith	Congressman John Jones
U.S. Senate	(or Congresswoman Jean Jones)
Washington, D.C. 20510	House of Representatives
	Washington, D.C. 20515

10. When the legislator replies, write a follow-up letter to reemphasize your position and give your reaction to the congressman's answer.

Congressional mail gets varying levels of attention, from the low attention given to form letters and petitions to the high attention given to people the legislator has met in person. When you want to influence the outcome of an issue by writing to your senators or your congressman or congresswoman, your tactical objective is to attain the highest possible level of attention. You can increase the attention given to your letter in many ways.

When and How Often to Write

Write your congressman whenever the notion strikes you, but don't write too often. Once a month is a good rule. If you write more often, congressional staff will start referring to you contemptuously as a "pen pal," and you will be taken less and less seriously.

You naturally will want to write before the legislator has to take action on the issue, and as early as possible in congressional deliberations on it, so that you encourage the legislator to take the right position before the opposition gets to him. Many votes have been determined simply by the fact that one side swung into action before its opponents knew what was happening. The best time to write is when you first learn that Congress is going to consider the issue, when little mail on the issue is being received by legislators.

The authors of this book strongly urge you to become a member of citizen groups active on legislative issues that concern you. Such organizations, through their publications, will tell you when to write to your member of Congress. The big decisions are often on inconspicuous details of a bill. If you wait to read about it in your local newspaper, you're not likely to hear anything until it's all over, because only the final decisions are "news" to most daily papers.

Whom to Write To

You are represented in Congress by two senators and one congressman or congresswoman. These three legislators have an obligation to consider your views. Don't be reluctant to write just because you believe a legislator is against everything you stand for. If you remain silent, you leave the field open to your opponents, and the legislator may get the idea that everybody back home agrees with them. Many crucial votes have come from the most unexpected legislators, because people on the losing side assumed they would follow the same old rut. This was a factor in the defeat of the supersonic transport (SST) subsidy in 1970 and 1971. Advocates of the SST program wrongly asssumed that they had the votes of several key Republican senators because they had supported the project before and because the Republican Administration favored it. Instead, the weight of public opinion led these senators to oppose the program.

You have three federal legislators to whom to express your views. The other 532 Senate and House members have no strong obligation to you, because they are not elected by you. Usually, if you write to a senator from another state or to a congressman whose district you don't live in, your letter will only be glanced at and then will be referred to one of your own senators or to your congressman.

But there are exceptions. When an issue that concerns you is being considered by a congressional committee or subcommittee of which your own legislator is not a member, feel free to write to legislators on the panel from elsewhere in your state or from neighboring states, and to the chairman and ranking Republican member of the panel. Your letter won't be as influential with these legislators, but it may shed new light on how the issue affects your region, and it probably will be answered. If convenient, send a copy to your own congressman or your senators so they will get the benefit of your views, since the measure will probably be coming to the House and Senate floors later on. Indicate that you are sending these copies by writing at the bottom of your letter "copy to Congressman ————." Letters to committee members will also convey the impression of widespread interest in the measure. Another exception is when a congressman from another part of your state is being mentioned as a candidate for a statewide office such as senator or governor.

Some legislators have become specialists in certain subjects, either out of personal interest or because the subject is important to their state or congressional district. An example is Congressman John Brademas (Democrat of Indiana), who is a national leader on education policy. Such specialists welcome, and answer, letters on their particular subjects from people all over the country, and from their correspondence often get new ideas or new information to support measures they are working on. You will find the names of such specialists by reading publications of citizen groups in your field of interest; look for the legislators who regularly take the lead on your issues as sponsors of major bills and as spokesmen for your viewpoint in speeches and articles.

The Format

Letters can be either handwritten or typed; it makes no difference as long as they are easily legible. (If you are writing as an official spokesman for an organization, be sure to use letterhead and typewriter; these signify the stature of your organization.)

Keep your letter short! If it's typed, hold it to one page, because anything more gets less attention. "There is no capacity in the average congressional office to read two-page, single-spaced letters," warns former congressman Jerome Waldie (Democrat of California). "At first I read all correspondence that came in, but I learned that I could not read two-page letters. When I got a two-page letter, I put it in the pile for the staff to read." If a letter is too long it usually is sidetracked into a "Read later" stack, sometimes not to emerge for days or weeks—often too late.

On the other hand, an assistant to one East Coast senator says, "Don't stop at one page if you have more to say that will really help, especially if it's about local impact." But don't go over one page if it's just more arguments repeated from a newsletter.

One way to convey more detailed information than a one-page letter will hold is to attach a page or two of background information. Give it a good, sound title, such as "Background on the Day Care Centers Program," "Resource Memo on H.R. 1234," or "How Stream Pollution Affects Crawfordsville." In this way you put into a short letter the meat of your position and what you want the legislator to do, and also provide more complete information that may be needed by the legislator or his staff. This technique is particularly useful when an issue is new and legislators have not yet heard much about it, when the legislator is a "freshman," or when you have a great amount of solid information on how the issue affects your community. Be sure to put your name and address on the background memo.

Treat only one subject in your letter. This ensures that it will be seen by the right staff member. If you try to cover six different issues in one letter, even if they are all in the same general field, your comments on four or five out of six may never be seen by the staffers who handle those topics. As a result, your comments on those issues will not be considered or tallied.

It doesn't much matter how you address your senator or congressman as long as you're civil about it. Time-worn usage is to address such a personage as "The Honorable," abbreviated to "Hon." But if you think this is laying it on too thick, or if you feel that the legislator is not very honorable, consider using any of the following: Senator John Jones, Congressman Sam Smith, Congresswoman Jane Doe, or Representative Jean Roe. The legislators won't even notice the difference.

Standard salutations to choose from, all equally correct, are:

Senate	House of Representatives
Dear Senator Jones:	Dear (Mr., Ms., Miss, Mrs.) Smith:
Dear Senator:	Dear Congressman Smith:
	Dear Congresswoman Smith:
	Dear Representative Smith:
	Dear Congressman:
	Dear Congresswoman:
	Dear Representative:

If you have met the legislator and feel you can use his or her first name, go right ahead because this will get more attention for your letter.

Setting the Stage

When you bring up the subject of your letter, be specific. Legislators and their staffs handle dozens of issues every day, and more than 20,000 bills are introduced in Congress every two years. Vagueness in your letter will usually result in delay and an equally vague reply, and is likely to cool the staff's receptivity to your opinions.

If you're writing about a bill already being considered in Congress, mention the popular name of the bill ("the education appropriations bill" or "the humane trapping bill") and, if you know it, the bill number ("S. 123," "H.R. 39"). Only if you lack these identifying data should you resort to general description, such as "a bill that would prevent the sale of national wildlife refuges." Such a description means that a staff member will have to make a phone call or two just to find out what bill you're referring to.

If your letter doesn't concern a bill but is about a recent action, event, or decision, be as precise as possible. Mention the date of the action and what agency or individual took it. This makes it easier for the legislator's staff to research the issue and thus easier for the legislator to take a position and assist you. Regrettably, some citizen organizations' newsletters and magazines are sloppy about dates, often citing events as "recent" or "in early February." Don't be shy about demanding greater precision from the editors. It's important to be precise in dealing with legislators and government officials because you save time and avoid misunderstanding; you also show that you're knowledgeable.

Show Your Awareness

It's easy for a legislator to look the other way when a staffer says, "We got a hundred letters in favor of a veto override on the education bill, but not many of them showed any real understanding of the situation."

In contrast, the legislator takes serious note when the staff member says, "We got a hundred letters in favor of a veto override on the education bill, and they're obviously from well-informed people who know your record on the issue."

Whenever you can, work into your letter a reference to something the legislator has done or said on the same subject or on a related issue. This indicates that you and the people interested in your issue are politically aware. Since you remembered the congressman's past performance, you won't be likely to forget what he does on the matter you're now writing about, either. Put this point in the body of the letter, rather than at the start, so your letter won't be routed to the wrong staff member. For example:

> Please vote for the tough Clean Air Bill reported to the floor by the Senate Public Works Committee. Your vote to allow the Concorde SST to land at U.S. airports was a disappointing action, because it will mean worse noise and air pollution. We've got to hold the line and, indeed, reduce the present pollution, as our own experience here in Centerville shows. A tough Clean Air Bill, without weakening amendments, will help us in our city by . . .

Sometimes your reference will be to an earlier vote on the same issue. For instance:

> Programs for the handicapped and disadvantaged children in our city schools are going to be cut back unless federal education funds are increased this year. I know you voted to sustain the President's veto of the education appropriations bill last year, and I was greatly surprised at that. I hope you will vote for full funding this year, because . . .

Perhaps you have no information at hand on the congressman's past record. But what has he said in the newspapers recently, or in his newsletter, or on radio or television? What can the public library's information desk dig up on his statements in the last six months? If he said something even remotely connected with your issue, you will gain by mentioning it.

For example, if he was lambasting federal spending and you are advocating a program that needs increased federal funds, don't despair! You can write him:

> I read your comments in the *Daily Tribune* today in which you urged cutbacks in federal spending. We certainly have to set priorities better so as to put money into the programs that really benefit the people. I want to ask you to vote for increased funds for the community mental-health centers program—at least $350 million, because . . .

Or, if the congressman was quoted as criticizing the President for budget cuts that are insensitive to citizens' needs, you can say:

> Your comments quoted in the *Morning News* really hit the nail on the head. The President is undermining the programs that help people the most. An example is this year's slash in the community mental-health centers program, which has helped thousands of people in our city. I urge you to vote for at least $350 million for this program, because . . .

Of course, the most telling things to mention are those that are closest to the topic of your letter, because these facts will stress the seriousness of your interest in the main topic.

It is worthwhile to keep a modest file of the legislator's public rhetoric, as quoted in newspapers from time to time, so you can quote it back to him. Suppose you're fighting to stop a proposed dam in his congressional district; you'll want to save anything he has said in favor of reducing government spending and quote it later in your letters, as in the following:

> Please oppose the Lost Creek Dam. Last October 20 during the election campaign you were quoted in the *Tribune* as saying, "It's time to stop the federal spending spree and return to the era of self-reliance." An obvious first step in halting the "spending spree" is to stop this absurd dam project, which would waste millions of

tax dollars, flood thousands of acres of productive farmland, and cause serious damage to the fishing. . . .

Your familiarity with the main subject of your letter, and with its current status in Congress, will also impress the legislator and his staff. Most opinion mail shows no such knowledge and contains little beyond a blunt request, as in the following:

Dear Congresswoman:
    Please support H.R. 5193 to enlarge the Redwood National Park.
Sincerely yours,
John Smith

Show your political awareness by mentioning recent congressional action on the issue. News media or public-interest newsletters can give you such information, and don't forget that great resource, the library. Consider this rewrite of the previous example:

Dear Congresswoman:
    Please actively support H.R. 5193, to enlarge the Redwood National Park. The hearings on this bill by the House Interior and Insular Affairs Committee on April 8 showed that logging on adjoining timber-company land is causing erosion and destroying trees inside the national park. If we fail to enlarge the park now, it will mean . . .
    I ask you to show your support by cosponsoring H.R. 5193 and submitting a statement for the hearing record. Please let me know what you will do on this.
Sincerely yours,
John Smith

When awareness of this kind is evident in many letters on an issue, the legislator and staff will quickly notice it. Such sophisticated, aware constituents can't be shrugged off as the one-liners can.

Ask for Action

    "Telling a congressman your opinion without asking him for specific action only invites him to find the most impressive way of doing nothing," says Marion Edey, a former House staff member who now heads the League of Conservation Voters. He may answer you, saying he agrees, but agreement with your opinion is not a commitment to vote yes or no on any particular bill or on the amendments that often make the difference between a good bill and a bad one.

If you write to one of your senators to complain that air pollution is making your neighborhood unlivable, he may agree and send you his latest speech against air pollution. But that doesn't commit him to any particular vote on the specific issues that must be decided by the Senate in adopting the Clean Air Act.

Speeches couched in generalities are great crowd-pleasers, and legislators rely on them to avoid bringing up more specific concerns that might turn on some people and turn off others. A generality can be interpreted to mean what each person wants it to mean. One often-heard generality, the cry to "reduce federal spending," to one person can imply cutting the military budget, and to another imply reducing the education and welfare budget.

Ask the legislator to do something specific. If you want him to vote for a certain bill, tell him so. But if he only votes for it, he is not doing much. By the time of the final vote to pass a bill, most of the controversies have already been resolved. The times when a legislator's support is most important are: (1) when the bill has newly been introduced and needs a showing of support to persuade the relevant committee to schedule hearings; (2) during deliberations of the committee; and (3) during floor debate, when weakening amendments are proposed by the bill's opponents.

These are some of the most effective ways you can ask a senator or congressman to support a bill; choose from among them, depending on the current status of the bill that concerns you:

1. Ask the legislator to cosponsor the bill. Cosponsorship simply shows that the legislator favors the bill as written, with the realization that it probably will be modified later as hearings and committee discussion bring new views and new information to bear on the subject. Cosponsors can be added at any time before the bill is reported to the floor; in the Senate, additional cosponsors are added to the original bill, while in the House the lead sponsor must introduce an identical bill with a new number carrying the names of additional sponsors.

The importance of cosponsorship lies in its influence on the committee that must consider the bill and in its effect on other members of the House and Senate. If a bill has a long list of co-sponsors of both political parties and from every state, the committee will get the message that the bill has broadly based support. If a bill has only a handful of sponsors, predominantly from one party or from one or two regions of the country, the committee will tend to regard it as unimportant and not likely to be approved on the floor. When a bill looks like a loser, no committee will devote time to hearings or markup sessions on it.

The list of cosponsors appears in the committee report when a bill is reported to the House or Senate floor. Legislators who were not on the committee and now are deciding how to vote on the bill will peruse the list to see whether legislators they generally agree with are cosponsoring it. The lead sponsors of the bill and citizen groups that favor it will also use the list to organize support for the floor debate, asking cosponsors to make speeches or buttonhole other legislators privately to seek their support. This is a vital function, because most bills involve floor amendments, either to strengthen the committee version of the bill or to gut it. The outcome on most proposed amendments is strongly affected by on-the-spot influence of one legislator on another, and the cosponsors can be the first line of support for those who favor the bill.

2. If no hearings have yet been held, **ask the legislator to request hearings on the bill.** This request is directed to the chairman of the committee or subcommittee to which the bill has been referred, because it is the chairman who controls the committee agenda. When a bill is being held without action by a committee, as often happens, requests from many legislators will help induce the chairman to schedule hearings, the first step in a committee's deliberations on a bill. If no legislators have asked for hearings, usually none will be held and the bill will go nowhere. The lead sponsor normally makes a request for hearings, but similar requests from other legislators will add weight.

A congressman need not have a strong commitment to a bill to request hearings on it, because hearings are basically a fact-finding forum, in which the committee explores the pros and cons of the bill as presented by witnesses representing different viewpoints. Hearings may involve testimony by other legislators, federal agency spokesmen, citizen groups and interested citizens, expert witnesses such as scientists or economists, and industry spokesmen. A request for hearings, while implying support for the bill, is really only asking the committee to get the facts on the measure.

If a legislator takes you up on this suggestion, he will usually send you a copy of his letter to the committee or subcommittee chairman. At this point, it is quite reasonable to ask the legislator to follow up by speaking to the chairman in person to reemphasize the request. One subcommittee chairman, Congressman Roy A. Taylor (Democrat of North Carolina), summed it up in 1974 when he told a group of conservationists, "We don't usually hold hearings until the affected congressmen corner me and ask for them."

3. Once the hearings are over, you can **ask the congressman to urge the committee to report the bill out.** After hearings, it is easy for a bill to fade into oblivion. There is no requirement that a committee take action on any bill; the burden of initiating action is always on those who favor the bill. If the committee members are generally against it—even though a majority of the full House or Senate may favor it—the committee can pigeonhole the bill without fear of contradiction. Procedures do exist to dislodge bills without committee approval, but these are rarely used successfully because too few legislators are willing to go against the will of the committee chairmen.

Delays after the hearings are therefore a serious danger. A legislator at this stage can write or speak to the chairman and members of the committee or subcommittee, asking for favorable action. This is regularly done by senators and House members who have an axe to grind—sometimes a major industry back home wants the bill, or sometimes it's a bill that will make the legislator look good to his constituents. Legislators who are advocating the general public interest do not make enough use of this direct approach to committee members. Your legislators should be urged to do it, presenting information on how the measure affects the people in their state or congressional district.

Your legislator's personal conversations with committee members are far more effective than letters to them, but of course he won't be able to send you any proof that he did speak to them as you asked.

4. When the bill is reported out for action on the floor, if opposition or hostile amendments are expected, you can **ask your legislator to speak with other congressmen,** seeking their support for the bill without weakening amendments. You can ask him to make a speech expressing his position.

You should be aware of a congressional dodge: many of the speeches printed in the *Congressional Record* were simply handed in rather than presented aloud. You can be sure that those headed "Extensions of Remarks" were not given orally. Many other unspoken speeches appear without this heading but with a large black dot (a printer's "bullet") before and after. If published a day or more ahead of time, these phantom speeches can be influential because legislators and staffers will read them. But if they are just handed in during the debate, they are purely for the benefit of constituents, since no one in the debate will know what position your legislator took.

5. Finally, and actually of least impact, come the votes on the bill. Always **ask your congressman to vote for the bill** and against weakening amendments. Also ask him to urge others to do so. Remember that in voting a senator is only one of 100 and a congressman one of 435. When a legislator takes one of the supportive actions listed above, he may increase his impact by helping to gain the votes of other, uncommitted legislators. Instead of having just one vote, he may have ten or twenty through his influence on others.

If you are opposing a bill that has been introduced in Congress, there also are ways you can persuade your legislators to help:

1. If no hearings have been held, **ask your legislator to write to the committee chairman** voicing his opposition to the bill. This action will register his position just as effectively as cosponsorship registers support. When opposition is expressed by many legislators, a chairman tends to be dissuaded from even holding hearings. Since opponents' names do not appear on a bill, as cosponsors' do, another effective action your legislator can take at this early stage, trying to head off committee action, is to write or speak to the committee members, seeking their help against the bill.

2. When the hearings are over, you can **ask the congressman to urge the chairman and committee members to reject the bill.**

3. If the bill is reported out by the committee, you can **ask the congressman to speak with other legislators** and seek their help in opposing the bill during floor debate.

Presenting Your Arguments

When you write a letter about an issue that is already being considered by Congress, it is unnecessary and impractical to include every argument that can be cited to support your position. The congressman has probably heard most of the arguments already. So include those that you feel are unique, that are most important to you, or that you think will best get the point across to your congressman, always stressing how the issue affects your locality or state.

The impact of a bill on your congressional district or state is of primary concern to your congressman and senators because the people affected are the people who elect them. Legislators are accustomed to handling issues on the basis of their impact back home. Every industry lobbyist knows this. On many issues, industrial lobbies in Washington send out the word to business firms asking them to contact their own legislators. The oil industry asks its local distributors, heating-oil dealers, and gas station owners to write to their legislators. The constant message to the congressmen is what these businesspeople think the bill will do to them and their communities.

Individual citizens can use the same approach, because senators and congressmen listen attentively to local-impact arguments. This can be easy to do when the issue is a national one. With federal aid to education, for example, it's easy to relate the issue to your city schools or your children. When the issue involves a part of the country remote from yours, the connection may not be as clear, but analogy and precedent can bring the issue home.

For instance, in 1966 and again in 1974 Congress considered and ultimately rejected the Bureau of Reclamation's proposal to build two dams in the Grand Canyon. Conservationists around the country writing to their legislators pointed out that if dams were allowed to intrude on one of our greatest national parks, then all other national parks could be threatened by dams, including those in the legislator's own part of the country. The argument was also made that the dam project would waste federal funds contributed by all the nation's taxpayers.

Use arguments that will appeal to the congressman's general philosophy. This means using common sense. If your congressman is a black liberal, you wouldn't do your cause much good by quoting George C. Wallace as an authority. If you have a senator who doesn't give a hoot about the environment but brags about his efforts as a watchdog of the Treasury, the way to get him interested in opposing a dam is to stress the wasted money. But of course make your environmental point, too, if that is your primary concern.

Citing local VIP opinion on the issue can help. If your newspaper publishes an editorial supporting your position, mention it in your letter and enclose a copy. For example:

> The *Daily News* just this week praised our local day-care centers program in the enclosed editorial. This good work is going down the drain unless the Day-Care Centers Bill is passed, because our city can't continue even the modest pilot program unless federal funds come through.

If a radio or television editorial is broadcast, call the station and ask for a copy, then send it to your congressman with your letter. If a state senator, mayor, or county supervisor has commented favorably on the issue, mention it.

Your awareness of national expert opinion on the issue can also make an impression. Suppose you favor legislation to bar fluorocarbon gases from use as spray-can propellants. When you read in the newspaper that a National Academy of Sciences panel has concluded that these gases are a threat to the earth's ozone radiation shield, you can mention this in your letter to the congressman and urge him to get a copy of the report and read it. Few congressmen will do so, but your mention of the new data may be followed up by his staff. Your letter alerts the legislator to the existence of this new information on the issue, and it shows him that you are well informed on the issue and therefore likely to remember what he does or doesn't do.

On issues that are already being considered before you write, your objectives are to register your opinion, show your seriousness, and insofar as possible link the issue to your congressional district or state.

When you are raising a *new* issue that your congressman is not likely to have heard about, your objectives include an additional one: to explain the basic arguments, preferably through a background paper or briefing sheet attached to your letter.

Ask for the Legislator's Position

Whenever you're writing to your senator or congressman for the first time on a given issue, be sure to ask what his position is. "He has a responsibility to tell you his stand," says former congressman Jerome Waldie, "but chances are he'll fail to do so if he disagrees, unless you've asked directly."

Your question can be as blunt as "Will you support this bill?" or "Will you oppose the Steiger amendment?" or "Will you co-sponsor this bill?"

Even if you already know his position from news stories, it is worthwhile to ask the question. If the legislator agrees with you, he and his staff will get satisfaction from being able to respond favorably, knowing that his position on the issue is pleasing his constituents and helping to build his reputation for the next election. If he disagrees with you, your question makes him realize that he's missing a chance to please another constituent. When these letters keep coming, a congressman's survival instinct may spur him to reconsider his position.

You can ask for a congressman's position even when you know he voted wrong a few months earlier on a related issue. You may even want to mention it.

I know that you voted last March for the gas decontrol bill. When it comes up again this month, I hope you will be a strong opponent of the measure, because it would result in higher gas prices. I just got my gas bill, and it was higher than ever before. Will you oppose the decontrol bill?

By asking this question you set the stage for the answer you want. It cries out for an answer of "Yes," and both the congressman and his staff know it.

Avoid the Pitfalls

Certain traits that often show up in congressional mail tend to undermine the impact of citizens' letters. By avoiding these common pitfalls you can make your letters more influential:

1. Don't mention your membership in citizen groups. Congressmen usually know the organization's position already. If you say you're a member of, say, Common Cause or the Sierra Club, the congressman's staff will write your letter off as something the organization told you to write. You don't add any influence to your letter by citing such organizations. Remember that the organization gets its influence from you, and not vice versa. What counts most is an individual citizen's own letter.

2. Don't apologize for writing, as in "I'm sorry to take time from your busy schedule . . ." You have a *right* to write to your legislator, guaranteed by the First Amendment to the Constitution, which protects "the right of the people peaceably to assemble, and to petition the Government for a redress of grievances." When you write to a member of the United States Congress, you are exercising that right, and your legislator has a responsibility to consider your letter.

3. Don't tell a legislator how influential you are. He won't believe it, because he thinks he knows all the influential people in the district or state. You will only be written off as a braggart. Instead, use your influence by persuading a few of your cohorts to write him about the same issue. For more ways to use your influence, see Chapter 7, "Organizing for Influence."

4. Don't overstate your case. Many legislators are experts at exaggeration, and they do it so well that they can't abide their constituents' doing it. From a practical standpoint, exaggeration in your letter will damage your credibility.

If a fact you want to mention sounds far out or hard to believe, you can make it more credible by citing an official source. For instance, don't say simply: "If the Concorde SST is permitted to fly to U.S. airports it will cause an increase in skin cancer." To the uninformed congressman, this would sound like exaggeration. Add a few details and it becomes believable: "If the Concorde SST is allowed to fly to U.S. airports, according to Secretary of Transportation Coleman's statement on November 13, 1975, it will cause 200 additional cases of skin cancer per year in the United States alone."

5. Don't make wisecracks or derogatory remarks about congressional staff, such as "I hope this letter isn't pigeonholed by your staff" or "I hope this gets past your secretary." Such remarks are a slap at the staff, whom you want to have on your side.

6. By all means be firm, but don't show anger and don't indicate blanket disagreement with the legislator's record. "People will write some of the ugliest, most intemperate letters you've ever seen," recalls Jerome Waldie. "This sets up a barrier to communication."

Displaying anger in your letter only makes the letter easier to ignore. The congressman will assume that you probably wouldn't vote for him even if he did what you ask. You want him to think of you as a potential supporter.

7. Neither offer election support nor threaten to oppose the legislator in the next election. Promises and threats smack of coercion and are resented. Congressmen get enough crackpot mail, but too little that is constructive and helpful. The best "threat" is the unvoiced one that is implicit in a pile of thoughtful letters asking the legislator to take a stand. He knows that the writers are going to be voting in the next election. You can best show your sincerity not by threatening to campaign against him, but by offering to provide him with further information on the issue. This attitude will pay off, even though your offer may never be taken up.

8. Don't be "Johnnie-One-Note," besieging the legislator and his staff with repetitive and almost identical letters on the issue. Be creative enough to think of a new reason to write every time, with occasional news clippings and supporting data enclosed. Make it an enjoyable experience to open your mail, if possible. Use a little humor, but never at the expense of the legislator, his staff, or the issue. If you find that you've been averaging more than a letter a month to a given legislator, back off and start writing some of your letters for friends to sign. Or use your time to organize citizens in your community on the issue. If you write too often, you'll be ranked among the "pen pals" or crackpots, most of whom could spend their time and energy far more effectively.

9. Don't send carbon copies or Xerox copies of your letters to save time. Some people write a letter to one senator and send carbon copies to their other senator and their congressman. This undermines their influence, because a legislator who is sent only a carbon never sees it, and his staff gets the impression that whoever sent it evidently didn't feel strongly enough about the issue to write the legislator personally. At the risk of getting writer's cramp or typist's knuckles, write to each senator and congressman individually, because it is the only way to be taken seriously and to get a good answer.

Make It Personal

Getting the highest level of attention for your letters is often a matter of demonstrating your prior contact—in person—with the legislator and his staff. We call this personalizing your letter. "Any way you personalize your letter will make a difference," advises Jerome Waldie. "Either it will be brought to the congressman's attention or it will get more attention from the staff."

There are several ways to do this. One of the best is to address the legislator by his first name. "Dear Bill" can be much more effective than "Dear Congressman Smith." And just how do you achieve a first-name relationship? It's easy, because politicians want constituents to know them at firsthand and therefore they make many personal appearances in the congressional district or state. All you have to do is to walk up to him during an informal moment and introduce yourself. There's no need to say anything about issues, and there may not be time anyhow. To find out when and where he will be appearing in public, call his local office and ask. Once you've met him, use his first name in your next letter and say you were glad to meet him at the event.

Another option is to get an appointment to see him when he is back home or when you're visiting Washington. It doesn't have to be a heavy meeting, laden with importance. An introduction, a handshake, and a few pleasantries will do the job—though it's even better to show your concern with the issues while you're at it. (Suggestions on this appear in Chapter 6, "Face to Face with a Congressman.")

Don't be overly formal by addressing the congressman as "Dear Congressman Smith" even though you've met him and could use his first name. If you don't use his first name in your letters, they will generally be routed to the staff instead of being read by the congressman.

If you haven't met the congressman and don't particularly wish to, visit his local staff and chat about your concerns. Then when you write to the congressman, say in your letter something like, "I had the pleasure of meeting with Sarah Jones, your assistant in Springfield." This will get attention because it shows that you have taken the trouble to call at his office personally. If the staffer was helpful, add a few words of praise; this will improve your reception, too.

If you've seen the congressman recently, mention it. He will probably not remember you unless you do. His staff is even less likely to know, because Washington staffers rarely travel to the home district. For example:

> When we met on April 23 at your "Town Meeting" in Ashland, you expressed interest in the education funding problem. Later I looked into the local situation and learned that the county school system has made plans to lay off fifteen teachers and cut back on teaching assistants. . . .

Or another example:

> It was good to see you at the Baltimore City Fair last weekend. I would like to raise with you a subject that has been very much on my mind—the sad state of public transportation in Baltimore. We badly need more federal funds for the subway system, yet it seems most of the federal transportation money still goes into highways, which is the last thing we need. . . .

If you know someone who is an old friend of the congressman, you may want to mention it, because this usually gets the congressman's personal attention. For instance: "Bob Bauer, who went to high school with you, urged me to write . . ." (Presumably you've engaged Bauer in a conversation about the issue, and asked him if you should write to the congressman.) Or: "Nora Lee, who knows you from your years in San Diego, is a neighbor of mine. I want to ask you to support the bill to . . ."

If You Are Under Eighteen

Although a senator or House member is elected by the voters, he or she *represents* all the people in a congressional district or state, including those who are not yet of voting age. Under the Fourteenth Amendment to the Constitution, the apportionment of House seats is based on "the whole number of persons in each state," without regard to their age. Citizenship is defined in the Fourteenth Amendment in these words: "All persons born or naturalized in the United States, and subject to the jurisdiction thereof, are citizens of the United States and of the state wherein they reside." So even if you aren't yet of voting age, your legislators in Congress should be representing you and they should consider your views.

Letters from citizens under the age of eighteen can be very influential. "That kind of mail is always very high-priority with me," says the administrative assistant to a Midwestern congresswoman. Legislators know that the response, or lack of one, to a young person's letter may influence that person's attitude toward Congress and toward the entire concept of representative government. They also know that young people grow up and vote.

Congressmen also realize that young people tend to receive less mail than adults, and are less involved in jobs and public causes. Therefore they may regard a reply from a congressman as something very much out of the ordinary. They may show the letter to their parents and to other students. The reply may be discussed in a civics or social studies class at school. If it's an unresponsive, noncommittal letter, the congressman is going to be spoken of unfavorably wherever the letter is seen.

If you're of high school or elementary school age, don't hesitate to write to your legislators on issues that concern you. There is no need to identify yourself as a student, unless you prefer to do so. Even though you don't yet vote, you may have more influence in the election than many people who do vote. You can spread the word about the congressman and help in his campaign, or help in his opponent's campaign. It makes sense to a congressman to heed your views just as much as those of people over eighteen.

Telegrams and Mailgrams

Only use a telegram or Mailgram when you think a letter will not get there soon enough. In most congressional offices, these are handled in the same way as letters and are given no more weight. Indeed, the typical short telegram is generally less influential than a letter because in fifteen words you can't fit in more than a demand to vote for or against a bill. You can't demonstrate your seriousness or the reasons for your position.

A Mailgram, on the other hand, is a useful medium when you want your opinion to reach the legislator the next morning. In a Mailgram you can send 100 words for a mere $2.95. "We ensure next-business-day delivery," says a Western Union spokesman. Mailgrams can be sent at any time, day or night, by telephoning the toll-free number listed under Western Union in your local phone book. Those to legislators are wired to a printout station in the Washington, D.C., post office, four blocks from the Capitol, and are delivered to congressional offices with the morning mail at eight or nine o'clock. (Business firms that have Telex or TWX teletype machines can send Mailgrams at even less expense.)

The overnight telegram (formerly called "night letter") was previously used often by citizens to reach congressmen, but introduction of Mailgram service has made overnight telegrams almost obsolete. Overnight telegrams are not necessarily delivered the next morning, because incoming telegrams frequently create a backlog at Western Union's Capitol Hill receiving stations when highly controversial issues are coming up for a vote. The stiff price also discourages their use: $4.45 for 100 words plus a delivery charge of three dollars.

The full-rate telegram (or "fast telegram") gets there first, but at a price! For a charge of $4.95 for a measly fifteen words plus three dollars for delivery, Western Union guarantees delivery within four hours after a full-rate telegram is received by the Western Union offices on Capitol Hill.

The "personal opinion message"—fifteen words for two dollars when addressed to the President, Vice President, or any senator or representative at his Washington office—has also been supplanted by the Mailgram, which is faster and gives you eighty-five more words for only fifty-five cents more.

Mailgrams are best used when the congressman has already received many letters on the issue and you want to reemphasize your position just before he votes on the matter.

Postal Cards

Postal cards, even when handwritten or typed, are among the least effective means of communicating with a congressman, because they are regarded on Capitol Hill as a sure sign of an organized, "pressure mail" campaign. Congressional staffers know that organizers pass out blank postal cards at a meeting where an issue is being discussed, ask those present to write a message to their congressman, then collect and mail them. Individual citizens who feel the urge to write usually write a letter instead.

Postcards also allow no room for real explanation of *why* the writer takes a certain position. They show little concern over the issue—else, why didn't the citizen take the time to write a letter? Postcards make an impact only through sheer volume, and each one is a drop in the bucket.

Telephone Calls

You can register your opinion by telephone, but this usually is effective only if the issue is already known to the congressman and his staff. If you haven't written a letter, a phone call will at least get you on record.

To phone in your views, call the congressman's local office. Most congressmen have at least one office in the congressional district, and senators often have one or two in principal cities in the state. Tell the staff member that you want to let the congressman know your views on the issue, give a couple of good reasons for your stance, and *tell the staff you would like a reply from the congressman.*

"If twenty calls come into the district office in a day, this is quickly relayed to the Washington office," says Jerome Waldie.

"You're looking for volume. This really worries them, because the staff in the district office are usually more politically oriented than those in the Washington office."

Some offices have arranged a telephone hookup that enables you to speak with the Washington office simply by calling the district office. This has the advantage of putting you on the line with the staffer who is most expert on your issue.

Certain congressmen have set up hours when they can be reached in person by constituents who call the district office. This often involves waiting on the line, but it is an excellent chance to bring your concerns directly to the congressman's attention.

In using the telephone, beware of overdoing it. One staffer for an Eastern congressman bemoans "my own albatross," a constituent who calls four times a week to chat about environmental issues. "Phone calls sap a legislative assistant's ability to work on issues," says this staffer. It's hard enough to get legislative work done in a crowded office and with a huge burden of work stacked up; the interruptions caused by unnecessary telephone calls can drive the staffer to a state of permanent annoyance with the entire issue. Overall, it is best to phone your views to the local office or write a letter to your congressman rather than pestering the harried issue staff in Washington.

Letters to the Editor

The letters column of a newspaper offers an opportunity to communicate with your congressman in public. The congressman rarely will answer, but your printed letter will get more of his attention than a personal one. It may also stimulate others to write to him. Instead of writing directly to your congressman, you write a one-page letter to the editor commenting on the congressman's stance on your issue.

The best way to break into the letters column is to cite one of the paper's recent editorials, news stories, or picture spreads related to your subject. If the congressman has commented publicly on your issue, you have a good entree. If not, try the indirect approach. For example, if the congressman has boasted of his efforts to cut government spending, you point out the irony of his failure to support reductions in the military budget. Inconsistencies seem always to catch the eye of the letters editor.

If the congressman does something good on your issue, don't lose the chance to do him a favor by praising him in the letters column. Send him a carbon copy so he'll see it even if the paper doesn't print it. Reciprocity is a principle congressmen believe in and apply constantly; take advantage of it when you can. Legislators need the goodwill that comes from praise in the letters column. Even letters from outside the congressional district, but within the state, can help your cause if sent to a newspaper that is widely read in the district.

Editors also accept letters not tied to recent newspaper coverage. A good news idea, well presented, usually ranks above the routine complaints about typographical errors and bad grammar. Editors look for news value and good expression.

Beware, however, of writing to the same paper too often. The crackpot threshold is lower here than in mail to a congressman, and you must avoid seeming to be interested in making the congressman look good or bad. The emphasis has to be on the issues. If you've had a letter in the *Chronicle* recently and want to write another one, either send it to the *Tribune* instead or ghost it for a friend to sign.

Letters to the editor will have their impact even if they never see print, because they show the editor that readers are interested in your subject. The results may include editorials and more thorough coverage in the news columns.

Give Praise

How would you like it if your friends wrote to you only to demand favors or to criticize your actions? If a friend did so, how much would you value that friend's opinion after a while?

Legislators are so battered by critical mail and demands for action that the rare letters of praise come as a cool breeze on a hot summer day. Legislators and staff alike are pleased to be praised. They assume that where there is praise there is also potential support for the next election campaign—at least a good word to your friends and maybe even volunteer time in the campaign. They will become more receptive to your future requests for action on the issue.

A note of thanks is in order when the congressman votes as you requested, when he cosponsors a bill you favor, or when he takes some other favorable action on your issue.

Too many people think they should not praise a congressman unless they agree with him on all issues. Not so! Your praise, if directed to a specific action on a given issue, cannot be interpreted as an endorsement of anything else. On the contrary, your praise may attract more of his attention to your issue and proportionately less to other issues.

When a senator or congressman who is not your own has taken a prominent role on legislation of interest to you, don't hesitate to write him a complimentary letter. Praise from different parts of the country can lead a legislator, especially a young one, to see himself as becoming a national leader in your field. This is to be encouraged, because one of the most difficult tasks faced by public-interest advocates is to engage the time, attention, and personal commitment of legislators as specialists on public-interest issues. Legislators who take positions favored by industrial lobbies are showered with gratitude, especially in the form of campaign contributions. Praise doesn't have a dollar sign in front of it, but it can partly compensate a legislator who chooses the public-interest road.

Praise helped to make an environmental leader of the late congressman John P. Saylor (Republican of Pennsylvania). Saylor took his first leadership role in an environmental campaign in the early 1950s against the Bureau of Reclamation's plan to flood Dinosaur National Monument, Utah, with a huge hydroelectric dam. In that battle, which he entered at first because of his belief that the project would waste the taxpayers' money, he came to enjoy being out in front, with a national reputation among citizens who opposed the dam. He became a specialist in the field of national parks, wilderness, and dams, and was known as the most reliable and effective environmentalist in the House until his death in 1973.

Legislators aren't won solely by either the carrot or the stick. Sometimes you have to use the stick to get their attention. But it's the carrot that leads them where you want them to go over the long haul.

5

If a Congressman Answers—
Follow-Up Letters

The postman just came, and now the ball is back in your court. The legislator has answered your letter. What do you do? Don't just sit there—or run gleefully around the neighborhood showing off the congressman's signature (which may have been signed by Mr. Siggie anyway). Prove to the legislator that you are serious about the issue and not just casually interested. Write a follow-up letter.

For every 100 people who write urging a legislator to take a position, at most probably one person writes a letter reacting to the legislator's response. Because so few people write to say what they thought of the answer, legislators naturally get the idea that any kind of answer will satisfy the folks back home.

Every congressman knows that a local citizens' group can stimulate a batch of letters by asking its members to "write your congressman." He realizes also that an organization cannot generate follow-up letters. When people write follow-up letters, they make it clear to the congressman and his staff that he is not experiencing a pressure-mail campaign, but is dealing with constituents who have a deep-seated concern about their cause.

Follow-up letters get more attention than most opinion mail because they cannot be answered easily by a roboletter. Usually a staffer or the congressman reads them, and an individual reply is drafted. Your follow-up letter will make a direct impression, with possibly more impact than your first letter.

Analyzing the Answer

Before writing a follow-up letter, read the legislator's reply carefully to see whether it really answers your letter. Does it tell you what the legislator's position is on the issue? Does it say what the legislator has done and will do about the issue? Or does it just repeat a string of clichés without getting down to the real point?

"The first thing to look for is responsiveness," says one long-time Senate staffer. "If a legislator takes a stand, consider yourself lucky."

Many senators and congressmen nowadays shun the use of noncommittal letters and insist on meeting constituents' questions directly. Even so, says former congressman Jerome Waldie (Democrat of California), "Eighty percent of the time the answer will be noncommittal, for which read 'I don't want to make a decision until I have to.' Either he hasn't decided or he disagrees with you. If he agreed, he'd say so."

The classic noncommittal letter, good for a chuckle among congressional staff, goes something like this:

> Dear Mrs. Black:
> Thank you for your recent communication.
> I appreciate having your views on this matter. You may be sure that I will have these views in mind when the matter comes before the House.
> With kindest regards,
>
> > Sincerely,
> > Member of Congress

The all-purpose noncommittal reply has generally been superseded by noncommittal letters that are issue-specific and are revised often to report the current status of the issue. Cranked out by automatic typewriter, these letters attempt to satisfy your interest in the subject by tossing you a few facts suggesting that the legislator is taking a personal interest in the matter. Actually, a staff member can find out the status of a bill by making a single phone call; if the status has changed, the staffer simply revises the roboletter. This is at least an improvement over the old-style roboletter that said nothing, because now there is a staffer who is up to date on the status of the issue.

An example of this new-style noncommittal letter is the following roboletter received by Pennsylvania residents who wrote to Senator Hugh Scott (Republican of Pennsylvania) in 1975 asking him to cosponsor a bill to protect three Western national wildlife ranges:

> Dear Mrs. ———:
>
> Thank you for your communication concerning the decision of the Secretary of the Interior to transfer three Western wildlife ranges from the jurisdiction of the Fish and Wildlife Service to the exclusive control of the Bureau of Land Management. You are not alone in your concern over the implications of this action.
>
> Restraining legislation (S. 1293) has been introduced which would, first, establish the Western game ranges by act of Congress, rather than by their present executive decrees, and second, award sole jurisdiction to the U.S. Fish and Wildlife Service. I am pleased that hearings on this measure are scheduled in the Senate Commerce Committee on May 21.
>
> When all the evidence is in and the merits of this case are known, I assure you that I will act in the best interests of wildlife and conservation.
>
> > Sincerely,
> > Hugh Scott
> > United States Senator

While Senator Scott's letter talks around the issue in a way that's calculated to make the constituent feel good, it completely avoids taking any position on the issue. The letter strikes a note of sympathy over the problem ("You are not alone in your concern . . .") without indicating whether Scott agrees or not. It mentions the current status of legislation and hints at support ("I am pleased that hearings on this measure are scheduled . . .") without actually taking a position on the bill.

In the end, the bill passed the Senate, but Scott never did take a position, and there was no record vote on it that would have required him to vote one way or the other. He saved himself a decision, but he also lost the chance to win the favor of constituents who had asked him to support the bill.

Consider the contrast between Scott's letter and the following roboletter received by Maryland residents who wrote to Senator Charles McC. Mathias, Jr. (Republican of Maryland) on the same issue:

Dear Miss ————:

Thank you for providing me with your thoughts concerning plans by the Department of the Interior to turn over management authority of the Kofa, Charles Sheldon, and Charles Russell game ranges to the Bureau of Land Management.

As you may know, S. 1293 has recently been introduced to establish these game ranges as part of the National Wildlife Refuge System. The bill is intended specifically to reverse the Interior decision to oust the U.S. Fish and Wildlife Service from management of these ranges and turn them over to the Bureau of Land Management. S. 1293 will establish the Fish and Wildlife Service as the oversight agency.

A study done by the Natural Resources Law Institute concluded that the National Game Ranges should be managed, not by the Bureau of Land Management, but by the U.S. Fish and Wildlife Service, which has the necessary expertise and inclination toward carrying out the mandates which established these ranges. I agree with this conclusion and have consequently cosponsored S. 1293 and will give it my fullest support when it reaches the Senate floor.

In order to prevent further management transfer, S. 1268 has been introduced to establish the "National Wildlife Refuge Service" in order to provide permanent protection for all units of the Wildlife Refuge System against transfer to other agencies, and against being sold or given away unless such actions are authorized by Act of Congress. I have also cosponsored this measure and firmly support it.

It was good to learn of your views on this matter. I hope you will contact me again on other issues of concern to you.

With best wishes,

Sincerely,
Charles McC. Mathias, Jr.
United States Senator

Mathias's letter, like Scott's, includes facts about the issue to impress constituents with his grasp of the subject, but he also commits himself to a position.

The terms used by legislators to avoid commitment make up a veritable waffler's lexicon. Some of these follow, with our translations:

"Legislatorese"	Translation
I will continue to monitor this situation closely. I am continually reviewing the project. I am following the progress of this legislation closely.	I'll forget about it until I'm forced to take a position.
I am taking the matter up with the authorities.	I've passed the buck to the bureaucrats in the executive branch.
Enclosed is the reply to your letter I received from the Bureau of ———. I hope this information is helpful.	I'm ducking this issue.
I will consider your views most strongly when the bill comes before the Senate. You may be sure I will give this matter my very close attention when it is considered by the full Senate.	I'll forget about it until I have to vote on the issue (and then I'll do as I please).
I will vote the interests of the country as I see them.	Don't bother me with your opinions.

Answering Noncommittal Replies

If you receive a noncommittal reply, write to the legislator again and tell him you want to know his position.

Avoiding commitments is a Capitol Hill tradition of long

standing, not an evil plot invented to defeat the bills you're most interested in. The noncommittal stance—what one congressman called "the strong neutral position"—is the easiest posture to assume because it requires no research and no thought and is supposed to alienate few voters. The special-interest lobbies have learned to overcome the problem by making the advantages of taking a particular position very attractive, with rewards often involving large campaign contributions or lucrative speaking engagements. Citizens have leverage, too: when a congressman hears his constituents forcefully asking him to take a stand and showing serious concern, he usually sees the value of a prompt commitment. Every legislator knows that when enough voters are concerned about an issue, a noncommittal position becomes a political liability.

Noncommittal letters sent out by senators and House members are one of the primary sources of public dissatisfaction with the United States Congress. Such letters are evidence to support the popular impression that you can't trust public officials because they won't tell you what they think. Noncommittal letters undermine people's confidence in their legislators, paving the way for challengers to win in future elections.

A few senators and congressmen make a fetish of remaining uncommitted until the floor debate. Some want to be able to trade their votes to other legislators for favors they will need later on. Some wait to see what special interests may seek their support on the issue and possibly fork over campaign contributions in return. Some want to avoid exposing themselves to pressure from industries or citizen groups that oppose their intended position. Others earnestly want to wait until all the facts are in. But most of the veteran issue-evaders are simply trying to make their job easier by avoiding the need for research on the issues and merely following the crowd when the issue comes to the floor.

And then there are the legislators who have a position, but won't reveal it to constituents who write in, taking the opposite position. There is a hoary tradition in Congress that a noncommittal letter is more acceptable than a letter disagreeing with the constituent's views. However, more and more legislators are coming to believe that a forthright answer wins greater respect from a constituent than a coyly noncommittal one.

There is only one situation in which a legislator is justified in being noncommittal: when he is asked about the specific details of a bill that is being considered by a committee of which he is not a member. In this case, the legislator's staff can't possibly keep up to date on the contents of a bill which may be fifty to 100 pages long and which is being changed from one day to the next by decisions of the committee. A senator or congressman who is not on that committee will never be involved in most of those decisions, since only the most significant issues are raised in floor debate and settled by votes on floor amendments to the committee-approved version of the bill. However, your legislators owe you a forthright statement of their positions on major amendments and basic provisions of a bill, even when it's before another committee.

If you get a noncommittal letter from your congressman, write back and tell the congressman his reply did not answer your question about his position. Do this diplomatically by starting with a friendly comment, such as:

> Dear Congressman Yin:
> I appreciate your thoughtfulness in answering my letter about the Consumer Protection Agency Bill, but you didn't answer my basic question—what is your position on the bill?
> This measure would help to overcome the big-business domination of government agencies by establishing a consumer advocate agency. . . .

A friendly but insistent tone is best. No anger—it would only undermine your effort and turn off both the legislator and his staff. Keep the legislator's letter rather than sending it back; the legislator will realize that if you were serious enough to write and complain, you may show it to friends and do some harm to his reputation in the community unless he shapes up.

One way to arouse more attention is to send a copy of your follow-up letter to the legislator's nearest office in your state or congressional district. The staffers in many of these local offices have the role of troubleshooters, on the lookout for complaints and problems. They will criticize the Washington office staff if noncommittal letters are provoking complaints.

In your follow-up letter you can make one or two good points about the issue or include a recent editorial from the local paper.

The same basic principles apply as you considered in writing your original letter.

An excuse long used by legislators to avoid commitment goes like this: "I can't take a position on H.R. 5512 at this time because it is still being considered by the committee, and it may be changed before it comes to the floor." You can respond to this evasion by saying that all you're asking is his position on H.R. 5512 as it was originally introduced. Or ask for his position on a specific principle of a bill, such as: "Do you favor the provisions of H.R. 13372 that would protect the New River from construction of the Blue Ridge power project?"

Legislators sometimes pass the buck by bucking your letter to the federal agency that handles the issue and requesting the agency's comments. You will then receive a noncommittal letter from the legislator, enclosing a copy of the agency's reply. This is supposed to impress you by showing you that your legislator can make the bureaucrats hop. But don't be awestruck; it's nothing more than evasion of your questions and can have little effect on either Congress or the agency itself. The bureaucrats have automatic typewriters, too, and they can send the same reply to dozens of legislators. They're glad to do it, because a legislator who uses their service is likely to follow the agency's line.

If one of your legislators goes through this paper-shuffling exercise, complain as in the following letter:

> Dear Congresswoman Himel:
>
> Thank you for your letter of May 7, enclosing the letter from the Office of Education in reply to my letter about the Impact Aid program.
>
> You didn't tell me, however, how you will vote on Impact Aid. If I had wanted to know the Office of Education's opinion, I would have written to them in the first place. Please let me know what *your* position is.
>
> Impact Aid is needed in our city because so many pupils in our schools are the children of military employees. The large military installations here keep so much land off the tax rolls that it would be impossible to maintain good schools without the Impact Aid funds. Twenty percent of our school district budget comes from Impact Aid . . .

If a Legislator Disagrees with You

Even thoroughly committed legislators change their positions when enough constituents have requested it. It happens every day on Capitol Hill.

If your legislator replies, saying that he disagrees with you, your next step is to write back promptly, refuting his arguments and once more asking him to take the position you favor. The legislator's reply may infuriate you by the irrationality of its arguments. If so, pound the table and swear a lot, but in your letter carefully conceal your anger, because it would only alienate the legislator and staff you're trying to influence.

If you fail to follow up, the legislator and his staff will have little reason to reconsider his position. They will get the impression either that his letter persuaded you of his position or that you didn't care strongly enough about the issue to pursue it further.

When follow-up letters arrive in a congressional office, the picture changes. These letters tell the staff that the legislator's position is bringing him into direct conflict with deeply concerned citizens. If the follow-up letters are thoughtful and courteous, but insistent, the staff will have to draft answers. The automatic typewriters won't be of much help when each letter asks for the legislator's reaction to different points. Thus your follow-up letters provoke thought that otherwise would not have been necessary.

When your legislator disagrees with you, you will want to cover at least these three elements in your follow-up letter:

1. Express thanks for the legislator's forthrightness in stating his position.

2. Tell him you disagree, and then proceed to refute his arguments. Go on to make new points, if you can.

3. Ask a question or two, so he and his staff will have to think about the issue and respond.

Aside from these basics, all the points in the previous chapter also apply to follow-up letters—except one. *Do not delay sending the follow-up letters;* if you adhere to the "one letter a month" rule in this case, the legislator may be led to believe you don't care much about your cause.

Your rebuttal of the legislator's arguments must be brief, to fit within the standard one-page letter, but you may go into more detail in an attachment if you need more space. You can also enclose supplemental material such as a report by experts or a favorable editorial in a newspaper or magazine. These enclosures will be seen by the staff, and may be influential if they are pertinent and reflect the views of people respected by the legislator or his staff.

In making your argument, try to cite any new facts you have (such as scientists' findings or a new example of local impact) or new evidence of local opinion on the issue (such as a newspaper editorial). When including new information, you have the chance to say something like, "I hope you'll reconsider your position in light of these new facts." Even if he has already seen the new information in the newspapers, only constituents' letters will force a legislator to stop and think about it. Bear in mind that it's embarrassing for a politician to do an about-face. New facts make it easier, but it's usually not the facts themselves, but the voters' insistence, that impels the legislator to change his position.

If the legislator's letter gives no reasons for his position, ask him to explain himself.

The questions you ask in a follow-up letter are vital, because you want the congressman and his staff to read your letter and devote some thought to answering it. **Types of generally useful questions include:**

- The did-you-know question ("Did you realize that our city schools will lay off teachers unless full funding comes through from the Education Appropriations Bill?")
- The have-you-consulted question ("Have you asked fisheries biologists at our state university to assess the impact on fishing of the proposed dam?")
- The whom-did-you-consult question ("Who told you that, as your letter states, decontrol would result in increased gas supply?")
- The can-you-back-that-up question ("What facts can you cite to support your claim that this bill will benefit small businessmen?")

Some legislators have an easy way out to save their having to answer your questions. This dodge is a reply cranked out by automatic typewriter, something like this:

> Dear Mr. Weiss:
> Thank you for your recent communication on gun control. Apparently we are in disagreement on this subject. However, I appreciate your taking the trouble to send me your views, and I hope you will continue to do so when matters of interest to you are before the Senate.
>
> Sincerely,
U.S. Senator

Don't settle for this kind of answer, any more than you would settle for a noncommittal response. Write again and tell the senator he didn't respond to the questions you asked.

If a Legislator Agrees with You

You're excited; today's mail included a letter from your congressman saying that he agrees with your position. Don't let it go at that. Promptly reply, expressing your thanks, thus reinforcing his stance by showing him the seriousness of people who take your position on the issue. This reinforcement will help him to protect his good stance against attacks by your opponents, and will contribute to building his long-range interest in the issue. Compliment him on his perception of the facts and arguments involved in the issue, and add new facts that may help him.

In your letter of thanks, ask him to take an active role in the issue, rather than merely waiting for the bill to come to a vote on the floor. He can influence his colleagues in Congress by cosponsoring the bill, by testifying when the relevant committee holds hearings, or by talking persuasively to committee members who are considering the issue. More detailed suggestions are given in Chapter 4, "Writing Your Letters."

If you wish, make copies of the legislator's letter agreeing with your position and hand them out to friends and associates. Tell the legislator you did so; he'll appreciate the favorable publicity even among your limited circle.

6

Face to Face with a Congressman

Ten Ways to Talk to Your Congressman

Your congressman wants to meet you, because he thinks it may help him get reelected. You want to meet him because it will help win his vote on legislation that concerns you. When you meet your congressman face to face, you have the chance to get your views across to him directly.

1. Get an appointment. Call the legislator's nearest field office and ask to see him on his next trip home. When you're in Washington, D.C., for business or pleasure, go and see him there.

2. Don't be awed by the congressman or by the impression he gives of omniscience. You probably know more than he does about your issue, because a legislator is a jack-of-all-trades. Act confident, even if you don't feel it.

3. When you first meet the congressman, **show that you're a friendly person** by complimenting something he has done. It's just a pleasantry, but it gets you off on the right foot.

4. Show that you're serious about your issue. Know your facts, and make your pitch concisely in five minutes or less. Start by telling the legislator what you're asking him to do, then give your arguments. Stress how the issue affects you and others in your community.

90

5. Be a good listener. Let the congressman ask questions as you go along, and answer them with hard facts and with understanding. You don't have to agree with his views, but you should show that you're willing to hear them.

6. Don't let the legislator evade the issue. If he changes the subject, tactfully bring it up again and ask how he plans to vote on your issue.

7. Don't assume the legislator is against your cause just because he asks a lot of hostile-sounding questions. If he's going to back your position, he'll need to know how to answer your opponents' arguments. Use the questions as an opportunity to tell him more about the issue.

8. If the legislator is on your side, **make him feel good about it** so he'll be willing to work harder for your goals. Make sure he knows how much the issue means to people back home.

9. Press for a commitment, unless the congressman is clearly opposed to your views. Ask whether he will vote for your amendment, whether he will cosponsor your bill, or whatever it is you want. You're entitled to know what he plans to do about the issue.

10. If you can't get to see the legislator in person, go and **see a member of his staff** instead. You can't press a staffer for a commitment, but you can do your best to persuade the staffer and show how serious you are about the issue, so he'll give a good report of your concern to the congressman.

Senators and congressmen want to talk with voters. That's one of your sources of power, whether you're an individual or a representative of an organization. Legislators have seen many colleagues go down to defeat in elections because voters got the feeling, "That congressman never comes to town; he's not interested in us." Indeed, many of the newer legislators got into Congress by challenging incumbents on that basis.

A legislator wants you to get a good impression of him and to spread that impression among your friends so they will feel that he's in touch with the voters. He thinks you will drop his name in your conversations: "You know, Phil Burton told me . . ." or "That Gladys Spellman really understands what we're up against . . ."

Thus the legislator's name goes out among the people, *on the strength of his association with you.* He gains more from this association than you do, because he needs the votes of your friends to stay in office. This is a paramount reason for the legislator to see you and to take your views seriously.

You need to see your senators and congressman to show them you're serious about your issues, to get their reactions so you know what else you need to do to promote your cause, and to press for their commitment to your position on legislation that is coming up for a vote. If you've never met the legislator before, a conversation also makes you a known quantity and puts you on a first-name basis, so you can write the legislator in the future and know that your letters will get more attention.

A face-to-face conversation with a congressman is one of the best ways to penetrate the cocoon in which he functions. Surrounded by his staff and by businesspeople and bigwigs back home, and in daily touch largely with other congressmen equally removed from the average citizen's problems, a legislator may become so isolated as to lose track of the real-world concerns of the voters. But when he sits down with you for a conversation, he is suddenly exposed to your concerns and has to deal with them. He knows that, in a conversation, you won't be satisfied with the easy answer of the letter, "Thanks for your views. I'll be sure to keep them in mind when the matter comes up for a vote."

In a conversation, your message is no longer heard only by the staffers who answer the congressman's mail. It is heard by the person who has the power. You now have the chance to impress the congressman with your concern and with your knowledge of the facts. You can try to convince him logically, answering his doubts point by point. You can find out what's on his mind. You can ask him for a commitment of his vote or his active support of your cause. In a conversation, he can't leave you unanswered in a month-old stack of letters.

It's easy to see your congressman, but somewhat harder to see your senators if you live in a populous state. The first step is to phone or write to the congressman's nearest office in your congressional district (or in Washington, if you don't know where the nearest office is) and ask for an appointment to see him next time he's back from Washington. It may be weeks before you get to see him, because congressmen average only six days a month back home. The meeting place may be the legislator's local office or it may be a "mobile office," a van used by many legislators to hold office hours in shopping centers or school parking lots in communities not served by local offices.

You can also see the congressman informally at events where he is trying to mingle with voters. Good access points include "town meetings" arranged by the congressman, public meetings and meetings of organizations at which he's speaking, county and city fairs, party rallies, community barbecues and clambakes, and political fund-raising receptions and dinners. Further ideas on where and how to meet your congressman are given in the last section of this chapter.

In the informal setting of a reception or a town meeting you can't go into an issue in depth, but you can introduce yourself, raise the subject, and ask the legislator, "May I come and see you about this?" He'll usually say yes, so you're all set to call his office and tell the appointments staffer, "I saw the Congressman at the county fair last week and he said to come and see him about the no-fault insurance bill. When would be a good time?"

Vans, local offices, radio talk shows, public meetings—all are the congressman's initiatives aimed at one thing: to meet the voters and especially to meet new people he hasn't met before. If you don't take advantage of these opportunities to tell him about your concerns, you have only yourself to blame if he votes against your views.

The First Time

A conversation with a congressman can be fun, because knowing how to make people feel comfortable, even important, is a politician's bread and butter. Besides making you feel good, the congressman will try to impress you with his sterling qualities and his omniscience. He may actually believe that he's an imposing public figure, and he depends on creating this impression among the voters.

A senator's or a congressman's whole environment seems designed to aggrandize him and make us voters feel at a disadvantage. His large desk, executive-style armchair, the flags behind his desk, the awards, plaques, and mementos displayed around the room, all attest to his elevation above the crowd. Carefully cultivated gray hair and well-cut clothes often complete the picture.

Don't be awed by it all. A legislator is just an ordinary man or woman and probably knows less than you do about the issue you want to talk about. If you've taken the time to study a subject, you may have the advantage. A legislator is a jack-of-all-trades. His only real expertise is usually in the subject matter of the congressional committees he serves on; if he's out of that subject, he's in deep water. Washington lobbyists capitalize on his lack of expertise by providing him with information that favors their viewpoint. You can take the same approach and be even more effective because you're his constituent and you're in a position to help or hurt him with other voters in your community.

Not that an uninformed legislator can't put up a good front! Congressmen over the years have adopted many ways of concealing their shortcomings, so that a voter who brings up an issue will go away with the impression that the congressman knows all about the subject and is in the thick of the action on it.

By learning some of the secrets of congressional conversation, you will be more successful in penetrating the legislator's defenses and getting him to do something to support your position.

Before meeting with a senator or congressman for the first time, have a serious subject and master it. This is essential because when you're starting to build your relationship with the legislator you have to show that you're serious, knowledgeable, and committed on issues that affect real people.

The congressman, when you first sit down with him, will be trying to figure out whether your issue is likely to be of concern to many other voters, whether he should do anything about it, and whether you yourself are likely to help or hurt him in future elections. Can he write you off as part of the die-hard 25 percent who would vote against him no matter what? Or are you and your friends part of the swing vote he needs to capture?

Sell yourself, and then you'll be able to sell the legislator on your issue. Don't let your desire for personal expression stand in the way of your influence. Few legislators are comfortable with students who come to a congressional office wearing old Levi's and hiking boots, and few regard such students as worthy of great attention. So consider dressing in more traditional business clothes, or dressy casual wear.

On a first visit, you can use the brief pleasantries at the start to establish yourself as a friendly person and make the congressman feel comfortable with you. A word of praise would be in order, such as: "Folks in our neighborhood liked your good work on the Consumer Protection Agency bill," or "People think you're so much better in touch with everybody than (name his predecessor) was." If you have a friend who knows the congressman, drop the name: "Joe Kowski said to say hello. He's a neighbor of mine," or "Sarah Edwards, who worked in your campaign, urged me to come and see you about this."

If you're shy, don't let it worry you; take strength from the good cause you advocate. Even among professional lobbyists there are many diffident people who overcome their shyness every day— a great contrast to the back-slapping, cigar-smoking stereotype we tend to have of the lobbyist. There are also ways to cope with shyness. When you enter a congressman's office, don't take a seat on the comfortable-looking sofa. The sofa would put you in a relaxed posture, below the congressman's eye level, a position that psychologically reinforces shyness. It's hard for anybody to make a forceful point when wallowing deep in an overstuffed sofa. Instead, sit in a chair, which will make you more wide awake and aggressive.

Act confident even if you don't feel it. You may summon up confidence simply by speaking up clearly and with conviction. By taking the initiative as soon as the pleasantries are over, you can give yourself a charge of confidence. For instance, say: "Congressman, I want to ask your help in support of the education bill." That way you've set the stage for what you want to tell him, instead of leaving it to him to drift into the subject.

Although legislators can be awesome, a simple image in your mind can deflate that awe. One environmental lobbyist, A. T. Wright, says: "I've always been a little on the shy side, but I've taken the view that a congressman puts his pants on one leg at a time, just like the rest of us. That homely vision of him may help you."

When seeing your congressman during his brief trips in the congressional district, expect five minutes with him at most and let the congressman extend the conversation if he wants to. To get your message across in this short time, you must be concise and hit the main points first, so you won't miss them if the conversation goes off on a tangent. During the discussion, hand the congressman something that sums up the issue or illuminates the topic—a fact sheet you've written up, a letter addressed to the congressman, or a pertinent magazine or newspaper article. This written material makes it easier for the legislator to pursue the issue afterwards, both in his own mind and with his staff back at the office. Whatever you give him should have your name and home address written on it.

Be a good listener as well as a good talker. This is one of the secrets of the best citizen-lobbyists, because it tends to evoke sincerity and directness from the legislator. If he knows you're listening thoughtfully, he'll be more willing to tell you what he really thinks about your issue, what political problems he may have with the issue, and even how he plans to vote on it. Being a good listener also helps build your relationship for the future.

There are a few pitfalls that you can easily avoid:

1. Hostility. You may feel hostile because you disagree with many of the legislator's positions on other issues. If you want to influence him on the issue at hand, you have no choice but to submerge your hostility, state your convictions, and ask for his support. Remember, nobody is all bad. By showing sympathy for the legislator's problems and allowing him the right to his own convictions, you'll give him the impression that you're a reasonable person whose opinions must be considered.

Some shy people unconsciously cover up their shyness with a show of hostility or arrogance. Neither will get you to first base. Instead, you'll be written off as one whose views can be safely ignored. Hostility never scared a congressman yet; it is usually returned in kind. It will never help your cause.

2. Taking too long. It's easy to go on chatting about the weather and about mutual acquaintances, and it's a natural thing to do in a normal conversation. It won't work when you're seeing your congressman. He almost always has appointments backed up behind yours, and if you take too long his attention will wander because he's worried about the other people waiting to see him. Keep the chitchat to a minimum and get to the point.

3. Tardiness. Being late for business meetings is a way of life to many of us. Being ten or fifteen minutes late to social engagements is fashionable. But being late to an appointment with a senator or congressman is a foolish blunder. If you're late you'll throw his whole day's schedule off, and very likely shortchange yourself and others who have been trying for weeks to get a few minutes with the legislator. Being late is inconsiderate, and that's the impression you will make on the legislator.

4. Overstatement. If you overstate your case in a conversation with a congressman, you're likely to be challenged on the spot and your credibility will be on the line. Be able to back up anything you say.

Presenting Your Case

First tell the congressman, in general terms, what you're going to ask him to do. For instance:

- "I think the day-care centers bill deserves your support, and I'll tell you why . . ."
- "Senator, we need that no-fault insurance bill, and I want to ask your support for it."

This way you've got the basic message across before the conversation has a chance to meander.

If the legislator interrupts to say that he agrees with your stance, you've saved yourself the time it would have taken to give the reasons for your request and you can get down to more specific points, such as *exactly* what you want him to do—cosponsor the bill, vote for a strengthening amendment, or whatever. If he doesn't jump in with an avowal of his support, chances are he'll hold off and let you talk. Most legislators who disagree with your general stand won't want to come down hard right at the beginning of the conversation.

Next, build your argument. Start with points with which the congressman can't fail to agree:

- (About a pollution-control bill) "Our river is so polluted that you can't safely swim in it."
- (About a health-care bill) "Our medical and hospital bills have been going up astronomically. You just can't afford to get sick anymore."

Try to elicit his sympathy and concern by making these truisms relate to the people in your community, showing how his constituents are affected by the problem. Give him a chance to say that he agrees.

Then move on to the arguments that he may not so readily agree with—how you propose to solve the problem—always striving to keep him with you. Let him interject remarks, but don't let him lead you off the track.

Explain what, if anything, is being done about the issue (by government agencies, corporations, or private organizations) and why this has not led to an adequate solution. Once he has agreed that there is a problem, the congressman's basic question is, "Why should Congress do anything about it?" By answering this question yourself in the course of your argument, you make it easier for him to agree with you and harder for him to challenge your conclusion.

On the other hand, if you're trying to stop a government proposal or program (such as a new billion-dollar dam or a new military weapons system), just turn the picture around and convince your congressman why the program is unnecessary or why the federal government should stay out of the issue. This argument will appeal both to legislators who share your views on this particular program and to those who see themselves as watchdogs of the Treasury.

Throughout your argument, relate your issue to broad public concerns in your state and congressional district, rather than just to yourself or your family. It's easy for a congressman to ignore your advocacy if it appears to be a selfish concern affecting a small group. Big-business lobbyists have long known this. They never argue that corporations should be given tax breaks in order to yield higher profits; it's always portrayed as a means of stimulating the economy and lowering unemployment. When you visit your congressman, use a similar approach to show what far-reaching effects are involved in your issue, and particularly what the effects will be on people who live in your congressional district and state.

Make the legislator realize the consequences of voting against your position—what would happen if your position were defeated.

- "If this national park bill doesn't pass, the greatest scenery in Alaska will be wrecked by development."
- "If this education bill doesn't go through, our schools will have to cut back immediately on these special programs."

The Congressman Reacts

A conversation with a senator or congressman has to be a real conversation, not a lecture or speech. You want the legislator to follow what you say, discuss it with you, and agree with you. In this respect it's like any discussion you've had with friends or associates whom you've tried to convince of something. You bring the other person along by involving him in the discussion so that by the time you've reached the conclusion, he's agreed too much to back out.

With friends, you usually get an unequivocal statement of their views:

- "Right on!"
- "I couldn't agree with you more."
- "That stinks!"

Many legislators will be frank with you, too. However, many of them also have the frustrating habit of not committing themselves. And there are many ways legislators may try to divert you from your purpose. Some of the most common conversational responses are the following:

1. The Philosopher wants to talk in generalities about the great concepts raised by your issue. He doesn't want to get down to details on which he might have to commit himself. If you go in to see him about the Day-Care Centers Bill, he'll ramble on about the problem of working mothers and how hard it is to get proper care for children, but he won't get around to saying how he plans to vote on the bill. If your purpose is to ask him to cosponsor a national park bill for Alaska, he'll tell you what great beauty he saw in

Alaska and how great our National Park System is, but he'll duck the question of cosponsoring the bill. Every time you try to bring the conversation back to the real topic, he'll lead you off on a new byway.

The only way to break the pattern, after more tactful methods have failed, is to bring up the issue bluntly and capture the congressman's attention by being firm. For example: If you favor the bill, you could say, "I'm here to ask you to vote in favor of this bill. Can you tell me whether you will?" If you oppose the bill, you could say, "I know you have a busy schedule, so I'll come right to the point: will you vote against this bill?" Whenever possible, phrase your question so the answer you want will be a yes. This puts a slight pressure on him in your direction.

2. The Elusive Intellectual always wants to consider both sides of the question, and you can't tell what he really thinks. Maybe he has already decided, but wants to show off his intellectual prowess. Or it could be he genuinely wants to explore the issue with you. Typically he'll interrupt your opening presentation with probing questions, he'll agree with you that there's a problem, but he'll have doubts that your solution is the best way to handle the problem. He wonders whether the bill you advocate may harm more people than it helps. A congressman who is trying to do this balancing act often is uneasy with the issue and doesn't quite know how to deal with it. By giving him good, reliable information, you can get a head start on your opponents.

If you're visiting the congressman when the issue is still new and the votes won't be coming up for weeks or months, you can afford to indulge his intellectual bent. Answer his questions cogently, do your best to allay his doubts, and try to find out exactly what is on his mind. If you can't answer his questions at the moment, tell him so and promise to look into them and write him in a few days with answers.

However, if the vote you're aiming for is coming up in a week or so, it's time for him to decide. Ask him, "Are you going to vote for this bill?"

3. The Patronizer wants to convince you that "Father knows best, and all you little citizens had better leave the decisions to us legislators." Prevalent among old-timey rural senators and congressmen, this type wants you to believe that everything will be all right because (a) the committee members are experts on the subject, (b) it takes great expertise and a national perspective to know what's best for the country, and (c) your views will be carefully considered. If you ask a Patronizer how he's going to vote, he may say that he always waits to read the committee report (or listen to the floor debate) before deciding, or that he has to weigh the views of many other affected people. (He may know perfectly well how he'll vote, but he isn't about to tell you so you can raise a stink back home.)

The Patronizer is seldom open to logical persuasion. Be firm in summing up your argument, and ask him to vote for your position. Then go home and organize pressure on him from friends, neighbors, and citizen organizations. For suggestions on organizing, see Chapter 7 of this book.

4. The Innocent is a legislator who shrugs off all responsibility for your issue. Typically he'll tell you to write to the congressional committee that handles the subject, or he will agree to send your letter to the committee. If he happens to be on the relevant committee, he says he wouldn't consider it proper to commit himself on an issue he will have to consider in committee. (This is one of the most transparent tricks in the book. Every important bill is introduced and pushed *by members* of the committee. And the leading opponents of a bill usually are on the committee, too. Being on the committee is no excuse for failing to take a stand.)

The Innocent blames everything on somebody else. If you've come to ask his help in defeating a proposed dam, he'll reply that if the Army Corps of Engineers favored the dam it must be all right, and who is he to question the experts in the Corps of Engineers? Or if consumers are getting ripped off by dishonest interstate land sales, he'll say that people ought to have enough sense to avoid being taken for suckers, and, anyhow, *state* laws are the way to handle the problem.

To get through to The Innocent, confront him with his responsibility. He is going to be voting on the issue; how is he going to vote? Or if you're asking him to initiate something, make it clear that the decision is no longer being made by the Corps of Engineers; it is *his,* and he is your last hope. Then organize pressure and news media coverage at home to make sure he knows that voters will hold him responsible for action or inaction.

5. **The Half-a-Loafer** always wants to compromise before the bell has rung for the first round. When you ask him to introduce or cosponsor a new bill, he'll try to convince you that you're asking for too much. "You should be content to settle for half a loaf," he'll say. "The committee will never accept this measure as it stands." Or he'll conjure up a picture of insurmountable opposition that will be stimulated by your bill.

Your best response is to point out that compromises are the business of congressional committees. Bills as first introduced must represent a strong position because they will be compromised during their consideration throughout the legislative process. If you start with only half a loaf, you'll end up with a quarter loaf—or less. It's an old motto on Capitol Hill: "Ask for what you want, rather than what you think you'll get."

6. **The Victim** is a legislator who blames his constituents for his unwillingness to support your position. It's not his fault. If you ask him to support a wilderness area proposal for a national park in his district, he'll say: "My constituents misunderstand the Wilderness Act, but they're dead set against wilderness and I have to go along with their views." If you ask him to support increases in education or library-aid funds, he'll say: "I'm certainly sympathetic, but my constituents just won't stand for any more increases in federal spending."

This is a sensitive area, because a legislator must be attentive to the views of large sectors of his constituency. But if you probe further you may be able to test his claim that he's being forced into this position. How many letters has he received opposing wilderness, or protesting federal education spending? Are any of the local politicians demanding that he take this position?

If there is an organized campaign led by a handful of your opponents in the district, a congressman can usually survive the issue. He can do a lot to avert criticism by taking the initiative himself to settle voters' concern, to answer fears that have been spread by your opponents. He has good access to the local citizens through his newsletters, newspaper columns, or radio broadcasts. Tell him you consider him a political *leader,* whose views will be respected in the district; he doesn't have to knuckle under to ill-informed opposition.

7. **The Doubting Thomas** is one who is basically opposed to your position on what he considers rational grounds, but he's willing to talk about it. He may think his information is more reliable than yours, or he may not think the problem is serious enough to warrant legislation. If you ask him to back the Consumer Protection Agency Bill, he'll agree that there is a consumer-protection problem, but he thinks it is being solved by the consumer-advocate agencies already set up in all federal departments, without needing yet another federal bureaucracy.

There's a chance you can still win The Doubting Thomas over, although some are actually more committed than they let on. Listen to his doubts carefully and try to respond to them. If necessary, take notes and get back to the congressman a few days later with more detailed written comments on the questions he raised. Ask whether he's getting pressure on the issue and how his mail is running on it. By organizing pressure and especially by reaching people the congressman respects and trusts, you may bring him around.

If the congressman seems to be rather firmly against your position, ask if he will keep an open mind so those on your side can present their facts and their views and hope to change his mind. (How can he refuse to keep an open mind?) Ask him, "Will you explain why you take this position?" Ask questions to find out what he knows about the issue, how deep his feeling is, who among his constituents favor his position, and whether he is getting any mail on the subject.

In discussing these factors you may be doing the congressman a favor, because a vociferous minority or a single VIP constituent may have put him on the spot, although he actually wants to support your position. Your reopening the question can give him an excuse to tell those who influenced him earlier, "I'm getting heat on this from too many people, so I can't do as you asked."

If the congressman advances facts you know are incorrect, tactfully restate your facts in more detail and this time cite the authority for your facts—scientific research, economists, government-agency reports, local VIPs, and so on. If you don't have this information at hand, promise to get more complete documentation to him promptly.

8. The Demagogue is a fully committed opponent who won't even listen to your opinions. There are a few of these in any subject area—ideologues who have spent years working for the very objectives you oppose. A constituent visiting Congressman Mike McCormack (Democrat of Washington) to argue that nuclear power plants are unsafe is in for a hostile, possibly abusive lecture from McCormack, a former nuclear scientist who is Congress's most outspoken advocate of nuclear power.

The lecture by a Demagogue usually begins with a catalogue of all the good things the congressman thinks he has done for your cause. Then he proceeds to demolish the position you advocate.

Most legislators at least concede you the sincerity of your convictions. A Demagogue probably won't. When you find yourself in the presence of a Demagogue in good voice, the best recourse is to change the subject or bring the conversation to a conclusion. You won't gain anything by getting into a shouting match with a congressman. On the contrary, you would only give him a chance to tell other congressmen that "one of those crazies came in and shouted at me about nuclear power," as proof of the irrationality of those who hold your views. Keep cool, let the congressman do all the shouting, and save yourself for another day and another subject.

9. The Good Guys are men and women who are on your side all the way. When you find one, don't rush off. Stick around and reinforce the congressman's position by telling how the subject affects his district. This may give him ammunition for the committee and floor debates, and it will make him feel good to know that voters like his position on the issue. If he starts telling "war stories" about what he's done on the issue, listen with interest and show him your appreciation. Your concern and your commitment will help to impress him with the importance of this issue among the hundreds of issues he must deal with every week. Talk over the ways he may be able to help support your position—by cosponsoring the bill, testifying at hearings, and so forth.

Seeking a Commitment

While the exchange of views and discussion of the arguments is the meat of the conversation, the goal of your visit is to get a commitment, a statement of how the congressman will vote or a promise to do something specific about the issue.

By the time you've discussed a subject with your congressman for a few minutes, you'll have an impression of his reactions. If you think he's on your side, leaning toward your views, or undecided, now is the time to seek a commitment. Ask whether he will vote in accord with your position.

Don't accept the standard noncommittal lines, such as: "I share your concern." "Your idea has merit." "I'm sure the committee will consider your comment." "I'll take a hard look at the question." If he gives you this sort of answer instead of a hard commitment, keep after him. Tell him you need to know what he's going to do, because your family and friends (or organization members) want to know.

If he doesn't give you a favorable commitment, ask whether he would like further information on any aspect of the subject. Ask if there are any political problems that would keep him from supporting your position. If so, perhaps you can help overcome these through local citizen organizations.

If he did give you a favorable commitment, tell him you and your friends will help him back home. This implies volunteer help or campaign contributions for the next election, so don't say it unless you plan to deliver on the promise.

If your congressman is clearly opposed to your position or is leaning against your position, don't press for a commitment. You won't want to force him into the wrong position when he might be undecided and influenceable.

Conversations with Staff

When you can't get a meeting with the senator or congressman in person, you will get to meet with a member of the legislative staff instead. In this case, the presentation of your case is much the same as though you were seeing the legislator, but a staffer can't be pressed for a commitment because he or she is not the one who does the voting, and a staffer may not know what the legislator's position is. Further suggestions on dealing with staff members appear in Chapter 13.

Where to See Your Congressman

Usually your visits with your congressman or senator will be in his nearest field office. If you don't know where it is, write him in Washington and ask. The Washington addresses are:

House of Representatives   U.S. Senate
Washington, D.C. 20515   Washington, D.C. 20510

More and more legislators are establishing field offices convenient to the largest population centers in their congressional districts and states. Staffed full-time by aides, these offices are the place to meet with the congressman during his trips home, unless he prefers to see you when his mobile office van is in your community. Call the field office weeks ahead, if possible, to arrange an appointment.

Eastern congressmen often go home every weekend; those from greater distances, once every few weeks. Voters have had more access to their congressmen with the expanded schedule of recesses or "district work periods" adopted since 1977, involving a week or more in the home district every few weeks throughout the year.

When you're in Washington, D.C., on business or pleasure, don't miss the chance to see your congressman and your senators. Many legislators are more relaxed, less rushed, and therefore more receptive in Washington than during the crowded schedule and rapid pace of their trips home. Write or phone ahead to ask for an appointment, but if you neglected to do so, call the office when you get to Washington and you'll probably be able to get an appointment. All senators' and congressmen's offices in Washington can be reached through the U.S. Capitol switchboard, (202) 224-3121.

Legislators are usually busy with committee meetings from 10 A.M. to noon and are easier to see during the afternoon. Most are in their offices or on the floor until 6 P.M. or later. Further suggestions on effective use of your Washington visit appear in Appendix A: "Your Visit to Capitol Hill."

Back home, senators and congressmen appear at a variety of

events that put them in touch with voters. You won't be able to go into issues in depth under these informal circumstances, but you can meet the legislator, raise the subject enough to elicit his interest, and ask, "Can I come and see you about this?" which usually leads to an office appointment. These informal encounters are also the basis for beginning to address the legislator by his first name. The following are some of the most common events in which legislators make themselves available to constituents:

1. **Town meetings** arranged by the congressman, generally in a school auditorium in the evening. Announced weeks ahead of time by mail, newspaper, and radio, these are the forums at which the congressman invites all citizens to come and voice their concerns about any topic. You can express your viewpoint when your turn comes, and ask the congressman for his position. You can also get a chance to shake the congressman's hand and introduce yourself before or after the meeting.

2. **Public or civic-organization meetings** at which the legislator is a speaker or a panelist. Announced in local news media, these are usually focused on a particular subject. Your best opportunities here are to ask questions during a question-and-answer period, if there is one, and to catch the legislator in the crowd before or after the program and get a brief word with him. A congressman's field office may be able to tell you whether he is scheduled to make such appearances soon.

3. **County and city fairs,** at which congressmen work their way through the crowds, shaking hands. A congressman's office can tell you when he plans to be at the fair and how you can meet him there. If his political party has a booth at the fair, the attendants may be able to tell you whether he's around.

4. **Party rallies, bull roasts, and community barbecues.** Ask your local party office whether such events are coming up.

5. **Fund-raising dinners or receptions** for the congressman or for other politicians of his party. In February every year, Republicans have Lincoln Day dinners while Democrats have Jackson Day dinners. You can get a few moments with the congressman during the cocktail hour or after the dinner. You don't have to be a member of the party to go. In many communities, the tab is twenty-five

or fifty dollars—well worth it because you not only get a brief word with the congressman, but it's in a situation that will make him think of you as politically active in his party. Washington lobbyists go to many fund-raising functions, of both political parties, every year as a means of building ties with legislators whom they want to influence. You can certainly do the same thing to get closer to your own legislators.

7

Organizing for Influence

Ten Ways to Organize a Legislative Campaign

Members of Congress are highly sensitive to organized opinion back home because it can affect their reelection chances. Even if it starts with just you and your neighbors meeting around your kitchen table, an organization can get results that you as an individual never could.

1. Invite a few people who share your concern over for a beer some evening, and chat about the issue and what you can do about it by working together. Decide what your specific goal is. Let the others contribute most of the ideas, so they'll feel committed to doing their share of the work.

2. Set up your campaign group either as a new ad hoc organization or coalition or as a project of an existing organization—whichever will make it easiest to build broad support in your community.

3. Plan your campaign. Assess your potential sources of support in the community—people and groups that will help you influence your congressman. Think about your potential opponents and what you can do to neutralize their efforts.

4. Get your bandwagon rolling. Involve every conceivable local organization in your campaign, and get each group to write to

109

your congressman stating its views on the issue, even if you have to draft the letter yourself. Don't stop with groups that are already interested in your cause; the more unexpected a group's participation, the more influential it will be.

5. Target your campaign. Make a special effort to get support from groups, individuals, and neighborhoods that strongly supported the congressman in the last election—"his people"—and from the "swing precincts" that could make or break him in the next one.

6. Have a continuing membership campaign, but keep the dues low. You need members to write letters to Congress, to spread your message all over town, and to enlarge your leadership cadre. You also need their dues to pay the bills.

7. Get plenty of volunteers involved actively, and train them to be leaders. Put new people to work on your committees and task forces, where they can do productive work and learn leadership skills at the same time. Give people responsibility, and they'll rise to the challenge.

8. Keep morale high. Use slogans, emblems, buttons, and T-shirts to help your people identify with your campaign. Create an environment that promotes friendships among your volunteers, so the campaign will be fun for them.

9. Publish a newsletter. You need one to keep people informed and interested, and to show local politicians and opinion makers that your group is a continuing presence in the community.

10. Stay one step ahead of bankruptcy. You can raise money through projects that also draw favorable attention to your group, such as a raffle, garage sale, scrap metal drive, or craft fair. Ask your more well-to-do members for money.

Senators and congressmen are highly sensitive to organized opinion, especially when it represents a broad spectrum of constituents and appears to reflect seriously held views. They know that a local citizens' organization can do a lot to help or hurt their chances for reelection, either by spreading favorable or unfavorable reactions to the legislators' actions or by providing volunteers during the election campaign. An organization represents something that won't go away. If voters were serious enough to organize around an issue, they won't forget what a legislator does about the issue.

A few people working separately in a congressional district can make an impact on an uncontroversial issue, but when you're confronting dedicated, active opposition or dealing with a legislator who won't listen, organizing is the only way you'll succeed. An organization, even if it's just four people who meet at your kitchen table once a week, does things that you alone can't do.

An organization gives the issue visibility in your community and makes it a local issue, which means that it will get more respect and attention from news media, politicians, and citizens. The association of a nationwide issue with local people and a local organization makes it easier for a legislator to respond, because his primary interest is in the impact of the issue on his constituents.

An organization is a vehicle for involving other people and organizations in the campaign. When people hear that Jane Jones is fighting for the Day-Care Centers Bill, they'll smile and say, "More power to her!" When they hear that a citizens' committee has been organized to work for it, some will be moved to join and help. People like to be part of something, and the existence of the organization gives them hope that something can be done about the issue. It helps to dispel their feeling of powerlessness.

An organization provides a structure for planning the campaign and assigning responsibility. The people and organizations whose support you want will more readily respond to a call for help from an organization than from an individual.

An organization can have stature in your community and state, perhaps as great as the stature of a mayor or governor. Because of this, an organization can do things that would be presumptuous or laughable for an individual to do, such as challenging a government agency's data, proposing a study, or hosting workshops and inspection trips. Having an organization can put you on roughly the same level as a senator or congressman, and thus able to deal with legislators on an equal basis, instead of as a prayerful suppliant. Stature doesn't come from being the oldest group in town; it comes from being recognized as a credible, active organization that can get things done.

Organizing is like being a parent. At first the children need you to feed them every couple of hours, but later they learn to raid the icebox without any help. Organizing can also be a hard push at first, but you'll find that as the campaign broadens, help will begin coming in from sources you never knew existed. The campaign acquires a life of its own, reaching into the nooks and crannies of the congressional district, involving people and groups you never would have thought of. With a modest investment of your own time and energy, you'll be a catalyst for a large outpouring of work by many people. Organizing can make you proud.

The First Steps

To start off, get together with one or two or a handful of people who believe as you do and think they want to work on the issue. Have them over for coffee some evening after dinner or at another convenient time. By talking over the situation together, you can energize each other with the conviction that together you have potential influence on your legislators' votes on the issue. Chat about what your goal is and how you can achieve it. The following questions cover the main points that must be covered:

• "What is it we want to achieve?" If your aim is to win your congresswoman's vote on a particular bill, this question is easily answered. But if you're trying to stop a federal project in your state, such as a dam or a freeway, you'll want to decide what you favor instead—perhaps a public park, or just leaving the land as it is. Being for something gives you a tactical advantage, and may open the door to new sources of support.

• "Who are potential supporters of our position in this congressional district?" Consider those who are already active and those who are not active but who have good reasons to be involved, such as a dimly perceived self-interest. Which of these will be most influential on your legislators? Some supporters will be obvious, others will be less so. For instance, on an education issue the local education association and teachers' union are obvious allies, but what about neighborhood associations and state legislators?

• "Who are our adversaries in this congressional district? Who will be trying to influence the congressman to oppose our position?" Consider what contacts you have within these adversary groups, because you may find people who share your views and will leak information to you. This is often possible when the adversary is a large organization or government agency.

• "How can we get our potential supporters involved actively?" This is the crux of the organizers' task. Consider whether you should set up an ad hoc organization for this fight, or whether you can use existing groups you're involved with to lead the fight.

• "Where will the money come from to cover the expenses of the campaign?" Starting is cheap, but printing and postage can mount up fast, so it's wise to think ahead.

Avoid coming on as the big leader. Let others contribute most of the answers, so they'll feel committed to further work. After a few hours of hashing over these questions, the answers will serve as your first action plan.

Framework for Organizing

You have several options in deciding how to structure your campaign. You naturally want a framework that will provide the best access to your potential supporters, make the best impression on the legislators you want to influence, and enable you to avoid spending your time on bureaucratic detail. These are some of the most often used and most effective formats:

1. An existing organization. If you are already active in a group that has a good reputation and that will give you a free hand to carry out your legislative campaign, start by setting up a committee or task force on the subject, and make that the core group for the campaign. This has the advantage of bringing into your campaign the goodwill enjoyed by the parent organization, the cooperation of closely allied groups, and possibly office space and funds contributed by the parent group.

There are several drawbacks to this arrangement. You can't easily build up a separate membership because people would have to join the parent group to affiliate with your campaign. Some leaders of the parent group may object to the controversial nature of your efforts, and you may have to spend time mending fences to keep the parent group from disowning you. Your opponents may be able to bring pressure on less-committed members and leaders of the parent group to moderate your stand. Some of your potential supporters may not cooperate because they are jealous, hostile, or distrustful toward the parent group as a result of past differences or basic philosophical disagreements, even though these do not affect the issue at hand. They may fear that your parent group will hog all the credit if you win and blame them if you lose. And if the parent group is a chapter or branch of a national organization, it won't have the authentic local stamp you need to make clear that your efforts are indigenous, not inspired by outsiders.

2. An ad hoc organization. This is easiest to set up, provides the greatest ability to act quickly and make tactical decisions when they're needed, is a good rallying point for people who care about the issue, does not greatly threaten existing groups whose cooperation you're seeking, and is undeniably a *local* group. To start one, all you have to do is choose a name, elect a chairperson, and get a supply of letterheads printed. Its main drawback is that it starts off without a reputation and without money in the treasury. These drawbacks are not hard to overcome, as thousands of such groups have proven.

3. An ad hoc coalition. Often used by organizers who are themselves active in an existing organization, this is a good structure for involving other groups that are uneasy about working directly with your existing organization. Instead of a group of individuals, this is a group of groups that support a single, readily defined objective. It ceases to exist when the issue has been settled. This is a good way to unite local groups in a campaign because it does not require that these groups actually join anything. Most local organizations can join another organization only after approval by their boards of directors. An ad hoc coalition can get around this technicality by not having a formal membership, but instead having the groups sign a joint letter or statement of position on your issue. Thenceforth the cosigning groups, if they wish, can be listed by the coalition as "cooperating organizations." The coalition shows their unity on the issue and is valuable as a way of bringing together groups that normally don't work together. Most of the actual campaign work is done by the cooperating organizations in their own names, and a steering committee or coordinator who is not identified with any particular group asks the cooperating groups to take on certain tasks and responsibilities.

The drawbacks of an ad hoc coalition are twofold. The ad hoc coalition is not well adapted to "battle" conditions because, unless the groups greatly trust the steering committee, the coalition has no power to reach compromises with legislators or issue reactions to day-by-day events in the campaign, because many cooperating groups will not allow a coalition to issue statements that imply the backing of the cooperating groups. And because it has no membership, an ad hoc coalition is hard to get money for, unless some of the cooperating groups will chip in enough money to cover the budget.

4. A permanent coalition. This is primarily useful when the same issue recurs year after year, as in the case of appropriations bills, and you want to avoid going through the organizing hassle all over again. It can also be used when you are trying to build long-lasting ties among diverse elements in your community. The permanent coalition operates by issuing policy statements signed by as many of its member groups as wish to endorse a particular stand. In this case, the coalition actually has member organizations, but any group may decline to participate in an issue on which it disagrees with the rest. As long as a group sees the continued overall cooperation as beneficial to its purposes, it will stay in the permanent coalition. Some permanent coalitions also have individual memberships and professional staff the year round.

Building Your Bandwagon

When you begin to seek allies, it is always helpful to have on your side one or two of the best-known groups in your field, such as on environmental issues, the local Sierra Club chapter or Audubon Society, or, on education, the local affiliate of the National Education Association or American Federation of Teachers. The endorsement of these groups for your cause reassures other organizations that it's a bona fide issue worthy of their attention, not just a selfish concern that you're promoting on your own. Get these groups to write a letter to the congressman or adopt a resolution, then take along copies of their letter or resolution when contacting other groups.

Organizations already active in your field should be relatively easy to involve in the campaign. At the same time you're approaching them, start working to broaden the campaign by involving unlikely sources of support, because these groups take longer to bring in.

The first request to make of any group is that it write a letter about the issue to the congressman or senators. Some organizations prefer to express themselves through formal resolutions, which have the advantage of showing that it's an official position of the organization, rather than something written off-the-cuff by one officer of the group. If this is the case, get the group to adopt a resolution at its next monthly meeting, and make sure the group sends a copy to the legislators. Offer to help draft the group's letter or resolution. A resolution can be simple, and need not contain lengthy *whereases.* The reasons for a particular stand can be put into a cover letter accompanying the resolution. The following simple resolution may serve as a model:

> *Resolved,* that the Oak Park Council for Better Schools urges the Illinois congressional delegation to support an appropriation of $800 million for Fiscal Year 1980 for the Head Start Program nationwide.

Once an organization has thus taken a stand on the issue, the group may be able to help in other ways through its membership when you have letter-writing or petition drives or other activities such as those described in Chapter 11, "Tactics for a Legislative Campaign." Some organizations like publicity. These should be asked to release their letter or resolution to local media so as to encourage others to join in. Other organizations prefer to stay out of the limelight and won't go further than to write to the congressman. As an organizer you have the responsibility to help each group do whatever it can, and then to make them feel good about having done so.

In your working committee, divide up the list of organizations so each of your leaders will approach the groups he or she has ties with or identifies with.

The broader the spectrum of organizations you get into the fray, the more clout you will have, because while a legislator is accustomed to disagreeing with one or another small sector of his constituency, he will not want to disagree with a cause that is supported by citizens from many different backgrounds. So make plans to involve groups that have not worked with your cause before but have good reasons for doing so now. It takes a long time to bring such groups into the campaign because they have never taken a stand on the issue before, they need time to consider it and get their board of directors to make a decision, and they need to get used to working with your organization. The best approach is to find an insider who will try to activate the group. Give the insider information on the issue, stressing why it should concern that organization. Offer your help—information, research, advice on publicity—and keep encouraging the insider's efforts.

In Montana, conservationists who opposed strip-mining approached ranchers whose land would be devastated by planned coal stripping. A few of the ranchers realized what was at stake and used the information, slide shows, and data on what stripping had done to Appalachia to organize many ranchers in a major campaign aimed at their congressman (and now senator), Democrat John Melcher. It worked, and Melcher became a leading proponent of a tough strip-mine control bill in Congress. Montana conservationists could not have done it alone, but by involving the unexpected allies, ranchers, who had the most influence in Melcher's district, they made a leader out of their congressman.

To get the most return on your time and effort, try to get help from two sources that are vital to the legislator's reelection:

• The organizations and geographic areas of his constituency that strongly supported him in the elections. If you can get support from these people, with whom the legislator expects to agree, you will validate your cause as a serious, respectable one deserving his attention. Even if these groups will only write a letter or cosign a statement, it's valuable to have their support because the legislator thinks of them as "his people."

• The geographic areas that are "swing precincts"—areas that could go either way in the election and therefore may determine whether the legislator will be reelected. Legislators tend to think that a single issue won't make the difference here, but if a lot of mail is coming in from swing precincts, it will be heeded more than the usual mail.

Other groups may try to absorb you or divert your efforts onto their own issues. Take this as a compliment; effective leaders are always in demand, but blunderers never are. Cooperation can be worthwhile, so it's good to help these groups up to a point. They will feel an obligation to return the favor. But don't let yourself be diverted from your project.

In a well-run coalition, whether it's called one or not, each group carries out tasks it is suited to and gets the credit for its share of the work. The groups have elbow room to use their own initiative, without having to check in with some coalition director. The coalition keeps the flame—the objective you are all working for—but authority is decentralized. Ideally, a campaign will reach the stage where you won't even know what is being done by your co-operating groups, but you will know that they are working for the common goal in their diverse ways. One group may be carrying out a letter campaign among its members, another may be using its businesspeople members to contact the legislator by phone, while a third is organizing support from members of the city council. People work best when they have authority, responsibility, and elbow room. Give them these, and your campaign will get maximum effort from all your supporters.

8

Care and Feeding of an Organization

Once you've decided to organize local support on a legislative issue, the techniques of running an action organization come into play. The techniques described in this chapter can be used for an ad hoc organization, for many campaigns that operate under the aegis of a permanent, general-purpose organization, or for coalition campaigns.

The aims underlying organization-keeping are simple: to find people who can help you, to motivate them, and to give them responsibility.

When you form an ad hoc organization on your issue, it's best to keep it informal at first. Many groups of this kind are not incorporated; most operate with a minimum of bylaws and other formalities that would be more important to a permanent organization. Choose a name that describes your aim and will appeal to the people you want to reach. There are several types of names:

- Names that stress what you're *for:*
    Citizens for Better Schools
    Committee for the Preservation of the Tule Elk
    Citizens for No-Fault
- Names that stress what you're *against:*
    Citizens Against Throwaways
    Massachusetts Coalition Against the SST
- Names that stress a general concept you favor, rather than a specific objective:

119

Eugene Future Power Committee
Consumer Action Now

- Acronymic names:
PANG (People Against Nerve Gas)
SOS (Save Our Salmon, Save Our Seashore, etc.)
GOO (Get Oil Out)

The first task of a new organization is to elect officers—at least a chairperson and treasurer—and form a steering committee, which could be those of you that are setting up the group. The second is to adopt a resolution stating your objective and urging your congressional delegation to support that objective, as in the following example:

> *Resolved:* Medford Citizens for Day Care strongly favors the Day-Care Centers Bill, H.R. 2966, now before Congress. We call upon the Oregon delegation in Congress to endorse this bill.

Send copies to local news media and to your senators and congressmen, with a covering letter that goes into the principal arguments for your position.

Decide what type of memberships your group will have. To recruit broad participation, keep the dues low, even as little as a dollar a year if you can get enough larger contributions to make this feasible. Some groups make the dues "whatever you can afford." Having low dues makes it easier to sign people up and build to a respectable membership figure within a few weeks. Will the members have a vote in electing the steering committee and in deciding policy? When you've decided these matters, adopt a resolution such as the following:

> *Resolved:* Midvale Citizens for Better Schools shall have the following nonvoting membership categories: regular members at dues of two dollars a year, sustaining members at five dollars a year, contributing members at ten dollars a year, and patron members at twenty-five dollars a year.

Have one of your members get membership cards printed and organize a membership drive.

Don't try to set up a grandiose organization with chapters in several cities or neighborhoods. These always take up so much time in bureaucratic squabbling and periodic reorganizations that you'll inevitably find your time being pulled away from work on the issue. People like to have their own organizations; they don't like to be subordinate to Big Daddy or Big Mama at headquarters. If you need similar groups in several places, you'll get a lot more done by suggesting that people form their own. This will be more impressive to your legislators, too. When a congressman gets letters from four different chapters of a Consumer Action Council, urging the same policy on him, he will assume that somebody at headquarters sent out orders to "write your congressman." When he gets letters from four different organizations—say, the Centerville Consumers' Committee, Riverdale Consumer Action, Citizens for Consumer Rights, and Midvale Consumer Council—he'll get the impression that people are thinking for themselves, and he'll be concerned about whether these organizations in four neighborhoods will help or hurt him in the next election.

As a new group, you have the problem of acquiring stature and credibility, both as a way of influencing your congressman and as an aid to membership recruitment and cooperation with other organizations. If you have a few local VIPs that you can enlist quickly, your group could gain stature fast by appointing them as an advisory panel and showing their names on your letterhead. Local politicians, college professors in relevant fields, religious leaders, respected citizen leaders, and businesspeople are among the likely candidates. Aim for those who will be respected by those you are trying to influence and by those you are trying to enlist in the campaign. Strive for full representation of your sources of support—men, women, majority and minority groups, different parts of town, all major political parties. Such a panel can be called an advisory board, advisory committee, or advisory council. Or, to save time, cut it down to an honorary chairman or chairwoman, or two honorary chairpersons. Announcing this panel of honorary officers may be good for a mention in the local newspaper, so save it for a couple of days after you have announced the formation of your group.

Building stature must begin right away, because it takes time to create influence. Professional lobbyists earn their credibility and respect over several years' time. A local citizen group has an advantage over the lobbyist and can gain influence faster because you are on the scene and are capable of doing the legislator good or ill among his voters. But you still must demonstrate that your group is one to be taken seriously.

Early in the life of any campaign organization comes an expansion phase, when you move from the original kitchen-table group to a broader division of labor. You have to structure your program to keep new recruits active and give them training. This is most often done by appointing functional committees or task forces. The word *committee* has a negative ring to many people, so *task force* has come into vogue. Whatever you call them, they can be set up for the major functions of your group. Perhaps at first they will cover Research (preparing a factual case), Cooperation (building a coalition), Membership (recruiting more people), and Information (publicity, newsletters, and handouts).

If your community is a relatively compact area, such as a neighborhood or suburb, consider arranging for some cheap office space, which could serve as a mailing address and work center. Having a convenient office makes the organization more a shared endeavor than if it is headquartered in someone's house or apartment. Free space may be available in a church, a student union building, a member's business place, or the office of a sympathetic citizen group. An office-warming party can be both a morale booster and a way of acquiring office equipment and supplies; circulate a list of needed items with the invitations.

You may be able to arrange for a shared telephone which another organization will answer when you're out. This makes your organization more accessible to the community. If news media and potential volunteers repeatedly call your home number and get no answer, they'll stop trying and will begin to think of your group as lightweight, rather than as a serious organization.

To Meet or Not to Meet

An action organization needs to have working meetings for those who are doing the work. You can get a lot done by telephone, but the greatest limitation of the phone is that it doesn't create an esprit de corps. Only in a meeting does the feeling of shared commitment and shared work emerge. Small working meetings also foster new ideas and new perspectives on the group's activities. If you don't have meetings, people will start to feel left out and may begin to lose their drive and consequently spend less and less time on the campaign as they turn their attention to more gratifying causes. People want to have a say in the group's plans, not just receive assignments over the phone from a chairperson who obviously has more power than they do.

Steering committee meetings, task force meetings, and meetings of ad hoc working groups all give people this important group spirit. If your campaign is coming to a head over the next two months or less, weekly meetings of your steering committee or core group—usually six to ten leaders—may be needed. If it's a longer-range project, monthly meetings may be enough. The more specialized committees or task forces, headed by your core-group leaders, will also need to meet often enough to keep spirits up and to plan and divide up their work.

The main business at a working meeting revolves around two points:

1. Evaluation. Are we getting results from what we're already doing? The group assesses the effectiveness of recent efforts and whether these efforts should be dropped or improved upon. For instance: "What contacts have we had with our congressman since our last meeting, and what did he say?" "Is our petition campaign petering out, or is it still getting enough new people involved?" "Did our approach to the city council members result in any endorsements of our bill? Is it worthwhile to keep trying with those who didn't endorse it?"

2. Planning. "What should we do next?" The group plots its future moves and divides up the responsibilities for getting these done.

In practice, these two points are best applied to specific elements of your program, rather than being featured as agenda items in their own right. But they must be kept in mind as the meeting goes through its agenda.

The chairperson of a steering committee or task force would be well advised to draft an agenda and send it a few days ahead of time to those who will be meeting. This serves as a last-minute reminder of the date, time, and place, and it stimulates creative thinking by those who are coming. The catchall item at the end of an agenda, "Other," is an invitation to participants to bring up matters that were left off the draft. When the meeting is called to order, the chairperson should ask for additions to the agenda.

The agenda of a working meeting is very different from the agendas you read about in *Robert's Rules of Order*. Here is a sample draft agenda for an imaginary group, accompanied by our notes on what *might* happen under each item.

Steering committee meeting, Citizens for Better Schools
October 3, 1977, 7:30 P.M.
2855 Oak Street, Centerville

Draft Agenda	**Notes**
1. Attendance	Chairperson observes who is present and absent. Secretary makes note of this.
2. Treasurer's report	The treasurer reports on the low state of the treasury, and the group divides the responsibility for finding new contributors.
3. Congressional contacts	The person responsible for liaison with the congressmen and senators reports the latest information on stances of the legislators and tells how much and what kind of visits and letters the legislators have had on the issue. Then the group discusses what new moves should be made to get more mail and visits. Responsibility for these is assigned.
4. Coalition building	The person responsible for creating a coalition reports on the status of that work. The group then discusses new approaches to be made to potential allies and decides who will contact which groups.
5. Parents' support	The person responsible for involving parents directly reports on efforts under way. The group discusses new ways to involve parents, such as through Parents' Night at

	local schools, and how this will be organized. Responsibility is assigned for organizing a Parents' Night recruitment effort.
6. VIP contacts	The person responsible for getting the support of city, county, and state officials reports on his group's efforts. The steering committee discusses this, and members agree to approach other officials.
7. Building our case	Head of the research task force reports on the opposition arguments that are still a problem, and how we can answer them. A member volunteers to get the school superintendent's staff to develop figures on services that will be dropped unless Congress passes full funding.
8. Publicity	Head of the information task force reports on successes and failures in getting the issue covered by local papers, television, and radio. The group offers suggestions and help.
9. Other	One member suggests a doorbell-ringing campaign for Halloween. She is assigned to organize this and prepare handout fliers.

Closed meetings are to be avoided because of the elitist, closed-door attitude they imply. It's better to announce meetings to your members in your newsletter. When other members show up, welcome them and give them work to do.

So far we have been talking about working meetings held by a core group, steering committee, or task force. These are essential to an active organization that hopes to have political influence.

Not essential, but often helpful, are larger meetings for your membership, built around a speaker, a film, or a social event. These meetings can be a means of recruiting new workers. They also give members a feeling of identity with your organization, a sense that the organization means something to them; this helps later when you're asking for letters to a congressman or are trying to replenish a depleted treasury. Membership meetings can also be a manifestation of political power if you can muster a large audience when your legislators are going to be on the program.

Whatever type of program you plan, the most crucial element of a membership meeting is to provide a context for informal socializing. If your members arrive at the scheduled hour, sit through a speech, and then go off into the night, you've wasted the evening. Instead, when a speech or film is the program, have refreshments afterwards—perhaps coffee and cake, tea and cookies, or beer and pretzels, depending on the group and the setting. This will keep people around and give them an excuse to get into conversation with one another. You have to get them talking, not just listening. A social hour gives your leaders a chance to circulate and ask people for their help on current projects. The leaders will find out what kinds of expertise you have in your membership, and the members will get a better impression of your leaders. Through social interaction your members will realize that they're part of an organization of knowledgeable, likable people, and this creates loyalty to the issue and to the organization.

Many organizations hold monthly potluck suppers or annual banquets, often preceded by a cocktail hour and followed by a short program. These provide even better social interchange, because everybody wants to be there in time for the food and they get into real conversation at the table. We have seen organizations that were dying of boredom come alive just from the institution of a monthly potluck supper.

At colleges and other large institutions there may be meeting rooms adjoining the cafeteria, and your meeting can be at lunch or dinner, a simple matter of "Bring your tray to Meeting Room B at 6 P.M."

The greatest pitfall of program meetings is trying to have them in a central location in a large city when most of the members and potential members live five or ten miles away. Few people will stay downtown for an evening meeting. You'll get better results by having meetings close to a neighborhood or suburb where many of your members live, even if this discriminates against members who live on the opposite side of town.

Regular meetings, if they are well publicized, can attract new people who will join and work for your cause. This is most feasible if your subject lends itself to varied treatment in an entertaining manner. Conservation organizations, for instance, have used program meetings featuring films or color-slide programs about interesting and endangered lands and wildlife. Field trips, outings, and bird walks serve the same purpose in outdoor organizations.

At each meeting, if the audience is not so large as to make it impractical, circulate attendance sheets so you'll have the names, addresses, and phone numbers of those who cared enough to come. These can be used by the task force working on the issue that was the topic of the meeting.

If you find that your membership meetings aren't interesting and are not serving their intended purposes, drop them. The leadership time and money that are spent on useless meetings can be used more productively on another part of your campaign.

The More the Merrier—Recruiting Members

"Only a handful of people really do the work. The rest are just dues payers." This often-heard complaint could not be more wrong! The broad membership of a citizen action organization has several vital roles in a campaign, and contribution of dues may be the least important of these.

The membership is a body of people committed to your cause. Joining is only the first step in that commitment. If members feel welcome in the organization and proud of it because of what they read in a newsletter, what they see at meetings, or what they read in newspaper stories about the campaign, they may agree to do more. Your membership is a primary source of people to write letters to your congressman and to visit legislators when this is needed. Members can spread the word to friends and neighbors by word of mouth and to the community at large by using bumper stickers and other "show-the-flag" devices. Members may be experts—or know experts in many fields—who can develop facts and arguments to support your position. Members have ties with other citizen groups in your community, from service and social clubs to professional societies, and they can activate some of these for your cause. Some of your members have good entree to local politicians and local business firms which have influence with your senators or your congressman. And it always helps to be able to tell a legislator you have a large membership; for example: "Citizens for Consumer Action is a group of 300 people in the Midville area."

The way to get the most and the best help in your campaign is to recruit a diverse membership and systematically cultivate that membership to find the people who will devote their time and skills to the campaign.

The first place to look for potential members is among people who are directly affected by the issue at hand. On education funding, parents and teachers are obvious candidates. In a campaign to stop a proposed dam, your supporters start with farmers whose land will be inundated, as well as canoeists and fishermen.

The second place to look is among experts on the subject, which may mean scientists, economists, engineers, anthropologists, physicians—any people whose work may have given them insight on your subject.

People will join more readily if they get the impression that your organization *can win.* Your handout material, newsletters, and membership blanks have to look good enough to make people think that your outfit is respectable enough for them. The old church mimeograph is not good enough in these days of cheap, attractive offset printing. Sloppy material will make people think, "Oh, no. Not another losing cause!"

Make it easy for people to join. Equip your members with handouts to give to friends, including a concise statement of the issue and a membership blank that clearly shows what the dues are and where to send the filled-out blank. Print membership blanks in each issue of your newsletter and distribute copies at meetings of other groups whose members may be interested. Ask friendly businesspeople, doctors, and dentists to leave a supply of handouts on their waiting-room tables.

If your issue affects a whole neighborhood, work up a mailbox-stuffer telling your story and including a membership blank, and have members deliver them to every house. To cover an apartment building, find somebody who lives there to deliver the handout to each door, or to get permission for your delivery crew to do so. Delivering these flyers can be a job for your less-skilled volunteers, with a gathering afterwards over coffee or beer to boost the workers' morale, giving them an immediate pat on the back.

Direct-mail solicitation seldom pays for itself in the first year of membership, unless you have a very good local mailing list of people you know are concerned about the issue. People are so tired of "junk mail" that usually only one or two membership applications come in out of every 100 sent out. The best ways for a local group to beat this low return rate are to get a highly respected local person to sign the membership-solicitation letter that is the heart of the mailing, to keep the dues low enough to be possible for most of the people who receive the mailing, and to enclose a postage-paid business reply envelope.

Take advantage of public hearings or meetings to call for citizens' support. Have someone attend city council, school board, or town meetings at which your issue is being discussed, and circulate a sign-up sheet in the audience, headed something like this: "If you would be interested in working to get more federal money for our schools, please sign up below."

Your opponents may do your recruiting for you. The U.S. Corps of Engineers, in public meetings intended to convince local people of the need for more dams, has often created an irate anti-dam movement instead as people realized that their property was going to be taken for projects that would be of little or no value to the public. If this happens in your issue, be sure somebody gets the names of those who attended, or as many as possible.

Better yet, have a respected local person stand up and address the audience, calling for a united movement—something like, "We don't have to let these bureaucrats get away with this. We can win this fight if we get organized. I urge everybody who's against this outrageous project to sign up on the yellow pads that are going around, and we'll organize a meeting for next Monday night to plan what we can do."

You can also carry your message to local civic clubs, which are always looking for programs for their meetings. Service clubs (Kiwanis, Rotary, Soroptimists, etc.), garden clubs, League of Women Voters, outdoor and hunting clubs, environmental groups, and consumer groups are possible audiences, depending on what your subject is. Once you have a few good speakers lined up—recruited from your membership and prepared on the topic—you'll be able to enlist widening support from other community groups, both in endorsements from organizations and in membership. A part of every speaker's routine must be to hand out your group's basic handout flyer, explaining the issue and containing a membership blank.

If some groups think the issue is too controversial, suggest a panel discussion—your speaker, another panelist from the opposition (you need not suggest their most articulate spokesman), and a moderator from the host group.

Your organization can also stage events that will involve the public. Groups trying to save a park have organized a cleanup day in which people turned out to rid the park of trash, old tires, and junk. Other conservation groups have staged a mass hike or walk to draw attention to a threatened area. For instance, New Jersey, Pennsylvania, and New York groups for several years had an annual hike to Sunfish Pond, imperiled by a power project. The event drew hundreds of participants from six states, and got news coverage in several metropolitan areas.

Have your organizing team get the names, addresses, and phone numbers of all participants. Your task force or committee leaders should be thoroughly involved, so they can recruit helpers for their projects and identify people with expertise that your organization can use. Don't omit the social gathering from these events. It could be a picnic during the hike, or a spaghetti feed after the hike or cleanup morning. Anything to draw your people together and get them thinking and talking about the issue will increase their commitment and participation.

For issues that are not outdoor oriented, more imagination may be needed. On an issue that involves your neighborhood, block parties could be the event that will involve people. On education issues, a bazaar to benefit the playground-equipment fund might work. What you're aiming for is a public-spirited, noncontroversial activity that will involve people at least marginally in your cause, so that you have a chance to enlist them more actively in your issue campaign.

Putting Them to Work

Have tasks ready for your new recruits. It's the responsibility of your leaders to have in mind plans for expansion of their work as new volunteers join the team—the sort of work that is covered by the oft-heard remark, "We'd do it if we just had another person."

Paper-shuffling donkeywork is a poor way to welcome a new person to your group. Granted, you've got untrained volunteers on your hands who don't have great skills to offer. But if you put a volunteer to work stuffing envelopes for his first day, you'll be extremely lucky if he shows up again. This type of paper work is better done by work parties including experienced leaders as well as novices, with coffee or beer and camaraderie to keep spirits up.

Victory at the end of the campaign is not reward enough for people who are working their hearts out for a cause. People need praise and recognition at all stages of a campaign, and they want to be doing work that clearly contributes toward the long-range goal. So if you have abundant volunteers and not enough work for them, put on your thinking cap and devise some ways of using their energy. A petition drive often fills the bill, but it won't keep them going forever, so have something else ready or resign yourself to losing a lot of help. It's true, a campaign does not always have endless opportunities for unskilled volunteer work, but the more you can use productively, the more people you'll have ready to give their all when the next big crisis arrives—a public hearing or a letter-writing campaign.

Elevating people from the unskilled level to more skilled tasks is a high priority for a citizen group, because there is always more work to be done at the skilled level than there are people to do it. *Training* is the key. Keep your new people learning—learning the facts of the issue and learning the techniques of leadership. Each task force or committee chairperson must emphasize training by having new people team up with more experienced people. On a publicity committee, for instance, Jim Smith, a novice, may at first be asked to type up, Xerox, stuff, and mail a news release that was drafted by Jean Day, an old hand. But after a week or two of this, Smith should be drafting releases under Day's supervision. After a month, Smith should be ready to take over the writing altogether, while Day is freed from the news release work and is assigned to get your issue onto radio talk shows and television interviews—a new project that couldn't be undertaken as long as Day had to spend all her time on news releases.

It's the same with political skills. Have a new volunteer go along when your experienced people go to visit a legislator or city council member. Next month your new person will be ready to lead such visits.

Leaders come from many backgrounds. Indeed, people without previous leadership experience may prove to be your best leaders because they will gain more satisfaction from a leadership role than others who have been leaders many times before. They will enjoy learning how to lead, and they will have the personal fulfillment of working with people toward an objective they believe in.

People without leadership experience bring other skills that can help in leadership—social skills such as the ability to make other people feel welcome, or individual executive skills such as those of a homemaker.

People enjoy having titles, and in a citizen group titles are easy to bestow. Not having one can be deflating, such as when you're asked, "What do you do in the Citizens' Committee?" and you have to answer, "Oh, I'm just a volunteer." In most citizen groups everybody is a volunteer, and it makes no sense to give titles to some but not to others. Titles can be based on the tasks a person carries out (Director of News Releases, Assistant Directors of News Releases) or on the general area of responsibility in which he or she works (Director and Assistant Directors of Information).

You can't afford to overload your most experienced people with tasks they can't possibly fulfill. This will gradually kill their interest, as the frustration of these unmeetable demands overcomes the satisfaction of working for a good cause. Assigning too much responsibility to the old hands also denies your new people the chance to learn and denies them the stimulation of having greater responsibility placed on their shoulders. Being given new responsibility is one of the best rewards a volunteer can receive, because it shows that you like what he has done and that you trust him to carry out the new task well. As a result, your volunteer will put even more effort into the campaign. Shared responsibility is what makes the best organizations work.

A leader who tries to do everything himself because he's the most competent person—what we call "the one-man band"—never builds a good leadership base because those who should be leaders never get to do the responsible jobs. If Bob Brown is chairman of the group, does the liaison with other groups, makes all the public appearances for the group, writes the news releases, and visits the legislators, then it's obviously Bob Brown's organization. To anyone involved, it's clear that the only other roles available are those of acolyte to Bob Brown, doing work that is too menial for Brown. Anyone who wants to help inevitably ends up stuffing envelopes or distributing petitions.

An organization of the Bob Brown type can give the illusion of being adequate while a campaign is just beginning and there isn't much happening. But at the peak of a campaign, when everything seems to be happening at once, Bob Brown simply can't do everything that must be done, and it's too late to recruit and train leaders to carry the load.

Bob Brown would be smarter to realize that, while he's certainly the most competent, there are other men and women who want to help, who have time on their hands, and who can be trained for leadership positions. A good leader is a good trainer. Brown would find that by spending more of his time training others, he will end up with a highly competent leadership cadre.

New leaders can be trained on the job by being assigned to work with more experienced people. Working together in committees or task forces, in which more and more responsibility is given to the less experienced, creates a cadre of leaders who have a stake in success and are therefore strongly motivated to continue their work even when the going gets tough. When your opponents have brought off a daring tactic that threatens to scuttle your objective and you have to show strong support overnight, leaders like these will work all night to save the cause. They won't do the same for good old Bob Brown, and he can't do it by himself.

Another leadership problem that stands in the way of developing broadly based leadership is the credit grabber, a leader who in effect says, "I did it!" and denies credit to others in the organization. It's essential to give credit unstintingly to all who helped, both at the final victory and in the events that form the building blocks of a victory. When your group holds a seminar or press conference, the people who organized it should get a public pat on the back. When a leader is congratulated on an effective campaign, he or she should immediately reply that it was a group effort and that the real credit belongs to all the citizens who worked together for this cause. Spreading the credit around rewards your leaders and members and cooperating groups while it also reminds legislators and the public that you have broad support and therefore are a political force in the community.

In enlarging your leadership group, you have to train people both in leadership skills and in the facts of your issue. People who are taking responsibility in your cause need to know the facts and arguments that underlie your position and how to answer opponents' arguments. The facts can be learned gradually through on-the-job training, but if you need to prepare a lot of people fast, consider holding workshops. Let's say you have forty people you want to prepare on the issue. Break this large group into five small groups of eight each, with a more experienced "resource person" sitting in with each group. Have the small groups choose their own chairperson and reporter, who takes notes on an easel-mounted pad. Instruct the small groups to come up with the arguments in favor of your position, then the arguments against your position that may be used by your opponents, and finally the refutation of those arguments. The resource people are there to help, but not lead, the discussion. It may take all day to go through the process, but when your people have finished it they will remember the arguments and facts. Knowledge you have struggled for will stick with you long after you've forgotten the content of a lecture. Some new and effective arguments may also be contributed by participants during this workshop process.

In another workshop situation, one of your members may play the role of a hostile legislator and ask all the tough questions, while your members try to respond accurately and persuasively.

Another type of workshop can aid your campaign both through discovery of new arguments and through exchange of leadership techniques. This is a one-day workshop or seminar on the issue, involving leaders of your organization and leaders from similar groups working on the same subject in other parts of your state or region. Generally held on a Saturday, when most people can attend, this kind of workshop consists of small group sessions during the morning to work on facts and arguments, and small group sessions in the afternoon concerning various techniques, such as

"Meeting the Media," "Lobbying," "Recruiting Members," and "Fund Raising." You'll see that each citizen group has found new solutions to the problems that all related organizations face. Your people who attend will be invigorated by the sharing of experiences and by the realization that your group had as much to offer as the others did.

Morale Boosting

In an issue campaign there is always a tendency for people to lose heart when they see that the campaign has not immediately attained its goal. If you let this discouragement grow, you will lose the time and commitment of active members and leaders as well as losing the financial support of their dues and contributions. To help your people survive the low times, use some of the morale-boosting techniques that have been successful for other groups.

An attractive membership card is the first morale booster your members receive. Charter membership has a special flair, so consider keeping your charter membership category open during your initial membership drive, and use special "Charter Member" cards.

Use a slogan, acronym, emblem, or graphic design on your membership cards, posters, flyers, newsletters, and other materials. This will stick in people's minds as a symbol of your organization.

Sell buttons or T-shirts showing the name, emblem, or slogan of your group. These help morale and also spread the word about your cause as friends of your members see them and ask what they represent.

Distinctive garb can build morale at a public forum. One example is the orange neckerchiefs used by North Carolinians who were fighting to stop a dam project on the French Broad River. When members of the Upper French Broad Defense Association wore the neckerchiefs to a government hearing, the bright color showed up clearly on color television news reports of the event, demonstrating graphically that the dam opponents were in the majority.

Morale can be aided by declaring a victory when you make even a little step in your progress toward ultimate victory. For instance, it's a victory when your city council endorses your objective or when you force a hostile government agency to release information they had tried to suppress. These small victories serve as milestones, showing people that you're making progress.

The best morale builder is the creation of friendships among your members and leaders. Working together is fun when people are friends, and the friendships will produce even more work. New recruits will come back if they have struck up a friendship at their first meeting, even when the tasks have been uninspiring. Friendships can be fostered by providing a social setting before or after meetings, such as having refreshments after a program. They can also be fostered by having parties, and if you need an excuse, have a party to raise money (at perhaps five dollars per person, using donated food and beer or jug wine), to start a raffle, or to introduce a candidate who is running for office.

Your Newsletter

Part of your morale-building program is your newsletter, which serves other purposes as well. It doesn't have to be fancy; an 8½ × 14-inch page, printed front and back, is a simple but effective format. Even this rudimentary publication helps to keep your members committed and proud both of your cause and of your organization, it trains your members by giving them new facts and arguments on the issue, it informs them of what has happened, and it urges them to take action—whatever specific action your steering committee wants, be it letters to a congressman or phone calls to the mayor. Your newsletter also shows local news media and politicians that you're an active, respectable organization.

The morale factor of a newsletter is one of its most important functions. You have to keep people informed of successes and failures and reinforce their allegiance to the cause by asking them to do things at regular intervals so they will feel both informed and involved. The newsletter should let them know how many attended last month's public hearing on the issue and how many testified for and against the proposal. What did Senator Doakes tell your group's delegation when they met with him? What have your opponents been doing? What new groups have endorsed your position? Include the dates in your news stories.

Fund Raising

Paying for the activities of a citizen group is not always easy. But when you're fighting against big industry or big government, it's reassuring to know that for every dollar you spend, your opponents will have to spend five or ten dollars. Citizen groups always get more bang for the buck because the issues are a matter of personal conviction, not just part of a nine-to-five job. Citizens work at nights and on weekends, they don't take two-hour martini lunches, and they contribute countless hours of time, skill, and experience. Can your opponents say the same? In a citizen group, a small treasury can do great things.

The first money in the treasury of a citizen action group usually comes from passing the hat at an organizing meeting, but you can't last long on what your kitchen-table leaders can afford to chip in. The second source is from selling memberships, and that's why the printing of membership cards and membership solicitation flyers is one of the first items of business.

At the same time the membership drive is under way, one of your leaders should have the responsibility of approaching people who favor your cause and could easily afford larger contributions of seed money—perhaps $100 to $500—to cover the costs of your membership drive, printed literature, publicity mailings, and newsletters. A few sizable contributions will get the show on the road fast. Then as long as you are expanding your membership, money will keep coming in in small doses. If this income is not enough, and it usually isn't, you'll have to go into other fund-raising programs.

Promotional items such as buttons, books, bumper stickers, T-shirts, posters, or greeting cards relevant to your cause can bring in funds, especially if you have volunteers who will sell them among friends or run a sales booth at a community fair or in a university union building. Have merchandise to sell that capitalizes on the latest fad of the land; if it's T-shirts one year, it may be beanies the next.

Special fund-raising events can also bring in money, especially when they attract the interest of the general public, who have not already been asked for membership dues or contributions:

- **Raffle.** Offer prizes that appeal to everybody, such as a vacation trip for two, and keep the ticket prices low enough to ensure that you'll sell a lot. Friendly businesses may be induced to donate prizes. You'll need lots of volunteers to sell the tickets. Check first to see whether raffles are legal in your community.

- **Garage sale, barn sale, or rummage sale.** You have to have good sources of donated merchandise, and enough buyers to buy it. One Oregon group, the Eugene Future Power Association, netted $900 from a two-day barn sale; others have done even better. In some cities there is a rummage sale center or thrift shop which different groups rent for a day or two, and this center has a regular clientele that will buy most of the items offered. Some groups put on one big sale a year, but collect and store items year-round.

- **Scrap metal drive.** You'll need a truck and lots of cooperation from neighborhood people, but if you've got them, this is a one-Saturday project that can net a tidy sum, as high as $1,000 to $2,000. The big gains come from having people who will let you cart off an old car hulk or heavy equipment that has been cluttering up their property.

- **Scrap paper drive.** This is a long-term project that brings in money slowly. It requires a lot of unskilled volunteer labor, which is hard to sustain over a period of months. Moreover, the scrap paper market sometimes is glutted and the price goes down. However, it can produce a significant sum for a small, active group. For instance, the small Dishman Hills Natural Area Association in Spokane, Washington, raised over $1,000 in 1977 from all its recycling collection efforts, which included paper (at $20 to $30 a ton), metal, and beverage bottles and cans.

- **Block party.** On a local issue, the sale of food and crafts at benefit block parties can add to your treasury, and the parties also provide a chance to rally your neighborhood to the cause and recruit new leaders. But don't try it unless you know that the neighborhood people are really interested.

- **Benefit concert.** If you have good performers who will donate their talent and an audience that will pay to hear them, you've got a chance to raise substantial sums. Rock, folk music, chamber music, and jazz concerts—all have been used by different citizen groups. Rely on local talent, because nationally known performers are constantly besieged by cause groups wanting them to do benefits. Watch your production costs carefully; unplanned expenses, such as paid advertising, could eat up half the receipts. And avoid commercial promoters like the plague; there are many of them around the country who produce benefits in return for a percentage of the take, but the usual result is that you net less than a quarter of the receipts because these promoters run up high expenses. If you can't run a benefit yourselves, don't run it at all.

• **Bake sale, craft fair, or art fair.** Held on a Saturday at a place with lots of pedestrian traffic—often a shopping center or downtown street or city park—these fund-raisers sell things made and donated by your members.

All of these fund-raising events depend on good publicity that identifies the event with your cause. The publicity responsibility should be assigned when the decision is first made to have such an event, and publicity plans should be made at least two months ahead of time. The organizing committee should check into pertinent laws and obtain necessary permits.

Most of the fund-raising methods described above are not dependent on the tax status of your organization, but when you seek large amounts as outright contributions, there is a crucial distinction. When a person wishes to deduct his gift as a charitable contribution on his federal income tax return, he can give it only to organizations that are qualified as charitable organizations under Section 501(c)(3) of the Internal Revenue Code. Under changes in the tax code enacted in 1976, many citizen groups may qualify for this category that previously didn't. However, groups with less than $500,000 annual income that spend more than 20 percent of their income on attempts to influence legislation will be taxed for the excess over 20 percent. If you plan to seek large contributions from people who will want a tax deduction, have a lawyer advise you as to your group's options. Don't let your lawyer or your big donors pull your organization's teeth by insisting that your group limit its legislative activity.

If your members like what the organization is doing, many will be willing to make extra contributions in addition to their dues. Special-appeal mailings, if they are not repeated too often, can bring in funds. A good time for special appeals is during November and December, when people are in a spending mood and when the well-to-do are figuring out how to use deductible contributions to put them in a lower tax bracket.

Try to tie special appeals to a need that has come up unexpectedly—a need to organize support for a forthcoming public hearing, to fight a new offensive by your opponents, or to send a delegation to Washington. Another approach is to list examples of what a contribution will pay for, since it's well known among fund raisers that people are more willing to contribute when they have a notion of what the money will be used for. For instance, one organization working against the B-1 bomber program listed the following in its fund-raising leaflet:

> $15 will produce and distribute 1,000 single-sheet leaflets
> $25 will produce and distribute 200 brochures
> $50 will produce and distribute 200 posters
> $100 will print and mail one issue of the Campaign Organizers' Newsletter

Don't neglect to include a postage-paid business reply envelope. These always pay for themselves because they make it easy to send in a contribution.

Besides mailing to your members, you can approach likely members personally, asking for money for a specific purpose or for general operations. When you find a person who wants to contribute a lot of money, you might wish to suggest that he or she make it a "matching grant," contingent on your matching it (dollar for dollar, or perhaps one dollar for three) through other contributions. Thus you can tell other members, "Every dollar you contribute means two dollars to the Better Schools Committee; every five dollars means ten dollars; every twenty-five dollars means fifty." This is a good way to increase contributions both through special-appeal mailings and through personal approaches.

A concerted program to get large contributions from members can take the form of a pledge club. The Northern Plains Resource Council, an antistrip-mining group organized by Montana ranchers, set up the "200 Club," whose aim was to get 200 people to pledge $200 a year. Variations on this theme might include one-year pledges of $100, which could make a big difference to a small action group trying to get an action program going fast.

Seeking funds from outside your membership must be done with good planning, because otherwise you'll waste a lot of time approaching people who have money but consistently turn down all except their pet charities. (They didn't get their money by being a soft touch for every good cause in town.) There are three good possibilities:

• **The believer.** A person who already agrees with your objective will give if he can be convinced that your organization is going to be effective in attaining that objective. An approach by someone he knows and trusts is the best way to open negotiations. He will probably want to see a budget.

• **Friends of a member.** When one of your members is highly respected in your state and has a circle of wealthy friends, your member might be willing to ask them to make a contribution to your group. The Kentucky Wilderness Council gained this kind of help from a retired judge, who signed individually typed letters (drafted by the group and typed on his own letterhead by organization volunteers) to a list of his old friends. They responded with several thousand dollars.

• **The beneficiary.** If there are businesses or organizations that would profit from a victory for your cause, they may be willing to contribute. However, you should decide whether you want such contributions, because these could impair your stature as a selfless, public-interest group. If you take industry money, your opponents might accuse you of being a front for selfish interests, and your credibility with the public and with legislators might suffer.

In each case the potential giver must be convinced of two things: that your project *needs* to be done, and that your organization is the best qualified group to carry it out because of your know-how, experience, and contacts.

Finally, and least likely for an organization devoted to influencing legislation, are grants from foundations and government agencies. University student groups can sometimes get modest grants from their student association, and the Ralph Nader-inspired public-interest research groups in several states are financed by a regular grant from student activity fees at state universities, as authorized by a special vote in student elections. Local foundations active on your subject would be sympathetic, but they cannot contribute to legislative action projects except for specific research or educational functions, and foundation executives verge on the paranoid when dealing with legislatively active groups because foundations are carefully watched by the Internal Revenue Service (IRS) to prevent them from supporting legislative action.

If you can get them, foundation grants can legally be used by legislative groups for strictly scientific and educational projects. They could pay, for instance, for preparation, printing, and distribution of a report on the impacts of inadequate health care in Central County, so long as the report was a research report and did not advocate legislation to solve the problems of inadequate health care. This is no great handicap, because your advocacy can be stated as openly as you like in other literature that is paid for out of your regular budget. There is no room for fudging with foundation grants; the money must be carefully accounted for to satisfy the foundation and the IRS.

For further information on fund raising, we recommend *The Grass Roots Fund Raising Book*, by Joan Flanagan, available for $5.25 postpaid from The Youth Project, P.O. Box 988, Hicksville, N.Y. 11802.

9

Your Publications

Your legislative campaign will depend on the printed word to transmit information, to inspire people to action, to give recognition to politicians and organizations that support your position, and to build the respectability of the cause you espouse. Publications to carry out these functions may be issued by an ad hoc organization, by a coalition, or by different groups that already exist in your community. While the suggestions that follow are presented as though for an ad hoc group with members of its own, they can also be applied to campaigns structured in other ways.

There are two main audiences to which a citizen group's publications must be aimed. The first is the group's own membership. These people are already somewhat interested in the issue; at least they've made the tentative commitment of joining an organization. You build on that interest by informing them regularly of what's happening on the subject, by inspiring them to care enough about it to become active, and finally by giving them cues for action—when to write letters and to whom, when to attend hearings, when to visit legislators, and so forth.

The second audience is the general public, or at least that segment of the public that might become interested in your issue. These people have not made the initial commitment of joining an organization, so you have the additional challenge of grabbing their attention long enough to arouse their interest and get them to make their first commitment, which might be a relatively simple act such as signing a petition or writing a letter to a senator. Getting their attention is the crucial point, because people are bombarded with dozens of demands for attention every day from advertising, from television, from their families, their work, and their play. "Why should I care?" is the question you have to answer.

In publications both for your members and for the uncommitted, don't mince words. Write vividly, using strong words and gripping similes and metaphors. Be sure of your facts and state them strongly. Of course, you'll also include the actual details. Your readers will need these facts when they write to their legislators, and you'll be respected by legislators and their staffs when they see that your supporters know the facts.

You can't afford to pull your punches in publications that are meant to arouse people. By doing so, you'll only make the issue look less urgent, and thus give your readers an excuse to do nothing. Besides, people are so accustomed to wishy-washy writing in newspapers, in magazines, on radio, and on television that they'll be entertained by a well-written piece of invective.

Essential to the success of the North Cascades Conservation Council, the group in the state of Washington that led the campaign to establish the North Cascades National Park, was its bimonthly magazine, *The Wild Cascades*, edited by Harvey Manning, which always contained some good old-fashioned invective. One of its best features was a column by-lined "The Irate Birdwatcher," spotlighting the latest misdeeds of the U.S. Forest Service and calling the agency's officials by nicknames such as "Logger Larry." The column was not only strong and to the point, it was funny. Humorous writing is not easy, and neither is invective if you've been writing punch-pulling prose for years. Once you start, it will become easier, just as any other kind of writing improves with practice.

One well-conceived phrase can be a battle cry for your campaign. You won't necessarily hit on one when you need it, but keep trying. In the 1975 campaign for legislation to keep the U.S. Fish and Wildlife Service in charge of the national wildlife ranges, the phrase heard around the country was Lewis Regenstein's charge that the rival agency, the Bureau of Land Management (BLM), then oriented toward livestock grazing, would turn the wildlife ranges into "feedlots for cattle and sheep." It was a daring metaphor that summed up environmentalists' concern that BLM would promote livestock grazing in the ranges and let the antelope, big-horn sheep, and other wildlife dwindle.

Include the names and addresses of your congressman and senators in every newsletter or flyer, especially when you're reaching lots of new people who have never written to these legislators before. It doesn't take much space, and it can be the little push that gets a person to sit down and write a letter.

If you can find an experienced editor among your members who will agree to be editor of your publications, you'll save much time and achieve impressive results at the outset. A writer who is frustrated by a boring job or who is at home raising children, a retired journalist, or someone who has edited a church or garden-club newsletter might fill the bill. An experienced editor brings skills that you need—how to design and lay out a publication, and how to deal with printers and with the U.S. Postal Service.

The Newsletter

A newsletter or small magazine, published every month or two, serves several functions that can hardly be achieved in any other way:

- It generates enthusiasm for the issue among your members.
- It gives members the facts they need in order to take action on the issue.
- It involves members in activities concerning the issue.
- It builds members' morale by reporting on what you've accomplished together.
- Every newsletter, when sent to news media and politicians, reasserts the presence of your organization and your issue in the community; otherwise the issue might sink out of sight.
- It rewards local, state, and national politicians and organizations that have helped your cause.

Since you want people to read your newsletter, the content should balance heavy, fact-laden material with lighter, more entertaining reading. Many of your members have joined out of passive interest in your cause; you still have to coax them into reading the newsletter and becoming more informed and more involved. Cartoons and humor will help by getting people at least momentarily engaged with the issue. When you chuckle at a cartoon about an issue, you feel closer to the issue and to the organization. Another likely source of laughter is the statements of your opponents, statements that may seem rational to them but sound patently ridiculous to your members. You can also poke fun at yourselves; a group that is sure of itself and its cause doesn't have to be superserious all the time.

Another balancing act the editor must perform is to show your readers proudly what their organization has been doing, and at the same time give due credit to cooperating organizations so they don't get the impression that your outfit is infected by the "We-did-it" syndrome.

These are some of the things to include in a newsletter:

• News on what's happening to your issue in Washington, D.C., and in your community
• Notices of your group's meetings and activities
• News about the group's recent achievements
• New arguments and facts
• Local case histories that support your arguments and make the issue dramatic
• Editorials
• Exchange of letters with your congressman and senators
• Pertinent quotations (yours or your opponents')
• Book reviews
• Reprints of good stories or editorials from local newspapers

In your coverage of recent activities, stress what local volunteers have done on the issue, so your less active members will identify with the campaign and feel drawn into it.

If your opponents have been active, tell your members. People are always more active when they know they're fighting wrong-headed or irrational opposition. Also cover your opponents' arguments, and give your answers to their new arguments as they arise. Your readers need to know how to respond to opposition arguments because these arguments will be raised by legislators and by friends and neighbors. Your supporters will lose interest in your cause if they can't answer them.

A newsletter should keep a regular schedule, but when something good happens for which your members can take credit, put out a special issue right away. This sort of newsletter rewards people and reassures them that they have power. It's important not only for those who helped in the fight, but for those who might help next time around. It gives them the idea that you have a winnable cause and a winning organization, and this makes them want to associate with the group.

If your campaign was strongly backed by a whole neighborhood, regardless of formal membership in your group, consider giving everybody the victory newsletter. It will recruit more people to join up for the next round.

The special issue is also a good chance to praise the legislators who did the right thing. Senators and congressmen always want favorable publicity. This desire is especially urgent for little-known House members from large urban areas, because such legislators aren't covered in major metropolitan dailies and they often don't have small local newspapers in their districts that will report their activities. Citizen-group newsletters that are read primarily in one congressional district are valuable to congressmen who labor under this handicap.

Choose a title for the newsletter that is not too far afield from the name of the organization. Otherwise people will remember the newsletter title and forget the organization—no small point when the organization is seeking contributions from members or is sending out membership renewal notices. The safest way to link the two is to include the name of the organization or its acronym in the title, and repeat the full name in the masthead, as in *Midvale Consumer Council Newsletter* or *SOS Report* (*Save Our Seashore*).

The Action Alert

An action alert has one purpose—to arouse people to do one specific thing. That one desired action often is to write to a congressman or congresswoman or senator. It may be to testify at a public hearing or it may be to circulate a petition. An action alert is stripped down to this one objective because at crucial points in your campaign you want the greatest possible response from your supporters: you want people to read the alert and then act.

This type of publication can be sent to your members and to members of other active groups that are already interested in the issue. Usually an action alert assumes of its readers a certain sympathy and familiarity with the issue. It may be two to four pages long, and is best designed as a self-mailer, without using an envelope that people have to open to get the message. A capsule headline on the address panel also helps to seize the reader's attention, something like "Senate Consumer Vote Set for April 10" or "Congresswoman Bean Is Wavering on School Funds."

The text of an action alert begins with a catchy headline summing up the issue, such as these examples from two action alerts: "Congressional Action Required to End Plutonium Threat" and "Proposed Power Plants Would Make the Grand Canyon Region a National Sacrifice Area."

Next, in a couple of paragraphs, state the problem vividly, give your group's position on the matter, and call for the desired action, including any names, addresses, and deadlines that are necessary.

Only after that should the text go into the background of the issue. This background section is where you give readers the arguments and hard facts they need to know about your issue. They may have read many of the facts before, but you'd better give them the essentials again; they'll rely on this action alert for the facts they'll use in writing, phoning, or testifying.

Quote authoritative sources—government agencies, experts, locally respected people—so your readers can cite these authorities or paraphrase them in their letters. Quote from good newspaper stories and editorials, too. Include something about the doings of your opponents and, if there's space, mention the opponents' main arguments, with rebuttals. If your campaign is one to stop a bill, outline the alternatives you favor. Your readers will want to know this, and they'll often mention the alternatives in their letters to Congress. Use photographs, maps, and graphs to illustrate your points. These also make the publication more interesting by breaking up the solid columns of text.

When you've finished the background section, end the action alert with a section headed something like "How to Help," "What You Can Do," or "Take Action Now." Here, repeat what you want readers to do and expand on it slightly. Always date your action alert, so readers will know it's timely. In an action alert, be attentive to things that will help your readers visualize themselves doing the requested action. For instance, when you want people to testify at a hearing, deemphasize the word *testify* and use the more familiar terms *speak, present your views,* or *tell the committee what you think.* The hearing itself will seem more approachable if you call it a "public hearing," rather than a "congressional hearing," to get the idea across that it's an occasion for the public, not just for officials or experts or lawyers.

If you can quote a respected local person to vouch for your request for action, it will make your appeal more believable and more urgent. An example at the national level was the remark of Congressman Morris K. Udall (Democrat of Arizona), quoted in the Wilderness Society's newsletter, concerning the House Rules Committee's rejection of the National Land Use Bill in 1974:

Almost without exception the Rules Committee members who ambushed us said they had not received a single constituent letter in favor of the bill. It is important that they get a bundle soon. Until this support is generated, it would be foolish to take H.R. 10294 back before the Rules Committee and risk another, perhaps final, defeat.

Think of people in your community who favor your cause and who will be believed by your readers, and approach one of them with a draft of what you'd like to quote them as saying.

An action alert can be published by a single organization, but when you're in a crisis, your best bet is to put it out under auspices of a coalition. The simplest method is to have one group do the editing and production, but list all the cosponsoring groups conspicuously on the action alert, mail it to members of all the groups, and divide the costs in proportion to the number of names on each group's mailing list. Some of the groups may insist on seeing the text before they join in, but it's often worth the extra trouble to gain wider participation.

Handout Flyers

Publications intended to be handed out to the uncommitted may be in any format that attracts favorable attention, but they must be short and easy to read, and they can't ask too much of the reader. You're trying to coax people into seeing your issue as a concern of theirs, and into taking that first step that gets them involved.

For an issue that affects a whole neighborhood, your flyer might be a single-sheet affair that's easy to stuff into people's mailboxes. For leafletting on street corners, it might be a half-page— shorter because you want people to get the message fast, rather than throw it away.

There's not much room for background details in a handout flyer. You can't afford to daunt the reader with a big load of facts when you're first trying to get him interested. That can come later. Use enough facts and authoritative quotes to show that you've got a solid case, but don't dump the whole load.

The crucial problem with handout flyers is that you want two things from the reader. You want him to take action and you want him to make contact with your group so you can get him involved again and again. One way to link these goals is first to urge the action you want and follow this with a coupon addressed to your organization, with check-off boxes such as the following:

☐ I am writing to Congresswoman Kovak, House of Representatives, Washington, D.C. 20515, asking her support for H.R. 2820.

☐ Please send me further bulletins on the Consumer Protection Bill, when I can help.

☐ I am enclosing $ ———— as a contribution to help organize support for the Consumer Protection Bill in Maxwell County.

Please mail this coupon to: Consumer Action Council, 325 Third Street, Maxwell, Miss. 38921.

Membership Flyers

Used to recruit members for your organization, membership flyers should be attractive, readable, and above all easy to use.

They should be of a size that's easy to carry in your pocket or purse, so you'll have them handy when you're with friends you want to enlist. And they've got to be easy for the new recruit to return with his or her check. You don't want anything to interrupt the reader's train of thought leading from the decision to join your group to the mailing of the membership coupon with a dues check.

It's a rule of thumb in membership recruitment that business reply envelopes always pay for themselves; you really can't afford to do without them. Whenever possible, use them with your membership flyers.

If you're contemplating a large-scale membership campaign and need 100,000 or more membership flyers, an excellent brochure with a business reply envelope attached can be manufactured for you by Webcraft (P.O. Box 185, North Brunswick, N.J. 08902, tel. 201-297-5100). For a flyer measuring 8¾ × 15½ inches, folding to 8¾ × 4 inches, Webcraft charges $25 per 1,000 in a run of 100,000. You provide camera-ready copy, and Webcraft makes and prints the brochure. This sophisticated format is not available from local printers. If 100,000 is too many, you may be able to combine orders with other citizen groups in nearby communities that will use the same format with different text and artwork; changing the plates in mid-run won't add much to the unit cost.

In the smaller quantities needed by many citizen-action groups, the best options are:

- Have regular wallet-flap envelopes printed locally, and fold them in with your membership flyers.

- Print your membership flyer on card stock, and make one panel a membership application in the form of a tear-off business reply postcard, with check-off boxes offering the choice of "Please bill me" or "My check for $ ——— is enclosed." The billing process means more work and you may lose 10 percent who don't pay, but the greater response rate usually more than makes up for it.

Some of the ways a membership flyer can be used are:

- Have your members give them to their friends and personally invite them to join.

- Have cooperating organizations mail them to their members as an insert with their newsletter.

- On a neighborhood issue, stuff them in people's mailboxes or slip them under doors.

- Hand them out at meetings of organizations that share your concern.

- Leave piles of them with a display on a table at your workplace, at a college or work-place cafeteria, or at meetings of relevant organizations.

- Include them as part of a direct-mail membership solicitation, usually also involving a cover letter and business reply envelope.

To get results, a membership flyer must:

1. Catch the reader's attention favorably

2. Express a point of view and get the reader to identify with that point of view

3. Persuade the reader that your organization is doing something effective to advance that point of view

4. Persuade the reader that your group needs help both in members and in money

Only then will a reader reach for his or her checkbook.

Some of these points can be communicated in words you write, but they are also communicated by impressions readers get from your flyer. Consider carefully the unwritten messages your flyer is transmitting, because they might contradict what your words say. A membership flyer that is too attractively printed (perhaps the typeface looks too posh, or the paper is too good) implies that you've already got plenty of money, so why should readers send you any of theirs?

The effectiveness of your organization may be hard to show when you're just starting. As soon as you can, get two or three respected local citizens to give you endorsements you can use in your flyers. Draft these endorsements yourself if the people agree, and work out a final version together.

You can give your membership flyer an action slant by asking readers to do something about the issue (say, "Write to Senator Harry Doolan and ask him to cosponsor S. 1522. His address is: U.S. Senate, Washington, D.C. 20510"). Or include a check-off box such as the following in your business reply envelope or membership coupon: "In addition to my dues contribution, I want to participate in the campaign for federal education aid. Please send me a special Better Schools Action Kit." If you offer a kit, be sure to mail it out promptly and include in it a good fact sheet, a list of things people can do to help, and possibly petition blanks and extra fact sheets to be distributed to friends.

Fact Sheets and White Papers

Unlike the publications discussed thus far, fact sheets and white papers are not intended primarily to arouse your supporters to action, and they are consequently very different in tone. When you write a fact sheet or a white paper, you are not standing on the soap box exhorting the crowd; you are standing next to a person, quietly laying out the facts in plenty of detail and answering his or her questions.

The audiences you're writing for in this case are:

- Your senators and your congressman or congresswoman
- Their staffs
- State and local politicians you hope to involve
- Editorial writers and in-depth reporters with the news media
- Your members
- The leaders of your cooperating organizations
- Leaders of groups you hope to involve in the campaign

A fact sheet is a boiled-down summary of the arguments, stated calmly but firmly, citing the principal evidence or authority for each argument. It is usually no longer than two to four pages, and it is set up in short paragraphs with subheadings, so that each point is easy to find on the page.

When writing a fact sheet, check your passion at the door. Your fact sheet is the first place a legislator's staff will look for the answers to questions raised by the boss or by your opponents, such as, "Why is this bill necessary? How much will it cost? Won't it hurt local businesses? Who supports it?"

You want a congressman's staff to be able to answer these questions by repeating just what you've written in the fact sheet. It should be that dispassionate. A fact sheet is not the place for demagogic value judgments about your cause. Save those for your action alerts, newsletters and flyers. See Appendix C for a sample fact sheet.

A white paper is the exposition of your arguments and facts in their full glory. Like the fact sheet, it should present the information calmly, but it can also include sections that editorialize in unabashed rhetoric. The latter should be clearly separate from the factual material, such as by presenting them as by-lined editorials or as policy statements of your organization.

Commonly ten to twenty-five pages in length, white papers may even include lengthy excerpts reprinted verbatim from original sources, such as scientific papers. Using such source materials increases the reader's confidence in the entire white paper.

A lengthy paper should be organized in sections. Principal subjects to cover are:

- A statement of what you advocate

- A capsule summary of the arguments in one page or less

- The background of the issue

- The arguments for your position and evidence for each. Often each major argument takes up a section of its own, so you can give plenty of detail, especially in the supporting evidence.

- Rebuttal of arguments raised by your opponents. If a flippant or outraged mood is appropriate in your case, this section could be headed something like "Ten Falsehoods Refuted." For a more moderate tone, set it up as "Concerns and Responses" or simply as "Questions and Answers," presenting each opposition argument as a question, such as, "Wouldn't the bill raise housing costs?"

- Quotations of what respected supporters are saying about the issue

- A list of organizations that support your cause
- A coupon by which readers can send in contributions and can order more copies of the white paper and other literature on the subject

There are various ways to issue a white paper. One is to have your organization publish it as a booklet with a catchy title, with photographs, charts, and graphs, and set in type or attractively typewritten. You can even put a price on the cover and sell them to your supporters; however, you'll encourage goodwill by simply asking for contributions to cover costs (for instance: "Suggested contribution $1.00 per copy; $7.00 for 10 copies").

Another alternative is to call it a report, which implies that you've investigated something. This would be the case if you've included information on local conditions or used local case histories. You might give copies to the city council just so you could entitle it "A Report to the City Council." Don't use the title to call attention to the legislators you want to influence; this would only annoy them. Indirect pressure is what you're trying to create.

A third possibility is to issue the white paper under auspices of a coalition. You may not get all your regular cooperating groups to join in, because some may disagree with certain of the concerns expressed in the paper and you're trying to make the paper comprehensive.

A white paper is a useful document in a legislative campaign because it covers all the arguments you're using. However, if your campaign is too fast-moving to allow preparation of such a lengthy paper, consider issuing shorter publications covering parts of your case. These can be issued at different times, whenever you get them done. Sections that lend themselves to this treatment are:

- **The arguments and evidence.** A major argument may deserve a booklet to itself, particularly if it's one you're having a hard time putting across. Detailed evidence and the very fact that you've devoted a whole booklet to it can help the argument along.
- **Rebuttal of opponents' arguments**
- **Quotations of respected supporters.** This can become a sizable booklet, such as the one issued by the Committee for Preserva-

tion of the Tule Elk, containing sixty-three pages of quotes from scientists, representatives of organizations, individuals, and even grade-schoolers, reflecting the diverse expertise and eloquence on behalf of the tule elk.

Include in each booklet a reply coupon or an address from which people can request further information and to which they can send contributions.

Petitions

A petition form is more than a page of blanks for people to fill in with names and addresses. It is one of your most direct ways of reaching the uncommitted. With it in hand, your volunteers will be approaching friends, neighbors, and people on the street to seek their signatures, and copies will be posted on bulletin boards where sympathetic people congregate. The petition itself should present your message in a way that will help win people's support, and one that will make your volunteers proud to be associated with the petition.

The petition will be used by newly recruited volunteers who don't yet know all the details of your issue. A person who has just signed, and who shows great interest, should be able to take a petition blank and get friends to sign. A good petition can stand on its own, without a big sales pitch to go with it.

The message itself should be short enough to read in a few seconds by a person who is thinking of signing. It must state your position frankly, so as to inform and convince the reader. Avoid making references to things the average reader won't understand. If your text raises questions without answering them, it will frustrate readers and put them off.

The text usually starts with something like this:

> We, the undersigned residents of Fort Wayne, call upon the Indiana delegation in Congress to support S. 1232, the Family Health Services Bill. The bill is needed in Indiana because . . .

Include at the bottom of the page an address to which signed petitions should be returned, and from which additional petition forms are available.

10

Spreading the Word: Using the Media

The mass media in your community—chiefly newspapers, television, and radio—are vital to your legislative campaign. They are your best route to the hearts and minds of the voters, they can establish your issue and your organization as respectable, and they can show your senators and congressman that a real issue has arisen in the community. What's more, the media will do all this at little cost to you in money. Instead of cash, you'll need time, patience, and plenty of creativity.

The primary goal of publicity in a legislative campaign is to inform people in your community about your issue in a way that will awaken their support and move them to express that support to their senators and congressman. The importance of the mass media lies in the fact that people rely on them for information on government and politics. A 1973 study by the Senate Subcommittee on Intergovernmental Relations showed that more people rely "a great deal" on television for this information than on any other source—65 percent. The next highest categories are newspapers, with 52 percent, and radio, with 39 percent. By using these media, you reach people through the news sources they are comfortable with and that they believe, rather than through less respected, less credible means such as leaflets and petitions.

Coverage of your issue in the mass media will also bring the subject to the attention of your legislators fast. Legislators and their staffs read local papers carefully and notice new issues reported there. Their field staffs monitor local radio and television to be

157

aware of what is being said about things that concern people. If your issue is featured, it will be noticed where it counts.

When your organization has participated in media coverage of your issue, the organization will become established as a respectable, believable news source, one that is prepared to comment knowledgeably on events concerning your issue. Once reporters know your group as a credible source reflecting a legitimate viewpoint in the community and having solid information, they will call you for comments when something happens. This redoubles your influence because legislators and local politicians will notice that the broadcasters and newspapers consider your group respectable.

Citizens' organizations have one big advantage over industry and government in dealing with news media. Citizen groups welcome publicity as a means of informing the public. Industry and government agencies often fear publicity and prefer to operate in secret, because their motives and actions cannot stand public scrutiny. Many times your opponents will probably try to influence your congressman by meeting with him in private, meanwhile saying nothing in public.

You can use publicity to make the enemy play on your turf. Once you've raised the issue in local news media, the reporters will seek the other side of the story from your opponents, whether they're ready or not. This takes the issue away from the closed-door meetings and exposes it to the light of day, to your advantage. By keeping up the publicity, you'll keep your opponents off balance.

To get your issue into the news, you have to make it interesting. The mass media are in business to sell a product, and they can't sell it unless their audiences are interested in what the media have to offer. For you this raises the basic question: what will make our issue so interesting that uninvolved people will want to hear about it? The question is most crucial when you're starting your campaign. Once you've been in the news, it's easier to stay in the news, but the interest always must be kept up.

Your campaign on a public issue is inherently more interesting than most community organizations' activities. Local charities such as the United Fund and Heart Association get lots of space in the newspapers and time on radio and television primarily because they capitalize on local angles—who benefits, who is leading the campaign, and what groups have made donations. You can make your issue a local one, too. Because yours is more controversial than traditional charities, it will be harder to break in at first, but by showing that people in the community share your concern and by doing interesting things with your issue, you *can* get into the news.

Getting publicity is a matter of cooperating with the media. You need them to carry your message to the public. They need you *if* you can provide solid news that will interest or entertain their audience. They don't need you if you can't. It's your responsibility to provide media with information in the right format and at the right time. They'll take it from there.

Following is a list of books that may help you prepare a successful publicity campaign.

Bibliography

Directories (Generally Available in Public Libraries)

Ayer Directory of Publications, published annually by Ayer Press, 210 West Washington Sq., Philadelphia, PA 19106. Price $54.89 postpaid. Covers daily and weekly newspapers, magazines, and ethnic, religious, fraternal, technical, trade and college publications, arranged geographically.

Broadcasting Yearbook, published annually by Broadcasting Publications, 1735 DeSales St., N.W., Washington, D.C. 20036. Price $32.50 postpaid. Covers all television and radio stations in the United States and Canada, arranged geographically, including station's format and names of principal staff.

Editor & Publisher International Year Book, published annually by Editor & Publisher, 850 Third Ave., New York, NY 10022. Price $27.30 postpaid. Covers all United States and Canadian dailies, arranged geographically, with circulation figures and names of executives and editors; contains lists of weeklies, foreign newspapers, and news services. An important feature is its listing of local bureaus of Associated Press and United Press International.

How-to-Do-It Books

Broadcast Media Guide for Candidates, by Thomas R. Asher and J. Victor Hahn, available from Media Access Project, 1609

Connecticut Ave., N.W., Washington, D.C. 20009. Price $4.25 postpaid. A handbook for candidates in public elections, focusing on the Equal Time Rule.

How to Be Heard: Making the Media Work for You, by Ted Klein and Fred Danzig, published by Macmillan Publishing Company, 866 Third Ave., New York, NY 10022. Price $9.95. An excellent general handbook for citizen groups; useful for anyone initiating a publicity campaign.

If You Want Air Time, available free from Radio Information Office, National Association of Broadcasters, 1771 N St., N.W., Washington, D.C. 20036. A brochure containing the industry's advice to citizen groups on using radio and television. Significantly, it fails to mention the Fairness Doctrine.

Radio: Get the Message, by Gary Marx, available from Radio Information Office, National Association of Broadcasters, 1771 N St., N.W., Washington, D.C. 20036. Price $1.00 postpaid. Detailed advice, endorsed by the radio industry, to citizen groups and local agencies on how to use radio's public-service opportunities. Again, no mention of the Fairness Doctrine.

Strategies for Access to Public Service Advertising, by Glenn Hirsch and Alan Lewis, available from Public Media Center, 2751 Hyde St., San Francisco, CA 94109. Price $3.00 postpaid. An excellent, practical review of the Fairness Doctrine and how to use it, with particular reference to public service announcements.

Government Documents

Applicability of the Fairness Doctrine in the Handling of Controversial Issues of Public Importance, available free from Public Information Office, Federal Communications Commission, Washington, D.C. 20554. The FCC's digest of its rulings on the Fairness Doctrine up to 1964.

Fairness Doctrine and Public Interest Standards, available free from Public Information Office, Federal Communications Commission, Washington, D.C. 20554. A 1974 report by the FCC resulting from a comprehensive reexamination of the Fairness Doctrine.

11

Tactics for a Legislative Campaign

Ten Ways to Put the Heat on Your Congressman

It often takes both persuasion and pressure to win a legislator's vote. You have to have the arguments and facts on your side, but you need to apply good old-fashioned pressure, too.

1. Make your cause respectable. Get scientists, economists, prominent local citizens, labor and ethnic leaders to speak up for your side.

2. Make your opponents' position unrespectable. Reveal who really benefits from their cause. Try to provoke them into "blowing their cool."

3. Make sure everybody knows your side is the underdog. You get more sympathy and help if you're seen as fighting a good fight against great odds.

4. Get help from friends in high places. Ask local and state politicians to talk to your congressman and to raise your issue in friendly local forums, such as the city council or county board.

5. Stay ahead of the opposition. Keep taking the initiative with interesting tactics that show you've got the facts on your side. Don't be sucked into a role of constantly responding to your opponents' charges.

6. Show public support through letter-writing campaigns, petitions, rallies, etc. Your objective is to make your issue so ubiquitous that the congressman hears about it everywhere he goes in his district, and gets letters and calls about it every day he's in Washington.

7. Get help from local VIPs who have special access to or credibility with your congressman. These include people who have power or money, people who are friends of the congressman, people who helped in his campaign, and people he respects. Get them to speak to the congressman.

8. Use all events for your purpose. Look ahead to holidays and ceremonial occasions, and plan ways to use them in your campaign.

9. Raise your issue in the election campaigns. Get the congressman's opponents to challenge his position, or his lack of one.

10. Build long-term influence by giving the congressman opportunities to learn more about your issue and to do something about it often, so he will come to identify himself with the issue. Praise him when he does the right thing.

An organization or coalition does not exert its influence primarily by direct contact with legislators, but indirectly, by stimulating many kinds of action by others that will in turn come to bear on those legislators. It doesn't do much good to have a spokeswoman for the Brownsville Citizens Association go and badger a congressman once a week; after the first couple of visits it's only harassment and is likely to influence the congressman against the association's cause. The group's time will bring far better results if it is spent planning and executing a variety of tactics that will produce pressure from different sectors of the congressional district.

Even an individual citizen can use many of these tactics by getting local organizations to undertake tactical projects. However, it is an easier job when you have other people who will share the load with you.

Never stop using your imagination. The tactics described in this chapter may work in your community, but tactics you have thought up specifically to fit your local situation will work better.

We urge you to use the principles laid out in this chapter as a basis for devising tactics that will be most effective in your locale.

Put the traditions of your community to work for your cause. If clambakes, say, are a local tradition, consider putting one on as a campaign event, with your congressman, senators, and local politicians invited to attend. If local people are generally passive, unaccustomed to picketing and confrontations with government officials, use tactics that at first require only passive support—attendance at public meetings or signing petitions. More active tactics can come later, after you've got people with you. On the other hand, in a city with an activist, protest tradition, passive tactics would not be effective because they would go unnoticed. Adapt your campaign to your own community's attitudes and traditions.

The underlying concept of all tactics consists of two simple points: (1) keep the pressure on the congressman so he feels it, and (2) use every possible event to do this.

Tactics are a way of chipping away at what would otherwise be a monolith. When you can't easily move a large rock, you can break it into smaller chunks and move them one by one. A congressman can be like that. You may not be able to gain his support by asking him directly, but if you go out and create pressures on him from several directions, his monolithic indifference will crack and you'll be able to move him.

Political pressure comes from a coalition effort. Whether or not you have anything that's called a coalition, you have to bring diverse pressures to bear on your legislator. These may come from citizen groups, individual citizens, business firms, local politicians, local government agencies, and news media. Pressure also comes from making the congressman accountable for what he does. Get the news media to cover the issue, so the congressman will know that the voters will hold him accountable for his actions.

Make It Respectable

It is a continuous process in any campaign to make your position more respectable than your opponents' position. When you're an advocate of change, it's an uphill battle because the status quo is generally considered more respectable. By the same token, when you're defending the status quo, you have to make your respectability obvious and simultaneously try to deprive your opponents' position of respectability. Both are done largely by having the right people express your viewpoint in the right time and the right place.

Who Is Respectable

The respectability factor explains why scientists, economists, and other "experts" have become so important in the legislative arena. Though they have little or no political clout, such experts can make your position look unassailable, or they can make you look like fools and crackpots. Every issue involves a contest between the experts on one side and the experts on the other, and the test is which experts are more respectable.

Prominent local people who are respected in your community are another category of respectability builders. Business leaders, labor leaders, ethnic leaders, and local politicians can help make your proposal respectable.

Your respectability can be damaged by your own supporters if the wrong people endorse the issue in the wrong place. This happened in California during the campaign for a nuclear-safety ballot proposition in 1976. Proponents of the proposition were striving to establish its respectability through endorsements by politicians and nuclear scientists when, to their consternation, a newspaper advertisement appeared, trumpeting an endorsement by the Doobie Brothers, a rock music group. If the Doobie Brothers had been smarter, they would have devoted their ad to a replay of the scientists' endorsement because, to the audience that needed to be influenced about the nuclear power issue, scientists had more respectability than rock musicians.

In planning your respectability tactics, first think over who is most respected on your subject in your community. Who will be most respected by the legislators? By your potential citizen activists and cooperating groups?

Aim for the unexpected, for people who would be assumed to be against your proposal. If they come out on your side, a congressman will conclude that this proposal has more support than he thought. As the Population Institute observed in its *Population Activist's Handbook* (New York: Macmillan, 1974), "Obviously, the most effective endorsement of a proposal to disseminate contraceptives to adolescents would be from the Pope. Failing that, Billy Graham and Shirley Temple Black might be best—despite the fact that they have no special knowledge of the problem. After all, 're-spectability' and expertise have never been really correlated in the public mind."

Besides experts, also aim for people within the social, professional, and political circles with which the congressman is associated. If he's close to labor unions and blue-collar workers, think of whom you can get from that sector. Another congressman may be close to the conservative business community in his city; to him a banker would be highly respectable. Check in the legislator's biography in the *Almanac of American Politics* to see what college, university, or law school he attended. If it was a nearby school, you may be able to gain respectability by involving faculty members from that institution. See what clubs and professional groups he belongs to, and consider whether there is a way you can associate the issue with these organizations—perhaps have a speaker appear at their meetings, or even win their endorsement for your position.

There are many local organizations that can add respectability to your position. Some types of organizations that can do so are:

- Religious groups and church committees
- Legal associations (bar associations and local law groups)
- Scientific associations
- Medical associations (American Medical Association's state and local affiliates and specialty groups in surgery, psychiatry, etc.)
- Other professional groups (engineering, anthropology, economics, etc.)
- University research centers (urban studies centers, population research centers, environmental studies programs, etc.)

Politicians and local government agencies are another category that will be covered at greater length later in this chapter.

How and Where to Use Respectability

When your inventory of respectability-building people and organizations is reasonably complete, start planning who can best ask these people and groups to help. If you have an organization, you'll find that some of your members know these "respectable" people and can approach them. If you're without a group, seek help from cooperating groups whose members and leaders are likely to have good access to people you want.

Decide what you want these respected people and groups to do that will make your proposal acceptable. To preserve their aura of respectability, it's best to have them act in their own normal sphere of activity and in a format normal to them, and keep your campaign group completely out of the picture. For instance, the best place for a respected businessman to endorse your proposal might be at a luncheon meeting of the Chamber of Commerce, while a scientist would be most effective if he made his remarks in a paper at a scientific meeting. Remember, the place can add to the respectability. To make sure the event is reported in news media, you'll probably need to help with publicity.

Some of the possible vehicles for the support of respected people and groups are:

1. A speech by a locally respected person before a respected local organization. This can be part of a larger speech, so if you hear that next week's City Club speaker is an acquaintance who favors your position, see if you can persuade her to work into her speech a few paragraphs backing your proposal, and then plan how to get the story to news media. If you have an expert but no organization to provide a platform, one possibility is to have a seminar at a local university, arranged by a friendly faculty member in a relevant department, so the story will come out like this: "Dr. James Robinson today warned that air pollution is costing Springfield residents $3 million a year in increased medical bills. Addressing an economics seminar at Jackson College, Robinson said . . ."

2. A study or research paper by a respected scientist, economist, or other expert or group of experts, published and released to news media. The best place to publish is in the journal of a professional organization, but since lead times are usually too long, the most practical possibilities are to publish it as a research report of the institution for which the expert works or to have the expert publish it personally. If your group pays the printing expenses, reporters will usually find out, so you might as well get credit in the author's ackowledgments. The less it's tainted by association with your activist group, the more respectability the research report will contribute to your cause.

If you lack an impressive institution to bring out the report, you can give it at least some status by having your expert present it to some official body and heading it, for instance, "A Research Report Submitted to the Albany City Council." In this case, the news release would start off, "In a report to the Albany City Council, economist Richard Black endorsed the proposed welfare reform bill . . ." Some respectability rubs off from the group to which the report is presented. As soon as the report has been released, make sure its author goes to give the congressman a copy and discuss it with him.

3. A letter from a respected local organization, released to news media. This can be addressed directly to the legislators you want to influence. You may have to help draft the letter, then stand back and let the more respected organization take the limelight. If the letter contains a resolution adopted by the organization, it will be even more respectable.

4. A letter from a respected local person. Written directly to your congressman or senators, such letters can make a big impact. They are usually not released to news media, because a letter between two VIPs is regarded as private correspondence and would not fall into the hands of reporters.

Respectability can become complex when your issue requires support from several mutually distrustful sectors of the public. In this case, move early to establish respectability with your legislators, and at the same time seek the endorsement of diverse people and groups that are respected by your diverse sectors of potential support. In California, for instance, opponents of the planned Butler Valley dam gained respectability by having four separate anti-dam groups organized to carry the issue to the four major constituencies they wanted to activate—commercial fishermen, labor union members, Indians, and local taxpayers in general. Each group could work for the endorsements of people respected by its own constituency and then get that message out to its people.

Respectability may be hard to establish when you're advocating a new concept that departs from conventional thinking in your community. You may not be able to get highly respected people to endorse your position at the outset. But that's only a temporary problem. Make do with what you can get, and this slim opening wedge will in turn generate cooperation from more-respected people. Gradually you reach higher levels of respectability.

In 1966, for example, opposition to nuclear power was distinctly unrespectable. Even the Sierra Club advocated nuclear power. Yet during the ensuing decade the opponents of nuclear power used respectability-building tactics so effectively—involving nuclear scientists, economists, consumer advocates, and former Atomic Energy Commission employees—that the nuclear power industry is now struggling to regain its respectability, after being turned down by many communities that were to have been the site of nuclear power plants.

Make Opposition Unrespectable

Work to deflate your opponents' public image, because they will be trying to deflate yours. If they can't do it by use of experts and VIPs, they'll try to tag you as a bunch of long-haired hippies or a pack of Communists—though most opponents are more subtle nowadays.

When your opponents are clearly black-hats to the legislators and to your supporters, take full advantage of this. Every time your opponents fulminate against you, it makes your position look better. For instance, in the 1967–68 campaign for the Redwood National Park, the logging companies' intemperate remarks and strong, overt opposition to the park only served to make the Sierra Club park proposal look more reasonable.

Point to the backers of your opposition. Who would benefit from defeat of your cause? For example, on dam issues the benefits are enjoyed by local construction companies and suppliers, the irrigation district, and members of the Chamber of Commerce. When you can show who benefits, you can begin to debunk the high-flown rhetoric of your opponents, who naturally claim that *everybody* benefits from the defeat of your position. An economist is a likely person to release this kind of information.

Your opponents may be using unfair methods to influence the decision makers. Do they entertain government officials lavishly? Do they take officials golfing, fishing, or hunting? Use caution if the congressman and senators are implicated, because you will not want to embarrass them if you still hope to win their votes. However, if they have been hostile, exposure of such favors might cool the buddy-buddy relationship, to your advantage. The hard part is finding out what compromising activities are going on. News reporters who follow local politics usually know a lot more than they can put into their stories, and a friendly reporter might give you some "background" that would put you on the trail of intriguing back-room dealings. People inside an opposition firm or agency may know of such abuses and be willing to let you in on the secret if they trust you not to tell where you heard it. The most responsible way to expose your opponents' unfair or illicit tactics is to have newspaper or television reporters delve into the matter and bring it out as straight news. Or get a public official or respected local person to charge unfair tactics. It's preferable not to make this charge yourselves, because it will be seen as self-serving and this will lower your group's respectability as well as your opponents'.

Point out wherever public money is being used to oppose your efforts. If it is, the taxpayers' money may be being used unfairly to propagandize on one side of the controversy. This can be an especially potent argument if your opponents include a federal agency, which can be accused of interfering in local decision making. To make this charge stick, you need to show that the agency has been doing more than just responding to invitations and questions. You need to show that it has taken the initiative, organized opposition, distributed biased literature, and given biased speeches to local audiences. The best person to challenge this kind of activity is a local official or highly respected person, but you can make the charge yourself if necessary, because it's usually considered fair to criticize government agencies.

A Primer for Underdogs

Confronting solid, entrenched opposition can be both a formidable handicap and a great advantage when you're campaigning for a congressman's vote. No matter how overwhelming your opposition seems to be—local industry, state and federal agencies, local officials—you *can* win. To do so, you have to get the people on your side, or at least the active citizens who will write letters and make phone calls for your cause. When people see your group as the underdog, they will be inclined to help you, as long as you're standing up for their interests or defending their views.

The Winning Underdog

You want to be the underdog so as to win the loyalty and support of your people, but you also want to win. These desires are not contradictory, because you are likely to be seen as the underdog long after you've in fact gained the upper hand. At first your opponents won't want to portray themselves as the underdog because they have reputations to uphold. The mayor, the president of the local factory, and the local spokesman of the Corps of Engineers won't want to admit that a mere citizens' group has power over them. Later in the fight, when they are the real underdogs, it's too late to claim underdog status.

Of course, if your position is in support of a federal agency's proposal, such as a new national park, your opponents will cast themselves as the underdog and try to cast you as minions of Big Brother government. This doesn't always work, but it gains them local sympathy. In California in 1967–68, when the Redwood National Park proposal was being considered in Congress, the timber companies that owned the land tried to portray themselves as underdogs set upon by the federal establishment. However, they simultaneously showed themselves as the top dogs and lost public sympathy by going ahead with logging in the proposed park area.

More recently major industries have tried, with more success, to portray themselves as the underdogs in fights with the U.S. Environmental Protection Agency over air pollution. But in states where clean-air citizen groups have been active, the industrial apologists have not gotten away with it, because when citizen groups are heard from, it's usually clear who the real underdogs are.

When you're an underdog, you'll not only attract more public support, more volunteers, and more contributions, but your people will work harder to overcome the opposition. When you lose that underdog spirit and people start thinking they've won, the campaign can be in real danger of losing its steam and giving opponents time to catch up.

Being an underdog can even help you in your direct approaches to your senators and congressman. Make sure these legislators know that you're operating on a shoestring, with volunteer efforts and nickel-and-dime contributions, because this will help them realize that your side is fighting for deeply held convictions, unlike many issues legislators face, which involve primarily paid lawyers and business executives.

There are tactics you can use that will capitalize on your underdog status to overcome the disadvantages of that status. It's a real case of raising yourself by your bootstraps. You use your opponents' imposing size and high visibility against them.

Try to get your opponents to lose their temper in public, where the news media will see and report it. Emotion on the part of government officials and business executives is frowned upon. It is only slightly more accepted in private citizens, so keep your cool. A shouting match is not what you want. An underdog is shouted at but never shouts back.

Provoke your opponents by asking them embarrassing questions about the issue. Sometimes the question of who would benefit can be asked repeatedly, in slightly different ways, with the result that the person being questioned gets peeved and begins snapping at the questioners. Likely forums for this sort of constructive provocation include radio call-in shows, panel discussions at meetings, and questions from the audience after a speech.

With some issues you can confront your opponents in a dramatic scene—standing in front of the bulldozers that are destroying a proposed park, or having a sit-in to prevent authorities from closing a school. If your opponents put on a public meeting to explain their proposal, have lots of people there to ask provocative questions. Let news reporters know that there will be some controversy at these events, so the exchanges will be reported. If your opponents blow their stack, you want the moment preserved.

Government officials and businesspeople are becoming more adept at handling criticism and confrontation. Often a public-relations person will be sent to represent the agency or company in public. Many executives have attended training seminars on how to keep cool in public. But many of your opponents will still see red if you press them. They can't seem to get used to the newfangled idea that ordinary citizens have something to say about national policies and programs.

Early in the controversy, before your opponents realize you're serious, they may try to win you over. They may invite you to a workshop, a conference, or an inspection trip—perhaps a trip to the site of a proposed dam you're fighting—or just a cozy meeting in a corporation's boardroom. Such meetings are intended to impress you and make you defer to your opponents' superior power and expertise. If you are invited to such a meeting, invite a reporter or two to join you. (Don't bother to clear this with your opponents because they can't very well refuse to let reporters in if you want them present. If your hosts bar the reporters, your side should walk out.) During the meeting keep calm, but after being "reasonable" for a few minutes of discussion, begin pressing your points and hope your opponents will blow up.

Good questions can be an excellent way to open an underdog campaign, even if your opponents won't rise to the bait. This is especially true in communities where confrontation is frowned upon, because questions seem less offensive than outright opposition. Write formally, on behalf of an organization (or several co-signing organizations), to appropriate local or state officials or to business executives involved in the issue, raising embarrassing questions as to how the issue affects local citizens. A list of as many as twenty questions can be posed in the same letter; the length makes it impressive. You should know pretty well what the answers are, because this is not a research exercise but a move to force your opponents out into the open. Release the letter to news media. Reporters may go straight to the addressees of your letter and ask whether they are going to respond. This ensures that you'll get an answer.

Tennessee citizens fighting a strip-mine project used this method to expose the issue in their community. The questions posed by KLEAR (Kentucky Lake Environmental and Recreation Association) included these:

- Is there enough housing for the 50 to 100 families involved in the project?

- How would schooling be provided, and how much would it cost? Who would pay?
- Are there adequate school buses for the influx?
- How would the strip-mine affect subsurface water?
- Would the company want to build a railroad spur to the project, and if so, where?

When the answers arrive, compile the responses and release them, with comments from your organization. If the answers are not forthcoming, or when the answers clearly show that your opponents are in the wrong, then this is your moment to announce your conclusions from the questioning, taking your firm stand on the issue. The delay in taking a stand until after you have questioned your opponents will impress people in your community who don't like to jump to conclusions.

If your opponents have responded, check their answers carefully to see whether they are misleading, inaccurate, or merely promises that aren't likely to be kept. Vague promises can be challenged by asking for details on commitments and plans. For instance, if a highway department has promised to relocate the families to be evicted by a proposed freeway project, ask where the new housing will be and how much it will cost.

When taking a firm stand, following a few weeks of questioning, research, and meetings, an underdog group can gain stature by releasing a list of the opposition's failures that have led to this stand. You're saying that you're opposing them only because your opponents have been unreasonable and have not moved to correct the problems that are implicit in their position. Such a list of grievances is a central part of the Declaration of Independence, in which the founders of our country stated their reasons for taking a firm stand for independence, and in opposition to the king of England.

Besides challenging your opponents' procedures, of course also include your substantive objections to the project, based on the best information you have so far and citing your most respected experts. If your group advocates an alternative to a project which you're against, stress it; in doing so, you show your position as being positive and constructive, for the benefit of those in the community who disapprove of negativism.

The Visible Underdog

One of the biggest problems for underdog groups is gaining enough visibility even to challenge their opponents. If your opponents are getting all the coverage in the news media, don't hesitate to show up at their news conference or public meeting, and challenge their remarks from the floor. Tell who you are and make your point concisely, in the form of a question. The reporters will probably pursue the point, and may also seek you out afterwards for further comment. At a news conference, avoid taking up too much time yourself, because reporters rightly consider this their time to ask questions. Reporters will be annoyed if you try to take over, but if you make a brief, pithy challenge to your opponents' assertions, reporters' interest will be aroused and they may welcome the diversion from the dull routine of taking your opponents' handouts and rewriting them. A little controversy can be fun both for you and for the reporters.

You can also gain visibility by bringing a well-known person to address a meeting—someone who can't be ignored by news media, such as a U.S. senator or congressman, a prominent state legislator, or a nationally known citizen leader. These may charge a speaker's fee of $1,000 or more, but they do get results in local media. Many struggling environmental groups around the country have got off to a good start by having David Brower, president of Friends of the Earth, address a special meeting. Senator Strom Thurmond (Republican of South Carolina) makes speaking tours around the country to address conservative groups. Every subject has its inspirational speakers who will inevitably be covered by local news media. If you get one of these personages to come, tell him or her what you have in mind, and get the speaker to plug your specific issue loud and clear. Set up special interviews for local radio and television stations, too.

In an underdog campaign, you should continually harp on the disparity between your side and your opponents'. You may be able to get a reporter to do a story on the amounts of money that have been spent by the two sides in the controversy. Your side won't have spent much compared to what a government agency or corporation spends to oppose you. Your opponents won't want to give out a figure, but if you keep track of their activities and make a conservative estimate of the staff time, printing, and postage that went into their visible activities, your reporter will have a figure to confront them with, and this may force them either to agree or come up with a different figure. Reporters like doing this kind of story, so it's worth a try.

When your opponent is a government agency, no matter whether it's federal, state, or local, consider challenging its use of tax money to propagandize on an issue that is still to be decided by the taxpayers. If the agency is not giving you all the information you have requested, you may charge the agency with suppressing information that is needed by the public and for which the public has already paid through taxes.

Underdog groups can sometimes use a lawsuit to draw attention to the issue and, you hope, gain a small victory. You can't force a congressman to vote your way by suing him, but you may be able to file suit against a government agency that has been suppressing documents you're entitled to see. Whether you win or lose, the suit reinforces your underdog role as long as you're suing Big Daddy government or a big corporation. However, keep your lawsuits to tangential issues such as suppressed documents, and avoid the central issue. If you sue on the central issue, and the lawsuit drags on for months, you will be handing the congressman a readymade excuse to remain undecided. With a lawsuit pending in court, a legislator can say, "I must wait to hear the decision of the court before reaching my own conclusions on this vital issue."

To file a lawsuit you'll need a lawyer, preferably one who believes in your cause and is willing to do the job for free. Even so, the expenses and court costs can mount up fast. Lawyers will sometimes tell you how much it will cost to prepare and file the suit—but watch out, because most of the costs come later, as the case goes into hearings, briefs, and counterbriefs. What began as a simple, inexpensive suit can cost thousands.

Going beyond these specifics, always try to give your campaign tactics and your publications a slant that will remind people that you're David against a Goliath.

A Cautionary Note

The difference between an underdog and a crackpot is in the eye of the beholder, so take care lest your group be regarded as the latter. People sympathize with an underdog and want to help, but they shrug off a crackpot with a "He must be crazy" shake of the head. **Your group could be regarded as crackpots for any of three reasons:**

1. **People think your arguments are not believable.** This is most likely to be a problem in issues involving technical or scientific information. You can minimize the problem by including experts and respected people in your initial tactics, so you enter the fight with a strong showing of credibility.

2. **People think your tactics are not serious enough.** This can be avoided by starting with substantial tactics, saving more witty or unorthodox ones for a later date.

3. **People think it's crazy to buck the authorities.** This is an odd one, but it's a prevalent attitude. Even in communities that are accustomed to activism and social protest, there are always some issues that people think are hopeless. And in some parts of the country it's considered almost un-American to fight against government officials or business interests. In either case, start as strongly as you can, using respectability-building tactics, and aim to pull off a couple of minor tactical victories early in the game. Even a minor victory can make people reconsider their apathy.

For instance, suppose you're trying to block a new government installation in farmlands near your community. If you can get the local school superintendent to admit in a news interview or in a letter that the schools could not handle the influx of new children, right there you've given people hope that it can still be stopped. As you win these little victories, people will start saying, "Those people sure have spunk." Their next step will be to get involved in the fight.

The Apathetic Underdog

An underdog of a different kind is the group that is not confronting substantial opposition in the community but still does not have the congressman's vote. If all the local support is on your side, you don't have a Goliath to fight, and it may be hard to get people aroused. For instance, if the public school system, the teachers union, and the mayor are all in favor of more federal education funds and there is no visible opposition group in town, why should Bill Green, father of four schoolchildren, get involved? He'll figure that with all that power at work on the issue, there's nothing he can do to help. He's wrong, but he doesn't know it.

You have to convince people that they do have power, and the best way to do that is to reach out through citizen groups that can approach people as equals. To keep Bill Green from feeling powerless, put the less influential groups out front, leading the public campaign, while the more powerful ones work within their own circles. The school system and the mayor should work quietly to influence the congressman, using their political contacts; the teachers union should get its members to write and phone the congressman; and the drive for broad public support should be led by an organization of concerned citizens—a "Citizens for Better Schools" or "Save Our Schools"—that can mobilize support of individual citizens through the service clubs, church groups, PTAs, and every other group in which people congregate throughout the community.

Friends in High Places

Presumably you're reading this book because your congressman and senators don't listen to you or follow your advice, and you want to change that. In case you haven't realized it, there are people in your commuunity to whom the congressman and senators do listen, and with whom you have influence. **These are your local and state politicians, and a few of them are listed here:**

- Mayors and city managers
- School board members
- City council members
- County executives
- County supervisors, commissioners, and selectmen
- Regional transportation and sanitary commissioners
- Members of the state legislature
- Governors, lieutenant governors, and state treasurers

Legislators in the U.S. Congress must beware of getting too far off base from the sentiments of their constituents. Local officials, who are closer to the voters, more wrapped up in the day-to-day life of the community, and more accessible to people, are a sort of early warning system for senators and congressmen. When local officials take a stand on an issue, the senators and congressmen notice it. When many local officials have taken the same position, a congressman will feel the need to get aboard the bandwagon, rather than end up as the lone dissenter from what looks to be a popular stance.

Reaching Influential People

Local office holders are easy to reach, and they are generally eager for good publicity on public issues. Among these are many young politicians on the way up, looking for popular issues they can use to show that they're different from the old, entrenched politicians. Working with them gives you a chance to get acquainted with the powers of the future, and at the same time influence your present national legislators.

Governors, mayors, and county executives are the most influential of these politicians, and they are accustomed to taking positions on issues. Going beyond these officials to involve other, less-exalted politicians is important, too, because it will demonstrate that your cause has broadly based support among local politicians. Lesser officials, such as state legislators and city council members, are not expected to be heard from on national legislation, so their support adds a persuasive element of the unexpected. All these people, from the governor on down, want your support and will want to say yes if they can.

The support of state and local politicians is one of the most potent advantages you can have, so it's well worth the time it takes to organize this support. Plan your approach to these officials carefully, by way of people who know them, are owed favors by them, or are in a position to help them in their political future. Young politicians can often be approached directly by leaders of citizen groups without previous connections, because young politicians don't yet have a big following and they may see your group as a potential ally in their move toward higher office. When you get to see a local politician, present him or her with background facts on the issue and ask for help, suggesting a specific thing you want him or her to do.

As you cooperate with local politicians, strive to build continuing relationships, so you can cooperate again on future issues without having to start from scratch. Politicians have good memories, but you'll only keep your credibility and respect if you tend the relationship every few months.

How to Use Influential People

Local politicians can express their support in several ways. The most effective is to see the congressman in person, either in Washington, D.C., or during the congressman's visit to the congressional district. A one-to-one conversation really shows a person's convictions and reveals how much he or she knows about the subject. Next best is a phone call. In either case, you may want to suggest the points your local politicians should cover in the conversation—substantive points you want to get across, and possibly questions as to what pressures the congressman is getting on the issue. A politician may get more forthright reactions from the congressman as to his current attitude toward the issue than you could, because there is a sort of professional bond among politicians.

After the visit or phone call, get your local official to write a follow-up letter to the congressman, reemphasizing the main points and perhaps adding a new observation that drives home the local importance of the issue. This letter reminds the congressman of the earlier conversation and adds an influential letter to his file on the subject, where it won't escape notice whenever the congressman or his staff go back to review constituent opinion.

The local politician need not be of the same party as the congressman. A member of the same party approaches the congressman as part of the party's buddy network, in effect warning him that the natives are restless about your issue. A member of another party approaches the congressman as part of a rival network, and there is an implied threat that the rival party may use the issue against him in the next election. Naturally a congressman wants to avoid giving his opponents a popular issue that can be used against him, and he can do this by adopting the same position as his rivals.

Less effective than direct conversation, but still influential, are letters from local officials. These can be particularly important in influencing senators from populous states such as California and New York, who are hard to reach because they receive such an overwhelming volume of letters and phone calls. In these cases, a letter would be a local official's normal way of getting word to a senator. In most other cases, a telephone call is a more normal way of communicating real concern, and a letter would be suspected of having been written just to please some constituent. (This in itself carries some weight, of course.)

If you have a local official who wants to help but isn't sure enough of the issue to embark on a real discussion of the subject, ask her to phone the congressman briefly to express concern and say that she'll send him a letter going into the details. However, you obviously can't do this if the congressman is an expert on the issue and is likely to argue with your local official when she telephones him.

Letters between politicians of the same party are usually not released to news media, because releasing them would be regarded as "grandstanding"—grasping for public attention on the part of the sender. Letters between politicians of different parties may be released, since this carries out the normal rivalry between parties. However, as a rule of thumb we suggest that such letters not be released. To get media coverage, you can come up with other events that won't carry the risk of interfering with this especially valuable behind-the-scenes influence.

Ask your local officials to speak about the issue in public. When a congressman sees that politicians back home are not only phoning him about the Day-Care Centers Bill, but are backing it in their speeches and television interviews, he will get the idea that there is real popular support for the measure. He'll realize that these local politicians think there is good political mileage in backing the bill.

For a start, you can always have your friendly politicians address some of the groups involved in your campaign. But more effective is having them speak to groups that are not known to be committed to your cause, even groups that might be expected to be hostile to it. A good forum for a speech favoring more federal education aid might be a meeting of the local Taxpayers' Union; a speech favoring strong antipollution laws could be given before the Chamber of Commerce. This unlikely combination of subject and audience reinforces the impression that you've got a safe issue that local politicians aren't afraid of advocating even before tough audiences.

Active politicians are continually speaking before diverse groups in the community, so it should be possible to use speaking engagements that are already booked. Help your politician draft her remarks on the topic, and offer your help with publicity. A news release by the speaker may do the job, or you may be able to get radio or television reporters to cover the speech. Make sure somebody sends the congressman clippings of the news stories so he'll know the speech was made. After all, that's the main purpose of the exercise.

The speech itself should not be directed at the congressman. Most local officials would rather leave the congressman out of the speech, but instead cover the issue—for instance, why the community needs the Day-Care Centers Bill, and why Congress should pass it.

Local politicians can also do a lot for your campaign through radio, television, and newspaper interviews. These people are newsmakers, and if they have something to say about an issue, you can usually find places for them to say it. All-news radio stations and talk shows are likely outlets, as are small-town and suburban newspapers. Access is more difficult in large metropolitan areas such as New York City, which lack localized media. From your work on the issue, you'll know which reporters are covering the subject for the broadcast and print media, and it's your responsibility to suggest that they interview friendly local politicians.

Once the interview has been published or broadcast, make sure the congressman finds out about it. Have someone send him a clipping of the newspaper interview. Have somebody mention a broadcast interview in a letter, or get the station to send him a transcript, if there is one available. Try to keep your campaign group out of sight, so the congressman won't think it's all your doing.

A mayor, county executive, or governor can declare a day or week devoted to your issue, such as Better Schools Day or Clean Air Week, and issue a proclamation that states the basic principles of the issue. You can't get down to details in a proclamation, but it can show where the signer's sympathies lie, and copies can be sent to your senators and congressman. You can also use the day or week as a focus for volunteer activities in the community—leafletting, petitioning, radio and television interviews, and so forth.

Local politicians can also raise the issue in their official bodies and adopt resolutions of support. A city council, a county board of supervisors, a regional transportation authority, a state senate or general assembly—all these can take positions on issues if there is enough consensus among their members.

State legislatures around the country adopt hundreds of "memorials to Congress" each year urging action on many issues. These have little effect on Congress as a whole, but they can be a significant influence on the senators and representatives from the states that have adopted them, and that's what you want. Don't put a lot of time into such resolutions, but if your politicians think they can do it easily, just draft them a good resolution and ask them to give it a whirl. For instance, citizens active in support of continued U.S. control of the Panama Canal did this, and succeeded in getting the legislatures of Alabama, Arizona, California, Delaware, Indiana, Louisiana, Maryland, Oklahoma, South Carolina, Tennessee, and Virginia to pass resolutions opposing any giveaway or dilution of U.S. authority over the canal.

Another possibility, when you have several local politicians who share your views, is for them to release a joint statement about the issue, perhaps in the form of a letter or telegram to all the U.S. senators and representatives from your state, stressing the local impact of the issue. A news conference could be effective in this case, since a number of public figures would be involved, and available to make statements for radio and television.

If you're lucky enough to have local politicians on your side when you first plan your campaign, ask them to approach the congressman and ask for his support even before you and your citizen allies do so. This way your position will have more respectability at the outset, and you'll have a head start on the whole campaign.

Political youth organizations in your community can also help influence senators and congressmen. The Young Democrats and Young Republicans are usually eager to prove that they can respond to modern concerns, thus dispelling the Old Guard image of the incumbent politicians. By taking a stand, these groups can add weight to your position. They generally have county and city clubs, as well as separate college clubs in some cases. Republicans also have separate groups known as College Republicans and Teenage Republicans.

In state and local governments, the agencies that do the day-to-day work in your subject area may have just as much influence as the elected officials. In subjects involving technical expertise, such as energy, health, and transportation, your congressman may take the agency directors and staff more seriously than he takes their elected superiors. The same is often true of the local representatives of federal agencies (regional directors, state directors, and so forth), who are expected to maintain good relationships with your senators and congressman. Get acquainted with people in relevant agencies (federal, state, county, city, and regional) so you gradually find out who is sympathetic and who is not, and the agency people come to trust you. Knowing the right people in the agencies can be crucial, because they will help you.

Don't neglect to reach out toward agencies that have an indirect interest in your issue. You'll have to show them enough facts to convince them that they should be involved, but once they agree, their support will mean a lot because it broadens your constituency.

What can agency people do to help? A local agency head may be willing to write or phone your congresswoman and express support for your position, explaining how it will help the agency's work. If the agency head agrees with you but won't stick his neck out, just get a friendly local politician to write and ask for his views. Then your politician friend circulates the reply to the congresswoman, senators, and news media. Or if a friend in the agency has facts that would help your campaign, he tips you off, you get a local politician to write the agency and request the information, and the politician releases the facts.

Know the right bureaucrat and he'll help you. The good relationships may start during the first investigations your group does on the issue. Be careful not to let them lapse when your researchers leave town or switch to another assignment. Somebody should have the responsibility of keeping in touch with friends in these agencies, and of finding more of them. An occasional lunch and frequent phone calls will keep you in touch.

Keeping Ahead of the Opposition

A legislative campaign involves moves by both adversaries, each trying to keep ahead of the other. While you are taking the initiative, your opponents will try to keep ahead of you in several ways.

They may try to provoke you into getting mad, which is the same tactic described earlier in this chapter in the section entitled "A Primer for Underdogs." They may try to destroy your respectability by showing that your people will gain financially from the proposal you advocate, by demonstrating that your position is opposed by respected authorities, or by portraying your people as hysterical, crazy, liars, or all of these.

Your opponents will try to change the subject of debate and concentrate on their favorite issue—one that makes their position look good. You have to shift it back, time after time, to the more important issues.

Your opponents will try to convince the legislators that *only you* are against them and that you have no support in the community. Combat this by keeping other groups and individuals actively and visibly involved in the campaign.

The biggest problem your opponents are likely to pose is that of sheer persistence. If they can keep putting out misstatements, half-truths, and predictions of disaster that would result from your proposal, they might be able to consume all your time just in responding to their charges. They might at least make you look defensive in that you're always responding to another of their allegations.

Don't be suckered into this losing game. Let them call you all the names they want to; those who throw tar inevitably get it all over themselves, too. Reserve your replies for erroneous statements of fact and for predictions with which you disagree. It's important to show that you have an answer, so your opponents can't make you appear unable to refute their arguments; but don't be lured into spending a lot of time responding to your opponents.

Lay traps for your opponents' material. Have friendly reporters slip you copies of their flyers, news releases, and speeches, so you'll know what they are saying. When a new argument comes out, write a rebuttal quickly and get it into the hands of your congressman's and senators' staffs and to reporters who are following the issue. Don't make a big issue of it by putting out news releases or setting up interviews. Instead, treat it as another futile move by your opponents, without merit and deserving little attention. But make sure the crucial people know you have an answer.

The best way to keep ahead of your opponents is to take the initiative. Keep developing new arguments and new evidence to support your arguments. Keep finding new sources of support and new experts to back you up. This will not only build your momentum continuously, but it will repeatedly throw your opponents off balance and consume their time and energy in responding to your moves.

Keeping in Touch with the Congressman

Most of the activities in a legislative campaign are intended to influence your legislators indirectly, by getting other organizations and individuals to express themselves. However, a central feature of every campaign is the direct relationship your organization has with the legislators. When representatives of your group meet with a congressman, speak with him on the telephone, or correspond with him by letter or telegram, they are building a relationship that can make a big difference both to your immediate issue and to related issues in the future. Through these encounters you put your group into the picture, so the congressman will see your organization as a group that must be considered when he is making decisions on your subject. At the very least you establish your group as an organization, made up of his constituents, that has something to say, has reliable information to provide, and is willing to listen to his viewpoint, too. At best, you establish your group as one that will make the congressman look good and will furnish help at election time.

When you've established a good relationship with the congressman, he and his staff will accept you, not fear you. You don't want to inspire fear, because this makes legislators defensive, as though backed into a corner with no way out. Fear usually stiffens a legislator's stance rather than changing it. Instead of fear, what you want is respect.

It is respect that opens the door at crucial moments in a legislative campaign. Suppose you've been working for a $10 billion education-aid bill and, two days before the vote, your opponents in Congress propose a compromise that would cut $1 billion out. You want to reach your congressman and tell him what's bad about the compromise, and you want to find out what he thinks of it. If your prior meetings have gone well (even if he hasn't agreed completely), you should be able to get him on the phone and talk it over. Or even better, when he learns of the compromise he may call you to ask what you think. This kind of access and willingness to talk is important. Without it, a legislator can feel perfectly free to decide, on the spur of the moment, to change his mind without consulting anybody and without being willing to discuss it with exponents of your position.

This kind of talking relationship is one of the reasons why senators and congressmen have always been close to business interests in their home states and congressional districts. Local businesspeople and business organizations keep in touch with their senators and congressmen regularly; they invite the legislators to address business luncheons and attend receptions. Many legislators came from local business and law circles, so they know many of the businesspeople. Legislators trust these people because they know them and have talked with them often.

The main purpose of seeing your congressman in person is to gain his respect and trust. When your organization has those, it will be easier to gain his vote.

Who Should Keep in Touch with the Congressman

An organization should have more than one person meet with the congressman, but only one person should be given responsibility for coordinating the organization's direct contacts with him. This person should team up with another person or two (who can assist and, if necessary, substitute for him) to plan continuous liaison with the congressman, such as attendance at campaign fundraisers, receptions, and neighborhood events at which the congressman will be present. They should also plan your group's local meetings with the congressman and get appointments for them, plan supportive activities (laudatory letters to local newspapers, volunteer help at election time), and organize research into who the congressman's friends and campaign contributors are. However, this person is not by any means a sole spokesman for the organization, but rather a member of a team of several people who may see the congressman from time to time on behalf of the organization.

There are too many drawbacks to having a single person represent your organization in meetings with a legislator. The one-to-one arrangement fails to show the diversity of people in your organization, it fails to provide the kind of expertise that members with different professional backgrounds can bring to bear on an issue, and it does not protect you against the blue-sky promises a legislator may make to one person but won't make to two or more. It also runs a risk that your lone representative will become such a buddy of the legislator that he'll compromise too easily in order to preserve their friendly relationship. To guard against these problems, whenever possible have two or three from your group meet with the legislator, have several different people attend the legislator's fund-raising events, and have people with different kinds of expertise speak for the group in their respective subject areas.

When to Approach Your Congressman

Make your first approach to the congressman early, before your issue has come to a boil in Congress. Your aim is to get the congressman involved in the issue well before the tough votes come up and before your opponents have mobilized their influence. Have something you want the congressman to do at this stage that is an easy step to take. Cosponsoring a bill is one example. Or, if your opponents include any federal agencies, you might ask the congressman to write to these agencies, asking them embarrassing questions.

In Washington State, for instance, one of the first things proponents of the North Cascades National Park did was to get their congressman, Thomas M. Pelly (Republican), to write and ask the Forest Service (which was logging off areas of the proposed park) a series of questions about their plans for the area. Pelly later became the first to introduce a bill to establish the national park.

When the congressman has done what you asked, make sure he gets a pat on the back from some of your people. Mention his help in your newsletter, and have people write and compliment him on his effective advocacy of the public interest.

From that time on, keep in touch by letter, telephone, and personal meeting, providing new information, sounding out his views, and asking what opposition he senses. An organization can be more persistent than an individual, because an organization is expected to be assiduous in communicating its views. Even so, watch for signs of annoyance or ill will, and back off if you're not welcome.

Staying in touch with your congressman is not just for your benefit. It's for his, too. He will be impressed by your sympathy for his problems, your willingness to hear his views and discuss them with him, and your ability to *help him* handle your issue. You can't afford to get your congressman out on a limb supporting your cause and then abandon him. If he is going to face criticism for his stand, you must help him weather the storm. It may be a problem of local auto dealers who oppose the Clean Air Bill, which you persuaded the congressman to support, or a problem of right-wingers who claim the congressman is aiding the Communists by voting for federal aid to education. If he's got problems with your issue, you'd better be ready to help him deal with them. Sometimes your help may consist of giving him the rebuttal to an argument used against him by your opponents. Or it may consist of getting some supportive letters into local newspapers to counteract abusive ones your opponents have been writing. You'll be respected for helping the congressman, and he'll owe you some goodwill for it.

Group Meetings with Your Congressman

Meeting the congressman in person is essential for an organization because it gives him an image of your group—what sort of people you are, how much you know about your issue, and how seriously you believe in your cause. He'll remember the group more easily once he has spent fifteen minutes or a half hour with you, and he's likely to be more influenced by your subsequent phone calls and letters.

Chapter 6, "Face to Face with a Congressman," described the basic principles applicable in any meeting with your legislators. An organization can use the methods of that chapter and go beyond them in the ways described below, to take full advantage of an organization's greater influence.

Whenever possible, an organization should be represented by two or more people when meeting with a legislator. This gives the legislator the impression that it's an *organization* speaking, not just an individual. It implies strength; it suggests that there are more like you back home. It will also avert the easy promises some legislators give to individuals, hoping the promise will be forgotten; a legislator won't be so free with promises he doesn't plan to fulfill if there are two of you to remember them.

A meeting of between two and six people with the congressman can also be advantageous in covering detailed arguments on several aspects of your issue. Your people at such a meeting may include experts such as an economist or a scientist, they may include nonexperts who have learned the facts and arguments on a specific topic just for this meeting, and they may include people whose own experiences dramatize the problems your group is trying to solve. For example, a meeting to seek a congressman's vote on federal aid for education of handicapped children might include a retired school superintendent (an expert), a housewife who has studied the local school budget in detail (a nonexpert), and parents of handicapped children who would be denied an adequate education unless the federal aid is approved. Your aim is to show the congressman that your position is correct for several reasons and that you can refute any argument he brings up against your position.

A group of Michigan college students used such a group meeting in 1970 to seek the vote of Senator Robert P. Griffin (Republican of Michigan) to stop the supersonic transport (SST) aircraft project. Griffin had previously voted for the SST subsidy. The topics were divided among the students, who then spent several days learning the facts, arguments, and rebuttals on their respective topics. One student took the topic of the SST as a waste of the taxpayers' money, another took the SST's noise impact on communities near airports, another the SST's possible effect on climate, another the question of the jobs involved in the SST project, and another the SST's impact on the international balance of trade. The students grilled each other with hostile questions until they found they could answer anything Senator Griffin would be likely to ask.

They then had their meeting with the senator, who found that these students collectively knew more about the SST than he did and were able to respond persuasively to every objection he raised. At the end of the meeting, Griffin said he was undecided, but he agreed to let the students come and discuss it with him again if he later decided to support the SST. Only weeks later, Griffin, in a speech in Michigan, announced his opposition to the SST subsidy.

The basics of a group meeting with a senator or congressman are:

1. **Keep the group down** to six or seven people at the most. A larger group is unmanageable in a discussion because everybody wants to get into the act and it becomes impossible to move quickly from one item to the next. Having people present who don't speak detracts from your effectiveness because the legislator will get the impression that some of your people don't know enough about the issue to discuss it. The group should consist of people who will actually talk about the issue. If you have a less well-prepared person who is an old friend of the congressman's or who has power in your community, include him or her, but one of these is enough.

2. **Have a "prep meeting"** to discuss the topics you plan to cover, decide who will present each topic, and go over what you'll ask of the congressman.

3. **Write an agenda** and give a copy to the congressman at the start of your meeting. This helps to prevent the congressman from leading you astray with anecdotes. Often legislators spin out pleasantries at the beginning of a meeting because they want to make everybody feel at home, not knowing that you have several topics you want to discuss.

4. **Have somebody in your group serve as an informal chairman** who will open the main subject, refer to others for their presentations, and draw the meeting to a close if the congressman doesn't do so. If the congressman talks too long about the weather, this person will have to interrupt him tactfully and say something like, "We know you have a busy schedule, so we'll explain our concern as concisely as we can."

Group meetings can be used to cover several aspects of one issue, as the Michigan students did in the SST case. They can also be used to cover several subjects that concern your group, in which case the issues should be divided among your people.

Group meetings are also used to show support by several organizations for a given issue, when you want to make a show of unity or demonstrate that a diversity of local groups are asking the congressman to take a stand. In this case, prepare a list of the names, addresses, and organizations of those attending the meeting, and hand it to the congressman as the meeting begins. Each person should reemphasize his or her organization's name when speaking. To convince the congressman that the several organizations are really serious about the issue, it's best to have each person make a presentation, even if some of them are brief—perhaps on different aspects of the issue or on the organizations' different perspectives or different experiences concerning the issue. Active participation is important, because if half your people sit quietly the whole time, nodding assent while the others do the talking, the congressman will think their organizations are not going to be active, and as a result their presence won't have much impact.

Group meetings involving several organizations are no substitute for the meetings each organization should have with the congressman. After such a unity meeting, the cooperating organizations should write their own follow-up letters and, perhaps a few weeks later, arrange their own meetings with the congressman. A unity meeting shows that you're all together, but it takes visible action by the cooperating groups to convince the congressman that you're all serious about it.

An organization whose concerns go beyond a single issue may wish to have a group meeting with the congressman and senators every two years to give the legislators an overview of current issues. Oregon conservationists have held these "seminars" before each new legislative session during the few weeks in December and early January when Congress is in adjournment and legislators are often back home. These occasions, involving about seven citizen leaders and one legislator, were highly educational for the legislators and they provided a chance for informal discussion outside the fast-paced, high-pressure environment of Congress in session.

Letters

Organizations can also get results from letters to senators and congressmen. When you have something to say, write. Mail from organizations gets more attention in congressional offices than mail from individuals. Senator Alan Cranston (Democrat of California), who receives 12,000 pieces of mail a week, rarely reads any letters except those from organizations and from VIPs, according to one ex-staffer. Cranston's staff reads and answers the rest and compiles mail-count data on it. Letters from organizations may have direct influence on Cranston because he reads them. In other offices the difference may not be as great, but it is always there, because an organization is assumed to represent a group of voters.

When you get a response, use it well. A legislator who writes to an organization knows that his letter is not confidential. One congressman, quoted in *The Job of the Congressman* (by Donald G. Tacheron and Morris K. Udall, Bobbs-Merrill, 1970), counseled new legislators: "You are now big news in your home district; and don't ever write anything to a constituent that you wouldn't be willing to see on page one of the local newspaper." If your congressman's letter shows his commitment or the lack of one, quote it, Xerox it, send it to your cooperating groups, release it to news media—use it in any way that will further your aims.

An exchange of letters with a senator or congressman can be a good way to confirm something the legislator has told you in person or over the phone. A simple letter from your group restating what you understood him to say, and asking whether your understanding is correct, may get you a written commitment. This still is no guarantee he'll vote right, because your opponents might yet turn him around. But a written commitment makes it far less likely that he'll jump ship.

Besides letters, an organization can send the congressman other materials that will influence him. Among these are:

1. Research reports related to your issue. A congressman may use these in his work, they may reaffirm his thinking or persuade him of your position, and they may inform or influence his staff.

2. Your testimony in other forums. If you speak at a City Council meeting about the school budget squeeze and you're trying to get the congressman's support for more federal education aid, send him a copy of your statement. It will at least reemphasize the issue and show what you're doing about it; it may even give the congressman new information on the local impact of education funds.

3. Local news stories that make a new point or show the congressman's involvement or your group's public-spirited activity. The congressman's district office may clip these, too, but do it yourself to be sure he or his staff see the stories that are important to you.

4. The newsletter and other publications of your organization. The congressman's staff will usually glance at these hastily, saving for him only those items that directly concern him. But sometimes your publications can elicit personal interest from a legislator or staffer. Congressman John D. Dingell (Democrat of Michigan), for instance, receives many conservation magazines and during his twenty-four years in Congress has made a point of looking through them—a continuous education that helped make him one of the most effective spokesmen for wildlife.

Right Before the Vote

When a crucial vote is about to come up, make sure your congresswoman hears from your organization directly one last time. At this point a congresswoman has to make up her mind how she'll vote. A good visit with her is best, to impress her once more with your group's knowledge of the issue and your seriousness, and to ask her how she plans to vote. She'll then know that you will hold her accountable for her right or wrong vote. A visit also gives you a last chance to find out any questions or arguments that are still bothering her and might lead her to vote wrong. Your opponents will probably save some of their ammunition until the last few days, hoping that you'll have no time to make a convincing rebuttal. Your final visit before the vote gives you an opportunity to counteract this tactic.

However, avoid being too persistent or too repetitive at this point. Congressional nerves get frayed as a big vote approaches, and you must avoid being an irritant. Let your group make its point and then wait in the wings while other groups take the limelight, thus showing once more that the issue has broad public support. You want a congresswoman, when she goes to cast her vote, to realize that it's not just the Committee for Solar Energy that wants her to support full funding for solar energy research, but it's the whole community, and that's what she'll think if she has been visited, called, and written to by dozens of citizens and citizen groups during the final weeks before the vote.

Frequently votes are delayed, and your "last visit" could turn out to be a month before the actual vote. When this happens, keep in touch by phone with the legislator's staff to find out when the vote will be. Ask the staff whether any new arguments have come up, so you can write or phone the congresswoman with a rebuttal.

When it's impossible to meet with the legislator just before the vote, use the telephone instead. It won't make the same impression of seriousness as a personal visit, but you can make your point and sound out the legislator's latest concerns about the issue.

A letter or telegram from your organization will also make a good final impression. Letters in the final days before a vote carry not only their inherent weight of influence, but they implicitly reaffirm the influence of all the mail that came in earlier and could otherwise be easily forgotten at voting time.

If your legislator is not strongly committed to your issue or is noncommittal right up to the end, you may want to prod her gently to make sure she shows up for the vote. In this case, if you know what day the vote is scheduled for, phone the congresswoman's office the day before, ask if she'll be there for the vote, and be sure the staffer you speak with knows your position on the issue. Then get several other groups and individuals to phone, in a similar vein. This will make it clear to the congresswoman that you know the vote is coming up and you expect her to be there.

Then, on the day of the vote, have a few others phone the congresswoman's office and ask if she'll be there for the vote.

Be cautious in using these reminder tactics. They are just that—reminders, not a whole new barrage of influence.

After the Vote

The week after the vote is a critical time for your cause. During this week a senator or congressman finds out whether his vote has pleased or displeased his constituents. You, of course, want him to reach the right conclusion on this point so he'll be willing to vote your way in the future. The praise or disappointment expressed by constituents after the vote is one of your most potent sources of influence, and it is highly worthwhile to organize a modest feedback campaign.

Thank your legislators if they voted for your position. A long-time conservation lobbyist, A. T. Wright, says: "Don't thank them for doing it because you or your group asked them to do it. A legislator doesn't want to feel that he did it exclusively for you or your group, he wants to feel that he voted in the public interest, so thank him accordingly."

Do your thanking while the vote is still fresh in the congressman's mind. If possible, phone the congressman's office after the vote and leave a message of thanks. But don't neglect to get a letter or telegram off promptly.

Let your cooperating groups know of the outcome as soon as possible so they can also thank the congressman. Your call will also make these groups feel rewarded and recognized for their good work on the issue.

Call the local news media and praise the congressman's vote. You may be quoted in their news coverage, and your praise will be appreciated by the congressman. Especially wanted by legislators is praise for their effectiveness, because this sort of praise impresses voters who may not even care about the issue involved. So if a congressman has helped your cause aside from his vote—perhaps by making a speech or by influencing other congressman—say that he was an effective legislator.

Except on earthshaking issues, local newspapers frequently get news of the vote long after citizen action groups have heard the outcome. How the local legislators voted often does not come through the wire services until days later. So you may be doing your newspaper a favor by tipping them off to a story with local impact.

Publicize the vote through your organization's newsletter, or put out a special bulletin praising the congressman's action. Your editor may be able to quote a sentence or two from the congressman commenting on the outcome; a call to his press aide or to the proper issue staffer should result in a brief, usable comment.

If the congressman voted against your position, the message in your phone calls, letters, and media contacts should be one of disappointment. In calling news media, restate the issue clearly so the public will realize what the congressman's vote implies:

> "Senator Alvarez's vote against the education bill was a repudiation of our city's fight to give our children a better education."

> "Congresswoman Kaplan's vote against the Clean Air Act is a vote for air pollution and against public health."

Avoid being angry. A show of anger would make you seem vindictive in your comments on the congressman's vote. Just be serious and tell how the vote was against the public interest.

Showing Public Support

In earlier chapters we explained how to organize for a legislative campaign. Now we come to the tactical aspects of organizing—what you want organizations, members of organizations, and the general public to do in your campaign. It's a matter of putting your organization into action. The purpose of these activities is to convince your legislators that your position has widespread support among the voters, and that it has more support than your opponents' position has.

This kind of public support is very different from the support expressed in an opinion poll, because it is opinion translated into action. People who have asked a congressman to take a stand have much more influence than people who merely respond to a pollster's question. The history of gun-control proposals in Congress illustrates the distinction. According to the national Gallup Poll in 1975, 67 percent of the population favor registration of all firearms and 27 percent oppose such a law. The active opposition of the 27 percent has completely nullified the large but inactive majority of gun-registration supporters.

Senators and congressmen are sensitive to active support rather than passive support because people who actively support a cause are the most likely to help or hurt the legislators in the next election. These people will not only cast their own votes but will influence others in their community—friends, neighbors, and co-workers—or will volunteer to help in the actual campaign of the legislator or his challengers.

In organizing a legislative campaign, it's your responsibility to encourage active public support for your objective in ways that will have the most influence on your legislators.

The Letter Campaign

The fundamental and inescapable element of a public-support program is letters. They are so important because they are a tangible, countable evidence of constituents' views. They must be answered, which means that a congressman or his staff must consider the issue at least long enough to decide on a response.

Even a modest number of letters can get attention. Congressman Lester L. Wolff (Democrat of New York), who gets a large amount of mail from his suburban district, is alerted by his staff whenever ten or fifteen letters a week are coming in on a new issue. In other offices with less mail to handle, the congressman will actually see these letters and they will thus have more direct impact. In the office of Senator Alan Cranston (Democrat of California), with a mail count of 12,000 a week, ten or fifteen letters a week would not necessarily reach the senator's attention, but the mail-handling staff would call your issue to the attention of the right issue staffer. A flow of ten to fifteen letters a week is not hard to achieve when you have started a concerted letter campaign.

To be effective, a letter campaign must have two important traits:

1. Persistence. A steady flow of letters is usually interpreted on Capitol Hill as evidence of a deep-seated concern. Mail coming only in spurts is seen as the product of a "pressure-group campaign." So a letter campaign should be planned to provide a continuing flow of letters, building to peak flows before a big vote or when the legislator is going to make a decision.

2. Seriousness. Most opinion mail received by senators and congressmen is ineffective because the letters repeat the same "canned" phrases. Such letters, clearly stimulated by organizations, are considered, but they have far less influence than those that show seriousness on the part of the letter writer, and more of them are needed to get results. When the letter writer includes his or her own thoughts, experiences, and observations, the letter will be taken more seriously. Therefore, a letter campaign must try to get people to write their own letters, in their own words, reflecting their own experiences.

When planning a letter campaign, it's worthwhile to find out how mail is handled in congressional offices you are dealing with, so that you can put your stress on types of mail that get the most attention. If your congressman reads all constituent mail himself, you may decide to try for a steady flow of mostly serious letters. But for a congressman who sees few of the incoming letters and relies on his staff to report on a large weekly volume, you may want to lay down a good, continuous base of letters so the staff will report heavy mail on the issue, and then concentrate on getting letters from local VIPs and organizations, since their letters are more likely to be among the few the congressman actually reads.

After you've gotten to know a legislator's aide through a few good visits or phone calls, ask the aide how the letters are handled in that office. Or suggest the idea to a friendly reporter, who might make a feature story out of the different ways your congresswoman and senators handle citizens' letters, both as to substance (do they reply frankly with a position, or just give a noncommittal brush-off?) and as to response time. Bill Keller, a reporter for the *Oregonian*, had friends send the same letter to all four Oregon congressmen (from addresses in their districts) and to both senators, and he based a feature story on the results.

Plan your letter campaign to fit the circumstances—your own legislators, your issue, and the people you expect to write the letters. The basic resources of a letter campaign are the members of your organization, the members of other organizations that are willing to help, and unaffiliated citizens who are interested or can become interested in supporting your position. A letter campaign consists of varied ways of reaching these three classes of people and getting them to write letters to the right legislators, conveying the right message.

It's not easy to get people to take pen in hand when you ask them to, even though they may fully agree with your goals. Most people are deluged with more demands for help than they can possibly fulfill, from their jobs, from their friends and families, and from organizations. To get people to sit down and write a letter, you have to inspire them with the conviction that the issue is important, convince them that they can influence the outcome, give them enough facts so they understand the issue and can demonstrate their understanding in their letters, and tell them to whom to write.

Members of your own organization can be reached easily through your newsletter or magazine. The newsletter can be used over a period of months to educate members on different facets of your issue and get them to identify with it. Then, at the proper time, feature a front-page story asking for letters to your congressman. A buildup of this kind accustoms your members to perceiving the issue as an important one and one they're involved in, so they will be more inclined to write when the big moment comes. Low-key requests for letters to the congressman or to other officials in the earlier stories help, too, because members who have written one letter on the subject will feel that they have an investment in and a commitment to the issue and will be more willing to respond in the crisis.

When time is short and there is no time to prepare your members through repeated coverage of the issue, a hard-hitting story on the front page can still get good results, but the response won't be as strong.

The drawback of newsletters is that members think of them as a routine monthly publication and get used to glancing through them and tossing them out. It is therefore impossible to rely on your newsletter as a means of activating the maximum outpouring of letters when the big push is on. Some newsletters routinely contain several requests for letters to legislators on different issues; these will be acted on primarily by members most interested in the respective issues. When you want all your members to write, you have to do something different to get their attention.

Action Alert

A special legislative bulletin, often called an action alert, is the way to get action from your members in one big burst. It is a call to action on only one issue. Usually two to four pages in length, it presents a quick once-over summation of the facts, the current situation, and a hard-hitting exhortation to write letters to the target legislators. To avoid having the resulting letters arrive in congressional offices all at once—and thus become less effective—you can stagger your mailing over days or weeks. Divide your mailing list as randomly as possible, so the congressman doesn't receive for the first week only letters from, say, people whose surnames begin with A, or people who live in ZIP code zone 20705. Editorial suggestions on action alerts appeared in Chapter 9, "Your Publications."

The three principal occasions when an action alert can be used are:

1. A bill has been introduced and you are asking people to write urging their congressman to cosponsor it (or oppose it). In this case, an action alert can be mailed gradually over several weeks' time to show persistent interest in the subject.

2. A crucial vote is about to take place, and you are asking people to write urging their congressman to vote for or against a bill or an amendment.

3. A public hearing has been scheduled, and you're asking people to speak at the hearing or send in letters for the hearing record.

The percentage of members responding to a call for action, either by newsletter or action alert, is seldom high. If 5 percent of your members respond to an action alert, you can count yourself effective—and lucky. Single-purpose organizations may achieve a higher percentage—but don't count on it.

You can boost the response rate by using reminder techniques. Most reminder efforts are made by telephone. After your action alert has arrived in members' mailboxes, have some volunteers telephone your members, call their attention to the issue, refer to the action alert, and ask them to write to Congresswoman Smith, urging her to support your bill. A friendly voice on the telephone can usually win a commitment to write, and this will be more binding, more self-policing, than a fleeting notion while glancing through an action alert. By making the calls over a few days' time you can spread out the mail for a more persistent impression on the congresswoman.

The most prevalent telephone reminder system is the "telephone tree," which spreads the task among many volunteers, making it fast and easy work, instead of loading it on a few people and taking a long time. In its *Population Activist's Handbook* (New York: Macmillan, 1974), the Population Institute offers the following advice on how to organize a telephone tree:

1. Divide your volunteers into groups of eight to ten, with branch leaders. Use logical divisions, like neighborhoods, if possible.

2. The principle of the telephone tree is that A calls B, C, D, and E. B, in turn, calls F, G, H, and I.

3. Each branch leader should have a complete list of his or her contacts, with all possible phone numbers and addresses and a stack of postcards to use when he or she can't reach them by phone. The leader should report all changes in the list to the organizer of the telephone tree.

4. To recruit people for a telephone tree, the organizer should announce it at meetings and circulate a volunteer sign-up sheet for it, and also advertise it in the newsletter and provide a mail-in coupon by which people can volunteer.

The telephone tree can only be used infrequently, unless your members are very committed and unusually tolerant of demands from the organization. You can't get across any complicated message, because the gist can easily get distorted or reversed as the message is passed on. But as a medium for a simple reminder, tied in with an action alert or newsletter, the telephone tree can be excellent. It can also be used separately, in a crisis, but the message has to be short and sweet, and it has to be about something your members are already familiar with.

Meeting to Write Letters

Membership meetings of your organization can be another occasion to get people to write letters, especially when your issue has been the main subject of the meeting. Pass out copies of an action alert or fact sheet containing the name and address of the legislator who is to be written to, provide assorted writing paper and envelopes, and allot ten minutes of the agenda for people to write their own letters. Then collect the letters, affix stamps, and mail them over the next few days. If your members live in different communities, it may be preferable to have them mail their own letters, to avoid having the letters postmarked from a community the writers don't live in.

Some localized organizations have "letter-writing socials." Those scheduled by Tennessee Citizens for Wilderness Planning (TCWP) begin at 7:30 P.M. at a member's home. Members spend an hour writing letters to legislators and government officials, then turn to refreshments and good fellowship—much of it involving informal discussion of current wilderness issues. One meeting is held each week, in different Tennessee communities where TCWP members live.

Letters from Outside Your Organization

You'll find the greatest number of letter writers for your cause outside your organization. In a letter campaign it is vital to keep expanding your circle of participation, because you need to involve people who haven't already written the congressman about the issue. One of the most influential things that can happen is the congressman's realization that he is getting dozens of letters from constituents he's never heard from before, asking him to take action on an issue that concerns them. You can achieve this by getting other groups to have their members write letters, and by going straight to the public.

Cooperation with other organizations is a basic and powerful tool in a letter campaign. Chapter 7, "Organizing for Influence," covered the methods of building a coalition of organizations to support your objective. What concerns us here is how to use that coalition in your letter campaign.

First, if your cooperating organizations have not written recently to your congressman on this issue, ask them to do so, and follow up in a few days to make sure it is done. You may have to draft some letters for them if they can't seem to get around to it.

After all, organizations that are not usually involved in your issue may be uneasy about writing letters because they don't want to show how little they know about the subject. By drafting letters for them, you get them over this hurdle. The only drawback to doing so is that the other groups will become more involved if they write their own letters.

Then tap the organizations for help getting their members to write letters to the congressman. There are three ways of doing this:

1. Most effective is to have the cooperating organization **ask its members to write.** Members identify with their group and may be accustomed to doing things requested by the organization. The group can send its own action alert to its members or ask for letters in a prominent story in its newsletter.

2. When several organizations want to help with the letter campaign but won't or can't put out their own action alerts, it is quite common to **publish a joint action alert,** cosigned and cosponsored by all the cooperating organizations and mailed to members of the several groups, with costs shared among the groups. As long as people see their own organization listed as a cosponsor of the alert, they'll realize that it's a legitimate effort. The long list of cosponsors helps to point up the importance of the issue.

3. An organization that will neither put out its own action alert nor cosponsor a joint action alert may be willing to **let you use its mailing list.** Use this list to mail a joint action alert even if the group lending the names is not listed, since the obvious coalition spirit and importance of the alert will overcome any bad reaction recipients may have upon getting an exhortatory action alert from an unfamiliar source. Another possibility is to persuade a prominent leader of the group to sign a short note which you will print as a conspicuous part of your action alert for this mailing. The leader can do this as an individual, saying something like:

Dear Friend:
    This special bulletin asks for your help on an issue of crucial importance to our cause of public health. Please help now by writing to Senator Schmidt in support of the Clean Air amendments.
                                        Sincerely,

If your issue is a popular and easily understood one, don't stop with interested organizations, but go for general public support in your letter campaign. Leafletting is one way to get the story out when there are many sympathetic people in a small area. A good leaflet is essentially an action alert written for the uncommitted, one that assumes no special knowledge of the subject. It is usually short—one to two pages—and its main message is "Write your congressman." Don't miss the chance to include a membership coupon for your group as part of the leaflet, so you'll gain the most interested as members and be able to involve them more actively in the campaign. Leaflets have to be printed and distributed by the thousands, because the response rate will be far lower than for other methods in your letter campaign.

A leaflet has to grab people's attention before they have time to throw it into the nearest trash receptacle. A dramatic presentation of the issue is essential. Clergy and Laity Concerned printed leaflets resembling play money as part of their campaign against the B-1 bomber program. The front carried a face value of $92 billion, a photograph of a B-1 bomber, and the legends "Stop the B-1" and "Ninety-Two Billion Dollars." The reverse carried the action message and a coupon to clip and return to the organization.

Leaflets can be distributed to an entire neighborhood by stuffing them in mailboxes or under doors. Most are handed out in public places, such as:

- Busy street corners
- Fairs
- Outside concert halls
- Outside fast-food restaurants
- Outside museums and libraries
- In university or work-place cafeterias

Teenagers are good volunteers to pass out the leaflets, since they tend not to evoke hostility or fear among the public. A good leafleteer smiles while offering a leaflet to a passerby.

A letter campaign may also involve letter-writing tables at a college or work-place cafeteria where you expect to find many people sympathetic to your position. The organizer of a letter-writing table sets up a table and chairs near the cafeteria exit, equipped with different kinds of writing paper, different pens, and copies of an action alert or leaflet explaining the issue. The organizer then approaches people as they prepare to leave the cafeteria. A modest display of pertinent photographs, charts, or diagrams also helps to attract interest and inspire your supporters.

Postcards

Compared to a letter campaign, a campaign of preprinted postcards is a Mickey Mouse operation and not an effective source of influence. However, if the people most affected by your issue are not given to writing letters and if there are lots of them, these postcards could be worth a try. They will be influential on a senator or congressman only if *hundreds* of them are sent in, because so little effort, commitment, or knowledge is required to sign one. There is no way to show seriousness with postcards.

Before launching a postcard campaign, consider whether the effort your group will have to expend to get 400 postcards signed and mailed could instead yield fifty good letters to the congressman; if so, forget the postcards.

If you decide to have a postcard campaign, you couldn't do better than follow the example of the gun-control opponents whose postcards have deluged Western senators and congressmen. In Montana in 1976, stacks of cards addressed to senators Lee Metcalf and Mike Mansfield,* both Democrats, were offered on store counters, in professional offices and barbershops, and in businesses across the state, and passed out at meetings. The printed text of the card to Senator Metcalf ran as follows:

Dear Senator Metcalf:

As a Montana resident I am writing to you and Senator Mansfield to strongly oppose additional federal gun-control laws.

I hope that your influence and vote will be used to oppose all new legislation aimed at further restricting the ownership of firearms and ammunition.

Sincerely,

On the reverse side the address was printed:

---

* Since that time, Senator Mansfield retired and Senator Metcalf died.

TO: Senator Lee Metcalf
Senate Office Building
Washington, D.C. 20510

For the greatest yield, have volunteers collect the signed cards and return them to your organization. Stamps can be affixed, and the cards can be mailed gradually, some each day. The legislators will answer most postcards by a roboletter, so those who signed your postcards with name and address will at least get a letter back. If you have kept a mailing list of those who signed, you may find it worthwhile to follow up later with an action alert or membership solicitation.

Petitions

Petitions have little influence on senators and congressmen, but they can be useful as a legislative tactic under any of these circumstances:

1. At an early stage of a campaign, petitions can be used as a consciousness raiser, to spread word of the issue throughout your community. The petition is primarily a tool; it provides the rationale for volunteers to meet people, explain the issue, and hand them a leaflet.

2. When your volunteer force is growing rapidly with people inexperienced at political work, a petition drive is a good way to involve them in an action role while you train them on the issue and on leadership techniques.

3. A completed petition consisting of hundreds of pages full or partly full of signatures can be the vehicle that gets your issue into the news media. Presenting a bulky pile or roll of petitions to a congressman can often get photo coverage in local papers and on television.

A petition can mean a lot if there is nothing to counteract it. For instance, early in 1977 Congressman William C. Wampler (Republican of Virginia) received a petition signed by some 1,600 of his constituents in Giles County, opposing the preservation of any wilderness in the county. Although this was a relatively small number, it determined Wampler's initial stance—in the absence of any evidence of support for wilderness. When wilderness advocates from his district later approached him, the congressman refused to introduce their wilderness bill and cited the petition as his reason for refusing.

To achieve a worthwhile petition you have to organize the petition drive well, to make sure volunteers are on the job getting signatures in the most productive locations. Also send each of your members a petition blank or two and urge them to fill these blanks, send them back to your group, and ask for more blanks. You may not get many signatures from this unorganized effort compared to the supervised program, but you will get more members involved and get them in the habit of approaching friends for help on the issue.

The Sierra Club's *Grass Roots Primer* offers sound advice on petition techniques: "Stand and hold out a notebook and pencil at arm's length, advancing and all but blocking the path of the would-be signatory, smiling genially. One feels gently compelled to grab them and sign." The *Grass Roots Primer* also points out that some types of people are better than others for this task. For instance, "A young mother with her child could fill two whole petitions while others got only two signatures."

Any petition drive should also include leafletting. When a person has just signed the petition, hand him or her a leaflet. The leaflet is your chance to get more help from a petition signer. It should urge the signer to write his or her own letter to the congressman, and it should invite the signer to join your organization, using a mail-in coupon. You could even include in the leaflet's text something like this:

> Thank you for signing the petition for Better Schools. You can make your views even more influential by writing a letter to Congressman William O'Hara, House of Representatives, Washington, D.C. 20515. Tell him why you favor . . .

Places to circulate petitions include the following:

- Street corners in downtown shopping areas
- Universities, colleges, and professional schools

- Entrances of parks, zoos, movie theaters, opera houses, concert halls, libraries, museums, and churches
- Folk-life festivals, craft fairs, county fairs
- Shopping centers, if you have permission

Shopping centers are a promising site for petition efforts, but the legal situation is different from most public places because shopping centers are entirely on private property. Under a U.S. Supreme Court ruling, shopping centers may refuse to let you circulate a petition unless the petition is directly related to the shopping center. However, you can always seek out the manager of the center and ask for permission.

Even on public sidewalks elsewhere in town, if you plan to station your petition workers outside a store, it's wise to call the manager ahead of time, check to be sure you won't be obstructing pedestrian traffic into the store, and ask the manager to call you if any problem arises. This goodwill gesture will get you off on the right foot.

How you use your completed petition can make a big difference. You should be able to get from it some attention from the news media and some influence on your congressman and senators. When your completed petition forms have been collected and assembled, hold onto them until you can plan a presentation that will get news coverage.

These are some of the occasions for presenting a petition to a congressman:

- When the congressman attends a membership meeting of your organization or one of your cooperating groups
- When you meet with the congressman at his local office
- When you meet with the congressman in Washington, D.C.
- When you testify at a congressional hearing

In case news photographers don't show up, have your own photographer take pictures of the presentation so you can put out a news release with photographs and also use the pictures in newsletters of your cooperating groups.

You don't have to leave the whole petition with the congressman. Tell his staff beforehand if you want to show it to other legislators later. The staff will want to look it over, but may be relieved that you aren't going to leave it around to clutter up the office.

In Rhode Island a bulky petition was a crucial tool in the campaign against the supersonic transport (SST) project. Senator John O. Pastore (Democrat) had voted for the SST subsidy for several years, but in 1970 he was running for reelection, and a citizen group, Ecology Action for Rhode Island, mounted a campaign to convert him. Part of the campaign was a petition drive, in which some twenty-five high school students circulated petitions. The resulting petition, bearing 1,600 signatures, was presented to the senator in his Rhode Island office by a delegation of young and middle-aged citizens. Dwight W. Justice, the young organizer of the Ecology Action campaign, had alerted the *Providence Evening Bulletin*, which sent a reporter and a photographer to witness the meeting. The next day's paper carried a photograph of Senator Pastore receiving the petition and a news story headlined "Pastore Favors SST Delay." Pastore waffled on the issue for weeks after this event, but continuous citizen action using other tactics won him over, and he voted against the SST, although his personal sympathies were still known to be favorable to the project.

For suggestions on how to write a petition, see Chapter 9, "Your Publications."

Face to Face

One of the most effective ways of showing public support is to have people speak with the senator or congressman in person. In Chapter 6, "Face to Face with a Congressman," we covered the principles of this type of contact. Your task as an organizer is to find people who care enough about your issue to actually get an appointment and talk to the congressman as individual citizens, rather than as representatives of an organization. This is more to ask of somebody than writing a letter, because it will take more time and it can be a more stressful situation. The best time to approach people with this request is when you're having a conversation. It might be during the social hour after a meeting of your group, or it might be over the back fence with a neighbor. You have to convince people that it's needed and worth doing, and that they *can* do it themselves.

What kind of person should you look for to go and see the congressman? Anybody who cares about the issue can make a favorable impression on a legislator. We offer only one caveat: people whose habitual dress or hairstyle is unorthodox would be well advised to adopt a more orthodox appearance for a meeting with a congressman, since a politician can too easily dismiss the obviously unorthodox as an extremist fringe element.

People who are going to visit a congressman need only care about the issue and be somewhat knowledegeable about it. They don't have to know all the answers or be able to refute every argument the congressman brings up. The main thing is to tell the congressman what they want him to do, why they believe this is the right thing to do, and not let him talk them out of their views.

People with experience or expertise in a relevant field can be influential, too. Suppose you find an economist in your neighborhood who favors your position on the Consumer Protection Agency Bill. He need not know all about the bill, but if he can go and talk to the congressman, attesting to the seriousness of the economic arguments for the measure, he will have helped significantly.

People who have leadership positions in other local organizations, even those completely unrelated to your issue, have influence, too. Holding office in a social club, professional organization, student group, or lodge shows that a person is liked and respected by others. Even if the organization takes no position on your issue, a leader can go to see the congressman as an individual, making it clear somewhere in the conversation that he or she is active in, say, the Washington Park Tennis Club. The congressman will realize that this person is in a position to influence other voters.

To illustrate this, let's suppose you're president of the Westmoreland Garden Club. Before going to see the congressman, discuss the issue with friends in the club who are sympathetic to your position. Then you can tell the congressman, "We've been talking this over—I and other members of the Westmoreland Garden Club—and we all are very concerned about the deteriorating quality of education in the public schools." Or: "I'm active in the Westmoreland Garden Club, and we've been discussing the schools problem lately. My friends and I think it's time to increase federal aid to the schools." Don't mention that you're the president of the club; that's too blatant a way of showing your influence. All you want to do in this situation is show that you're active in an organization, rather than a loner who never talks things over with anybody else.

In organizing a program of individual visits to a senator or congressman, work for a steady flow of visits, week after week, whenever the legislator is available. The persistence will make an impression on the legislator, and you'll be able to get feedback as to what the legislator is telling people and replan your tactics accordingly.

More impressive, but harder to arrange, are brief, casual encounters with a congressman, what we call "street contacts." In this type of contact, the congressman is greeted by people on the street who tell him, for instance, "We sure need that law to stop nuclear exports. I hope you're planning to vote for it." Such encounters carry weight because they are unexpected and because this is not the kind of contact that is normally inspired by an organization. Street contacts give the impression that your issue is known and important to the proverbial man on the street, rather than a concern of a small, elite group. A few street contacts can mean a lot, especially if you're having trouble getting the congressman to notice the issue and take it seriously.

If you can find out where the congressman is going to be during his trips back home, prompt some of your members to be on hand where he may be mingling with the crowds—on the street, at factory gates, at county fairs, at political rallies, or at receptions. Ask your people to walk right up to the congressman and tell him what they think about your issue.

Another good place to have your issue mentioned to senators and congressmen is at political functions attended primarily by the faithful Democrats or Republicans. Among them are campaign fund-raising receptions and dinners, county and state party meetings and conventions, and party rallies. People who attend these functions are the campaign contributors, campaign workers, and local politicians who can help get a senator or congressman reelected. When an issue is repeatedly mentioned to a congressman by different people at a party function, all urging the same position, he'll start to see it as a reasonable issue that he ought to take a stand on.

Like a street contact, an encounter at a political function is brief, and you have to get the point across fast. The legislator may be greeting people in a receiving line—in which case you'll have to reduce the message to one sentence—or he may be circulating informally during a cocktail hour. To find out about such events, call the congressman's local office or get friends who are active in the political party to let you know. When the purpose of the event is to raise money, you won't have any trouble with invitations, because they'll welcome anybody who can pay the tariff. Just find out what it costs, what organization is putting it on, and carry on from there. If you can't afford the tickets yourself, perhaps a wealthier donor who favors that political party will buy the tickets for you. Most citizen-action groups are tax-exempt and therefore cannot contribute to partisan campaign funds, but individuals always can.

If your congressman or congresswoman already knows you, your presence at these political events will show him or her that you and your group are serious about participating in politics, rather than dilettantes who scorn party politics. If you're still an unknown, your issue message will make its own impression.

By building your network of supporters among people who are active in political parties—as convention delegates, block leaders, and the like—you'll be able to have them raise the issue at party functions which they would be attending as party workers, rather than in the more suspect role of advocates of your particular cause.

Besides getting individuals to see the congressman or senators, get your cooperating groups to call on the legislators. By presenting their own reasons for favoring your position and stressing who their membership is, each organization makes the congressman think harder about why he should favor your position. Keep hitting him with different groups, so that he is continually surprised to discover yet another element of his constituency endorsing your position and demonstrating their concern by seeing him in person.

Work quietly behind the scenes to instigate these meetings, and let each group handle its own contacts with the legislator. If you show yourself in connection with these groups, it will undermine their impact because their actions may be tainted by association with you, the issue advocate.

"Actions"

Public support can also be shown through "actions"—picketing, mass protests, and the like. These don't necessarily require a cast of thousands; sometimes a dozen is enough to draw attention to an issue. An action, at its best, is a vivid dramatization of your issue by your supporters. Its purpose is to get your issue across to the public and to your senators and congressman through television, radio, and newspaper coverage. An action can be much more than what is conveyed by the word *demonstration*—a crowd carrying signs, marching around in a circle. An action can take the form of a picket line, a confrontation at a hearing, a mass march, a skit, a game, a stunt, or whatever your group thinks up. Try to invent new things, because these will get the most attention from news media and the public.

An action can be especially effective when your issue is not being noticed by your community, or when the issue is too legalistic or technical to be easily grasped by the public. An action might be able to simplify the issue and make it dramatic. For instance, in Pittsburgh, citizens were fighting Duquesne Light Company's practice of charging consumers for taxes the company never paid—an overcharge of $17 million, according to the People's Power Project. To dramatize the issue, members of the project staged an action to protest these "phantom taxes." Held outside Duquesne Light's headquarters, the action consisted of picketing by citizens dressed as phantoms, in white sheets and masks, carrying signs saying: "Phantom Taxes, $17 Million," "Refund Tax Overcharge," and "Duquesne Light Rips Off $17 Million in Taxes." The action was highly visual and got the issue onto local news media.

Actions used as part of a legislative campaign can focus on a local example of the issue, on local opponents of your position (if the public will clearly see them as "the bad guys"), or on local politicians who have opposed your cause. While your purpose is to influence your congressman or senators, the target of an action should be a local person, company, or agency that you believe is acting wrongly or irresponsibly.

In planning what kind of action to put on, base your thinking on what your people will be comfortable with and what they will enjoy. This is the advice of Michael Troutman, Environmental Action Foundation's expert on actions. Troutman points out that outraged people enjoy having a direct confrontation with the opposition, while more straitlaced people prefer actions involving less anger and more humor.

In the outrage department, Troutman cites residents of neighborhoods affected by "red-lining," banks' and insurance companies' practice of denying insurance or mortgage loans to entire neighborhoods. The outraged victims of red-lining have confronted bankers on the sidewalk, engaged them in shouting matches, and wrapped them in red crepe-paper streamers to symbolize red-lining.

Less angry but no less pointed was the action by members of Citizens United for Responsible Energy (CURE), an Iowa group, who appeared at a hearing of Iowa's Energy Policy Council to present officials with 200 dirty socks, symbolizing the dirty socks used to plug radiation leaks in a Japanese nuclear-powered ship.

"If there's any rule for effective actions, it's 'Be Creative!',", says Troutman. "Almost any group has a person who thinks creatively." Just as an indication of the range of possible actions, consider these examples:

1. Protesting the lack of rat-control measures in poor neighborhoods in Washington, D.C., activist Julius Hobson threatened to trap large numbers of rats and release them in the posh Georgetown residential area. He then drove through Georgetown with cages of rats atop his car, to make the threat more dramatic.

2. To call attention to the need for repeal of laws that restricted the sale of contraceptives, the Rochester, New York, chapter of Zero Population Growth had a tall man appear on the street in a stork costume, carrying a sign, "On Strike Against Unwanted Pregnancies."

3. To dramatize the unreliability of nuclear power, citizens might stage an awards ceremony in which the citizen group presents a bushel of lemons to the local power company.

4. To exemplify local water pollution problems, a citizen group might collect a bucketful of foul-smelling effluent from a factory's outflow pipe at the river's edge and present it to the chairman of the board.

5. Annually on the anniversary of the Supreme Court's decision legalizing abortion, opponents of that decision have staged a protest rally in Washington, D.C., for which thousands of people have been bused to the capital city. Participants called on their senators and congressmen, leaving red roses as a symbol of their cause, and asked the legislators to support a constitutional amendment prohibiting abortion and to end federal funding of abortions for the poor.

6. To demonstrate the hazard of radiation escaping from nuclear power plants, Californians released 2,000 helium-filled balloons at a power plant site, with this attached message: "As easily as this balloon reached you, so could the radiation from Diablo Canyon Nuclear Power Plant (if the plant goes into operation)."

An action becomes more effective when its participants are of an unexpected sort. Demonstrations by casually dressed college students are pretty routine stuff, although they still have an impact. Greater impact comes from a demonstration wholly of farmers dressed in their work clothes, or businesspeople in business dress. A congressman or senator thinks that farmers and businesspeople seldom get so concerned about an issue that they'll adopt so unorthodox a tactic as a demonstration. This unusual factor will also attract better coverage by news media.

Schedule your action with two points in mind: to get the best media coverage and to get a good turnout of your supporters. For evening television news and morning papers, a noon-hour or early-afternoon time is your best bet, if your people are free at this time. Do some checking beforehand to avoid times when other major events are scheduled. If the governor is speaking in your town at the same time you're picketing the school superintendent's home, you know where the reporters are going to be.

Sometimes an action can be tied to a newsworthy event put on by your opponents. If an association promoting a new dam holds a meeting, for instance, opponents of the dam might put on an action outside the meeting place. Reporters will be on the scene to get your opponents' story, and will generally cover your side, too, as long as it doesn't look insignificant or too far-out. Bear in mind that a demonstration has less respectability than a meeting, but you can partly make up for this by having respectable-looking, articulate spokespeople in your action.

Population activists took advantage of their opponents' Ohio Pro-Life Convention in Cincinnati in April 1977. To counteract the antiabortion message from the Pro-Life Convention, the rival Coalition for Abortion Rights called a press conference, issued a declaration stating their views on abortion, hired an airplane to circle above the antiabortion rally towing a banner reading "Keep Abortion Safe and Legal," and also picketed the Pro-Life Convention.

One of the first steps in planning an action is to check with local police as to pertinent laws and regulations and permits that may be required. Some communities require up to two weeks' advance application for a permit, and some have regulations governing the size and construction of signs used in demonstrations.

An action requires signs and handout materials. The signs should be homemade, not because these are cheapest, but because they show that your cause is a citizens' cause, an underdog cause. A sign-making session a few days before the event can be a morale booster and an occasion to take stock of your efforts to get a good turnout. Use humor in your signs, both to poke fun at your opponents' position and to show that your group has a healthy sense of humor along with its serious commitment.

Here are some examples of signs used in various actions:

1. Retired and disabled textile workers fighting for better protection against "brown lung"—the disease caused by inhalation of cotton dust in textile mills, which reduces the victims' breathing capacity—used these signs in their picketing:

Cotton Breathes But We Can't

Spartan Mills Took My Breath

Blue Jeans for You—Brown Lung for Us

2. In the campaign against nuclear power, these signs have been used:

No Nukes Is Good Nukes

Uranium Now, Leukemia Later

Better Active Now Than Radioactive Later

For best appearance on television, the predominant colors used in your signs should be reds, blues, and greens.

Handout materials for an action can include background packets to be given to reporters and leaflets to be given to passersby. Reporters should get from you at least a prepared statement explaining why you're there. One or two of your people should be prepared to be interviewed for radio and television news and be able to sum up your message in forty-five seconds or less. The person in charge of publicity for your action can usually suggest to reporters who would be good to interview. A practical division of labor is to have one person in charge of the action and another person responsible for greeting the reporters and giving them the information and photo and interview opportunities they need in order to make a real news story out of your issue.

The leaflet for general handout use should be a page or a half-page in length, summing up the issue, urging people to take some specific action (such as writing to your congressman), and including your group's address and, if there's space, a membership blank.

Rallies

A rally lacks the vivid, dramatic quality of an action, but it may be another way of demonstrating support for your cause, and is far more likely to muster a large crowd. A rally—sometimes publicized as a "celebration" in order to emphasize the positive and escape the aura of political rallies—usually depends on well-known speakers and entertainment features to attract a crowd. Good publicity through posters and handbills during the preceding days and a good location (often in a park or public square) are basic. The program may include rock or country music groups interspersed with inspirational speeches from diverse supporters of your cause. Exhibits and displays may be mounted by your cooperating groups. Some highly visual elements should be included, to give television and press photographers what they need to make a story.

For instance, in a celebration whose theme is protection of your local river, the event could be at a riverbank park, and one of the visual elements might be the arrival of a flotilla of fifty canoes that have paddled from the next city as a sign of support.

Opinion Surveys

Public support can also be shown by an opinion survey, if you're sure public opinion is heavily on your side. A poll designed and directed by qualified survey researchers can influence your legislators and also be a morale booster to your activists, since it reassures them that local citizens are really behind your cause in spirit, if not in action. The opinion survey should be organized by a professor or researcher in sociology, psychology, or political science who knows survey research methods. A poll taken inexpertly, using a biased sample or slanted questions, can be easily demolished by your opponents, so it is important to have your poll done right.

This is also danger in a poll. If the results do not support your position, you may not be able to keep this fact quiet. Reporters may hear about the poll—perhaps from an opponent who happened to be polled—and beat a pathway to your door, demanding release of the results.

Boycotts

Boycotts, though rarely used on legislative issues, can be effective as an educational tool, making people in your community aware of the issue as it affects them in their buying. **A boycott is feasible only if you can identify one of the following:**

• Retail businesses that are responsible for the problem your legislation would solve

• A product sold by retail businesses that is clearly tied to the problem

Suppose you're fighting for a bill to prohibit gas-guzzling automobiles; you might consider boycotting auto dealers that handle cars getting less than, say, fifteen miles per gallon.

A boycott need not be a blanket "don't patronize this store" appeal. It can be precise, pinpointing the products you are boycotting. This has been the approach of such national boycotts as those against nonunion grapes and lettuce.

An effective boycott can use a large number of volunteers and can get your story out to thousands of people who would not otherwise have known about the issue. It can also get publicity that helps to build sentiment behind your legislative goal.

The principal methods of boycotting are:

• Picketing, leafletting, and talking to shoppers at entrances to stores

• Publicity in newspapers, on radio and television, and in posters and bumper strips

Citizens' Hearings

When you feel you have excellent public support that can far outshine the opposition, one means of showing it is by holding a citizens' hearing. This is an unofficial public hearing, organized by your people, at which anyone who wishes to can speak on the announced topic. The statements are transcribed by a stenotypist or court reporter, and the written transcript is submitted to the relevant senators and congressman.

An outstanding example of the citizens' hearing took place in Eugene, Oregon, in 1971, concerning rival proposals to preserve or log French Pete Creek, the last untouched river valley in the Oregon Cascades. No congressional hearing had been held, despite repeated requests to the Senate Committee on Interior and Insular Affairs by Oregon citizens and by the state's U.S. senators. So the Oregon Citizens' Committee on Interior and Insular Affairs came into being and organized a citizens' hearing. A vast majority of those speaking at the hearing favored saving French Pete, but opponents were also heard from.

Frank J. Barry, then a law professor at the University of Oregon and one of the organizers of the hearing, says: "The advantages of the hearing were very substantial. Not only were the activists given a focal point, but many people who were 'unorganized' showed up. One elderly woman, who had not been in French Pete since she was a girl, came to the hearing. She evidently had never spoken in public before. After listening to other witnesses, she made notes on a piece of paper and eventually got up to tell about a secret place in French Pete she used to visit years ago. It was quite a touch."

The hearing was held before rotating panels of citizens, instead of a single chairperson, and it was conducted according to the rules of the Senate Interior Committee. A local court reporter had been hired by the Citizens' Committee to take down all the statements. The transcript was not only submitted to Senators Mark O. Hatfield and Robert Packwood (both Republicans); Packwood had it printed in full in the *Congressional Record*. This citizens' hearing was a turning point in the fight to save French Pete, because it showed that public support was there. The logging plan was subsequently sidetracked, and legislation was enacted in 1978 to preserve French Pete as a wilderness area.

The keystones of a good citizen hearing are:
- Rigorous fairness by the hearing officer or hearing panels
- An overwhelming turnout by your supporters

Be sure to get plenty of advance publicity out, and get the news media to cover the hearing itself. To plan the best presentation of your position, consult Chapter 14, "Your Role in Congressional Hearings."

Town Meetings

In some parts of the country, official town meetings are held annually in which residents can propose resolutions for adoption by the townspeople. In March 1977, at thirty-six town meetings in Vermont, opponents of nuclear power plants proposed local resolutions forbidding the construction of atomic power plants and the transportation and storage of nuclear wastes within their towns. The resolutions were adopted in all but one of the town meetings, sending a firm message to Vermont's elected officials about local sentiment on nuclear power.

Using Very Important Supporters

"All animals are equal, but some animals are more equal than others." That's how George Orwell put it in *Animal Farm*. The tactical question in a legislative campaign is how to get help from those who are more equal than others—what we call VIP support.

This goes beyond the topic discussed earlier in this chapter, how to use respected local citizens to build respectability for your cause. The topic here is how to get those who have special access to your senators and congressman to influence them directly. This access may exist because a person is powerful, has money, is a friend or business associate of the legislator, or because he or she has been a campaign contributor or campaign worker. Or it may be simply that the person is respected by the legislator.

Finding VIPs

The first step in seeking this kind of influence is to draw up a list of those who have helped the congressman or been close to him. Then work over this list to find which ones may be sympathetic to your cause and which can be approached by members of your group. **Among the most basic components of this raw list—what might be called the Congressman's Inner Circle—are:**

1. Campaign contributors. The report of a congressman's campaign committee listing his contributors may be ordered from the Public Records Office, Federal Election Commission, Washington, D.C. 20463. The copying charge is ten cents a page. The contributor pages, which appear in the committees' quarterly reports, may be ordered separately. The same reports are supposed to be filed with the secretary of state in your state capital.

2. Campaign manager and other principal campaign workers. These are reported to the secretary of state in your state capital.

3. Former colleagues and business associates. Read the congressman's official biography in the *Congressional Directory*, his listing in *Who's Who*, and newspaper clipping files in the office of your local paper. After noting what jobs he had, work outward

222 | HOW YOU CAN INFLUENCE CONGRESS

from there to find who was working with him: who else was in his law firm, who else were directors of his corporation, who else was on the faculty when he was a professor, and so forth. Many legislators are involved in businesses while in Congress, too.

4. Friends. With whom does the congressman play golf or tennis? What families does he stay with when he visits in the congressional district? Whose parties does he attend? The newspaper clipping files may help, and if you're on good terms with the social columnist for the local newspaper, you may be able to get the answers fast.

5. Former congressmen, senators, governors, and other officials who are respected by the congressman. Find out who launched your congressman on his political career and who fostered it along the way, and you'll have a few names of people who can influence him.

The second list to prepare and comb for potential support contains the names of those who are not necessarily closely allied with your congressman but who unarguably have money or power in your community and therefore have access and probably influence with your congressman. **The list—what might be called the Local Power Circle—begins with these:**

• Top executives of the biggest businesses in town, including both the operating officers and chairmen of the boards
• Labor leaders
• Minority-group leaders
• Religious leaders
• Education leaders, such as university presidents
• Social leaders. While not known for their attention to substantive issues, those who give the biggest parties in town may have excellent access to a congressman.
• Business leaders active in groups such as the Chamber of Commerce, board of trade, and civic festivals (Rose Festival, Music Festival, etc.)

- Businesspeople active in social-service and cultural groups such as the Jaycees, Heart Association, or symphony association

- Spouses of businesspeople. Though not usually involved in power politics, business spouses who are active in cultural and social events usually know the congressman and can be effective by raising the issue with him.

- Retired people who have money or power. These people can be especially helpful because they may have time to work on the issue actively.

How to Approach VIPs

The hardest part of working up VIP influence is figuring out how to approach the VIPs. You can't approach them cold on behalf of, say, Citizens for Better Schools, because if they don't like your position and resent being approached, they'll probably fire off letters to the congressman advocating the opposite of what you want. A congressman's closest supporters are likely to be highly sensitive and may write to warn him that a campaign is afoot.

The best approach is through people who know the VIPs— friends, colleagues, neighbors, people who go to the same church, attend the same concerts, or belong to the same country club. If your campaign has enlisted diverse support groups, some of them are likely to have useful contacts with the VIPs you want. It takes patient work with leaders of your cooperating groups, perusing the target lists, to hit pay dirt.

The best results come from a good contact with one of the Congressman's Inner Circle list. Next best is the larger Local Power Circle list, which can be worked continuously if you can get people who move in that sphere of society to keep plugging away. One or two socialites can get their friends to keep raising the issue with the congressman week after week. A top business executive can get his or her colleagues to phone or write the congressman, one after the other. A good team effort can produce a small but powerful flow of contacts by people in the Local Power Circle.

A mailing to campaign contributors might work when the issue is one on which you're sure the legislator's backers agree with you. If Congresswoman Green ran for office as a friend of better schools with the support of teachers' groups, but she's now wavering on the education appropriations bill, this kind of mailing could provoke a healthy barrage of letters from her campaign contributors. But don't let your mailer give away the fact that it was sent to the contributors' list. Use the same approach you would in a mailer to anyone in Green's district who is concerned about schools. Somebody will inevitably send the congresswoman a copy of your mailer, and she'll be irate if she thinks that you've approached her contributors.

Using All Events for Your Purpose

Many events can be used to gain an advantage for your issue. By applying imagination and foresight, you can identify and exploit situations that are not of your own making, but which lend themselves to your campaign. To have your subject raised in unexpected times and places can be both newsworthy and persuasive to your congressman and senators. When legislators keep hearing about the issue, when they can't seem to get away from it, you're well on the way to winning their votes.

Events that evoke dissatisfaction among your potential supporters can be turned to your purpose. For instance, when a natural gas shortage hits your community, the time could be ripe to build support for energy conservation measures.

Functions attended by large audiences can also be used to advance your issue. For instance:

• At high school and college graduation ceremonies, speakers can advocate your cause. If a senator or congressman is present, the message gets across directly, but if not, a little advance publicity work can get the issue into the news media. A good example was Stephanie Mills's valedictory speech at the 1969 commencement of Mills College, in which she announced that, as a response to the overpopulation problem, she planned not to have children. Her speech shocked many people, and it got nationwide attention for the population issue.

• At a stockholders' meeting, sales conference, or convention, a few well-chosen remarks by a sympathetic speaker, backed up by good publicity work, can get attention for your issue.

Tactics for High Schools

High school students can participate in regular citizen-group activities supporting your legislative campaign. But they often are not given enough responsibility by adults. If you're a high school student and encounter this problem, consider the special opportunities you have to further the cause through activities in your school.

These are some of the tactics used by high school students:

1. Get interest clubs to adopt a position statement or resolution on your issue and send it to your congressman. The Cleveland High School Science Club in Portland, Oregon, for instance, endorsed the Wilderness Bill in 1958 and submitted a letter for a congressional hearing on the subject. Most interest clubs have no rigorous bylaws that would prevent them from taking a stand. All it takes is a student to write and propose one and talk a majority into voting for it.

2. Have students and teachers in a relevant field do research on the issue and release the results to the congressman and to news media. To support a tough pollution-control bill, a biology class could do an inventory of plants and animals in a polluted stream. To support a consumer-protection bill, a home economics class might compare the BTU output and prices of rival brands of air conditioners.

3. Have a class field trip to an affected area in your community, write it up as a report by your class, and release the report to legislators and news media. Ask members of the class to write their own letters to the congressman, too.

4. Suggest devoting a class period to the issue, either as a debate or as a panel discussion with questions from the class. Then ask your fellow students to write their own letters to the congressman, and hand out a one-page flyer containing pertinent facts and telling whom to write to.

5. Bring up the issue whenever you can tie it in with the subject of the class, and arrange for other classmates to do so too, so you won't be written off as a nut on the subject. For instance, when studying business letters in English class, suggest that the students write to the congressman and two senators concerning the issue—or divide up the class so one-third writes to each legislator.

6. Have delegates to the student government propose a resolution on the subject, to be adopted as the recommendation of the student body association, and then send it to the congressman and to news media. The faculty may tell you it can't be done. Check the association's bylaws to find authority for the action you want to take.

7. Have delegates to the "youth state"—the annual or biennial mock government held in many states—propose a resolution on the subject. In Idaho, a student delegate recently proposed a resolution favoring wilderness status for the River of No Return area, and it was approved by the youth legislature and publicized around the state, much to the consternation of the timber industry, which wants to log off part of the tract.

8. Consider forming your own student organization around the issue as a means of enlisting other students actively in the campaign. Chapter 8, "Care and Feeding of an Organization," gave more detailed ideas on this point.

9. As a consciousness-raising tactic, organize a "studies week" on your issue, such as the Population Studies Week held in a Portland, Oregon, high school. Other variants on this theme include Health Studies Week (pollution, medical research, etc.), Consumer Studies Week, and International Relations Week (foreign policy issues).

10. If your school library is deficient in books on your issue, get a few students together and go to see the librarian, presenting a list of basic books that could be added to the library.

11. A high school group can also testify at congressional hearings, visit and correspond with legislators, organize letter campaigns, and use many other tactics common to adult organizations.

Studies Week

The basic plan for studies weeks comes from the Population Institute's *The Population Activist's Handbook.* By keeping the program on a "studies" basis, you avoid the implication that it's a biased program. But then you follow up by organizing advocacy groups afterwards; your opponents may do the same.

A studies week is a multimedia program, including films, seminars, and speakers. First, plan your program and get a few other students involved. Then take the proposal to a sympathetic teacher and ask his or her help in getting it approved by the principal. Involve diverse elements of the school to get the issue into many classes.

A Population Studies Week commonly involves biology, social studies, health, and mathematics classes, while English and foreign-language classes may use population as a topic of composition exercises. Art and photography classes may get an early start by making posters for a studies week, and the school newspaper may devote special pages to the topic.

Funds for a studies week may be available from the school or from the student government to cover the costs of films and the fees of guest speakers.

The studies week may be newsworthy in your community. Send out news releases, but make the "for release" date *during* the studies week, so your opponents can't pressure school officials into calling it off, if you think this is a risk in your community.

12

Preparing Your Arguments

Without good arguments your cause is dead. You need arguments to win the help and influence of other citizens, and you need arguments to influence your congressman.

In a legislative campaign, an argument is simply a reason why legislators should vote a certain way. Arguments are not necessarily the greatest determinant of a legislator's vote. A congressman may decide to do as you ask simply because you and your co-workers have built political support in his district for your cause. Yet even when he supports you for such political reasons, the congressman needs the arguments to justify his decision. He needs to justify it to himself, so he can feel comfortable with it. He also needs to justify the decision to the public if he is challenged by your opponents or by a rival candidate in the next election.

An argument must be logical, but it can also appeal to emotion. The logical content should predominate. An overemphasis on emotion runs the risk of alienating legislators and turning off many citizens who will feel patronized or demeaned by a purely emotional argument. People are generally flattered to be approached with a logical argument.

The combination of logical and emotional content was shown in the campaign against the SST subsidy. Opponents of the project argued that the government should not spend $1.2 billion to develop an airplane that would be patronized only by wealthy businessmen and the Jet Set. This argument had its logical side (Why spend all that money for a questionable purpose?) and its emotional side (an appeal to prejudice against the rich).

When you carry out a legislative campaign you need persuasive arguments, backed up by the most impressive evidence you can get. To meet this central need you'll have to find the information and put it in a form that will enlighten and inspire people. On many issues you'll be able to get the arguments and background information from national organizations that are active on the subject. Then it's your job to recast these arguments in terms that will mean something to your community. For instance, if you're working for an increase in federal aid to public libraries, you can get national arguments from the American Library Association, but then you'll have to find out how the increase would help your local libraries, because this is what will mean the most to your congressman.

Congress often deals with subjects on which there is plenty of information, none of it presented effectively in the form of persuasive arguments. The SST issue initially was one of these. The SST subsidy had been approved year after year during the 1960s, despite the efforts of Senator William Proxmire (Democrat of Wisconsin) and Congressman Sidney R. Yates (Democrat of Illinois) to turn the tide, armed with ample information. Only in 1970 and 1971 was the SST finally rejected by Congress, after that information had been disseminated to citizen leaders all over the country, through a citizens' coalition effort, and these leaders had forcefully presented the arguments to their legislators, using many of the tactics described in this book.

The House Commission on Administrative Review (the "Obey Commission") reported in 1977:

> Members complain that their offices are deluged with substantive information—both a large volume and a wide variety—often more than can be processed for legislative use. Too much irrelevant and undigested material is presented in hard-to-read reports, transcripts of hearings, unsolicited position papers and so forth. Offices do not have the time or the staff to sift the wheat from the chaff, and much of the information is therefore unusable.

Information itself is not an argument. In a campaign for an air-pollution control bill you might have a four-foot stack of scientific reports on the health effects and property damage caused by air pollution, but all this information won't do your cause any good in that form. No congressman or senator is going to read those reports, and few will even know they exist. The information must be put into argument form. Then you can cite those reports as the authority behind your arguments, and you may even be able to use them ceremonially at hearings or news conferences to impress people with the weight of your arguments.

Kinds of Arguments

There are basically four kinds of arguments used in legislative issues:

- **Social good:** how your proposal will enhance people's lives
- **Economics:** how your proposal will make (or save) money, make more jobs, or stimulate more business
- **Ethics:** how your proposal is morally right and the opposing position is wrong
- **Science and technology:** an assertion that certain facts are true or a prediction of what will happen

A fifth kind of argument is often used in connection with the Senate's consideration of the President's nominees to federal judgeships, Administration posts, and regulatory commissions—the *personal argument*, concerning how a person is or is not qualified for the job.

To support the arguments, three kinds of evidence can be used:

- **Uncontestable facts:** those your opponents won't challenge
- **Contestable facts:** those you'll have to defend
- **Opinions:** the predictions or recommendations of experts and respected people

This chapter tells how to prepare your arguments, how to accumulate evidence to back them up, and how to present your arguments and evidence.

Preparing Your Arguments

The first step is to make an inventory of your arguments. Include every reason you can think of in support of your position. Then decide which of these arguments will be most persuasive to your senators and congressman and to the people in your community whose help you will need to influence these legislators—the public at large, active citizen groups, local politicians, local government agencies, local news media, locally respected citizens, and so on. Having chosen the most usable arguments, you'll be able to concentrate on preparing these thoroughly, giving less attention to the less usable arguments.

The entire inventory should be made not by you alone, but by your core leadership group, because it concerns the arguments all your leaders will rely on during the campaign. If the leaders have contributed to this basic preparation, they will have a stronger commitment to the campaign that follows. Besides, they may offer effective new ideas or different perspectives.

Inventorying All Arguments

After inventorying your arguments, proceed to inventory your *opponents'* arguments. Here again, consider which of these opposition arguments will be most influential on your legislators and on your opponents' cobelievers in the community. Then take stock of your responses to these arguments—how can you refute them or defuse them?

Don't neglect to think over how your opponents will respond to your arguments. If they have a strong rebuttal of your best argument, you'll need to prepare a strong rebuttal of *their* rebuttal.

As you review the arguments, consider how good the evidence is for each argument. If you have believable and authoritative evidence for an argument, chances are it will be taken seriously; if you don't, it won't. However, you can build up evidence by putting people to work researching the subject.

The argument inventory is a planning tool, showing you:

- Which of your arguments are not refutable

• Which of your opponents' rebuttals need a prepared rebuttal

• Which of your arguments rest on slender or unimpressive evidence and therefore need further work

• Which of your opponents' arguments rest on slender or unimpressive evidence and therefore are vulnerable

Also review your argument inventory to see whether you have arguments in all four categories—social good, economics, ethics, and science and technology. If not, you may be missing a chance to broaden your appeal and thus gain more support.

Review the arguments to see if you have made a strong case that the issue affects your congressional district and state. Local-impact arguments are among the most effective when you're dealing with members of Congress, so don't neglect this subject if you can possibly make a good argument.

Support for Your Arguments

As part of your inventory process, draw up a list of your potential sources of support, and indicate which arguments will be needed to bring them into action.

After preparing this list, based on your knowledge of potential supporters, look at the subject the other way round, to discover new sources of support that you hadn't thought of before. Go through your arguments, asking yourself, "Who in our community would be concerned about this argument?"

This inventory process will give you a head start on your campaign, because you'll know where your strong points and weak points are. However, preparing your arguments is a process that never stops. During the heat of your campaign you may discover new sources of support—perhaps an affected neighborhood you had not known about, or a labor union that is concerned about your issue. When this happens, put somebody to work preparing the arguments and evidence that will bring this new support into action. On the other hand, your opponents may spring a new argument on you, in which case you will need to prepare a persuasive rebuttal fast.

This sort of argument preparation under pressure is normal to a legislative campaign. But you'll always do better if you start your preparations early and, as a result, can put all your group's time and effort at the peak of the campaign into tactical projects that will yield political support, instead of into research to plug the holes in poorly prepared arguments.

The argument inventory should be started at one of your group's first few meetings around the kitchen table. You can't afford to wait for ultimate perfection before kicking off the campaign. Indeed, the first things your group does in public should bring more supporters into the fold who can help with the argument-preparation work. From start to finish, you must keep developing new arguments and new evidence, and keep poking new holes in your opponents' arguments. If you rest on your initial arguments and facts, people—especially politicians and news media—will start thinking your case is weak. Keep asking yourself, "What can we do for an encore?"

Dredge deep for good arguments. Citizen groups often base their campaigns on a few shallow arguments, and they run into trouble when the heat is on. Opponents will use their superior staff and money to try to defuse each of your arguments, and they will probably succeed in defusing some of them. By having plenty of arguments early in the campaign, you can afford to lose some.

If your opponents are likely to rely on technical or economic arguments to defeat your cause, your best bet is to put your own technical people and economists to work on the issue as soon as possible, preparing arguments of your own on the points that will be challenged.

Propose an Alternative

When your objective is to defeat something, such as a dam or a wrongheaded government policy, make one of your arguments the advocacy of an alternative. If you can avoid it, don't let your opponents paint you as irresponsible "aginners," because that can damage the credibility of all your arguments and may deprive you of community support you need in your campaign.

Many, many people who share your views will hesitate to join in a campaign that is purely against something. People will say, "They're just too negative!" The attitude seems to be that being against things is immature, irresponsible, and unrespectable. Remove this obstacle by advocating an alternative, and you'll open the door to all those who distrust "negativism" but otherwise would love to help.

The opponents of nuclear power, for instance, had great difficulty getting their point across in Congress in the early 1970s because the nuclear industry had so expensively and successfully convinced legislators and the public that there was no alternative. Antinuclear groups kept arguing that energy conservation and solar and wind energy were viable alternatives, and by 1976 these were taken seriously enough so that Congress began to look more critically at nuclear-power issues, abolished the Joint Committee on Atomic Energy, increased appropriations for solar and wind energy research, and weakened the Price-Anderson Act's federal subsidy of insurance for nuclear power plants. The growing acceptance of the alternatives to nuclear power was a major factor in this turnabout.

A good alternative is simply your answer to the question, "What should we do instead?" An alternative should not be a compromise; it should be what you really favor, presented so it looks at least as attractive as what you oppose. **Several types of alternatives have figured in legislative campaigns:**

1. An alternative that fulfills the purposes of the thing you oppose. An example occurred in the campaign, in the late 1960s, against a transmountain road that would have cut through the wilderness of Great Smoky Mountains National Park purely for sightseeing purposes. Conservationists in Tennessee and North Carolina who were trying to get their congressmen and the Department of the Interior to drop the road project proposed as an alternative a "Circle-the-Smokies" scenic drive, using existing roads, that would provide some 215 miles of sightseeing (compared to thirty miles on the transmountain road) and would connect with a dozen existing access spurs into the national park. This alternative let the local congressmen and federal officials off the hook by showing that the destructive road project was not the only way to satisfy the demand by local businesspeople for more tourist opportunities in the Smokies.

The alternative need not serve *all* the purposes of your opponents' plan, but it should serve some of the most important or attractive ones. If you can make your alternative look as good to your legislators and to the public as what you're against, you'll be in a good position to win your campaign.

2. An alternative that fulfills different purposes from those of the thing you oppose. Citizens opposing the State Department's plan of transferring the Panama Canal to the Republic of Panama advocated as an alternative a modernization plan for the canal, involving construction of additional locks to increase the canal's shipping capacity. Based on a project that was begun before World War II, the modernization plan was partly a response to the Department's advocacy of a new, sea-level canal, but was more importantly a positive move by those who opposed "giveaway" of the canal, and made them appear less negative.

Another example has occurred in many fights against freeway projects. If the land has already been bought up for the highway project, the freeway fighters propose to make it a city park instead of a freeway. Thus they gain the support of those who don't like to see the money go to waste, but think a park is better than a freeway.

3. A "do-nothing" alternative that makes a positive, attractive proposal out of doing nothing. For instance, the do-nothing alternative to building a dam is *not* to build the dam, and instead to preserve the free-flowing river that exists there now. The do-nothing alternative to building the B-1 bomber might be to reduce the burden on the taxpayer.

The Congressional Viewpoint

One of the most important results of your argument inventory will be the selection of arguments that will be most persuasive to your congressman and senators. You can make some good guesses, based on what you know of their past performance, and you'll learn more as the campaign progresses through your conversations with the legislators themselves, with their staffers, and with local politicians who know them. You will also learn about this from research on your legislators, which is discussed later in this chapter under the heading, "Research on People."

You may find that your three legislators are interested in completely different aspects of your issue. Perhaps your congresswoman will be most influenced by economic arguments, one of your senators by arguments concerning social benefits, and the other senator by ethical arguments. In this case, you'll have to include all three types of argument in your grass-roots campaign—indeed, diverse arguments will attract wider support among the public—but stress different arguments when you meet with the legislators or arrange for local VIPs to call on them.

Whatever arguments you use may reach the congresswoman's eyes or ears, so avoid using any argument that will poison her attitude toward your cause. For instance, if your congresswoman is strongly unsympathetic toward the style of anti-Communism reflected by the John Birch Society, you're very likely to lose her attention completely if you argue that your opponents are "tools of the international Communist conspiracy." Look instead for other arguments that will fit in better with her outlook on foreign policy, or rephrase the argument as a question of "national security."

Debunking the Opposition

Just as important as having good arguments for your position is being able to refute your opponents' arguments. You need a good rebuttal not only for the legislators you're trying to influence, but for news media, local politicians, and even your own supporters. If your most committed volunteers keep getting asked by their friends, "How can you support a bill that would put 150,000 people out of work?" they will need to have a good answer, or you'll lose them.

There are several ways to handle opposition arguments:

1. Challenge the evidence the argument is based on. Never trust your opponents' facts. Go through them with a fine-toothed comb, looking for errors, misstatements, and faulty assumptions. Numerical data may have been based on faulty sampling or have been extrapolated from similar situations elsewhere. Get your experts to analyze opponents' facts and figures and shoot holes in them, if possible.

For example, in the campaign against the SST subsidy, the

proponents of the SST claimed that 150,000 jobs were at stake. But when economists looked into this figure at the request of anti-SST groups, they found that only 20,000 workers were actually to be employed in the prototype program then at issue. SST proponents had taken a blue-sky figure of 50,000 workers that might be employed if enough SST aircraft were eventually ordered by the airlines, and had multiplied that figure by three, a standard multiplier reflecting general community services such as grocery stores, barbers, and taxi drivers patronized by the 50,000 workers.

Perhaps your opponents are relying on a barrage of statistics to carry them through; there may be less to their data than meets the eye. By putting their figures into proper perspective, you may be able to undermine their biggest claim. In the 1974–75 fight over preservation of Hells Canyon in Idaho, Oregon, and Washington, electric power companies argued that more dams should be built in the canyon to supply power to the Pacific Northwest. Conservationists took the power companies' figure and showed that the dams would provide only enough additional power to cover one year's growth in regional power consumption.

You can also challenge opinions and predictions that your opponents are using as evidence for their arguments. To do so, you'll need experts. If you can recruit experts with more stature than those cited by your opponents, you'll be in good shape. But even if your experts are of less stature, you may be able to build them up through good use of the news media, good choice of a forum in which your experts will present their opinions, and by having your experts stress points that will appeal to those you want to influence.

An example occurs in the nuclear power issue, which has involved a continuous battle of experts for and against nuclear power. The stature was at first heavily on the side of nuclear power proponents, who boasted Nobel Prize winners such as Hans Bethe. But as a growing cadre of nuclear scientists without Nobel Prizes, such as John W. Gofman, Frank von Hippel, and Thomas Cochran, have appeared in many parts of the country, at citizens' conferences, and on television, stressing the view that nuclear power is not safe, their stature has grown to the point where they are now taken seriously by the public, by news media, and by government decision makers.

In responding to your opponents' arguments, strive to give

your senators and congressman an alternative, equally authoritative source of information and expert advice, so they can justify turning their backs on the information and advice your opponents have given them. Scientists, technicians, and other experts can serve this purpose, and so can government agencies—local, regional, state, or federal.

2. Challenge the assumptions your opponents' argument is based on. Suppose you're working against a proposed dam which your opponents argue is needed to prevent floods from causing loss of life and property. If you can't disprove your opponents' figures on past losses of life and property (challenging their evidence), you may be able to challenge the assumption that the dam is the only way to prevent these losses. You might challenge the assumption that this advantage is worth the multimillion-dollar cost of the dam. You might also challenge the assumption that the dam will really prevent the losses. Assumptions can be the most vulnerable spots in an argument, because they are supposed to be accepted without question. If your opponents are smart, they will have built their arguments carefully to avoid relying on unproven assumptions; but if they haven't done so, they may be wide open to your challenge.

Every challenge to your opponents' assumptions should be made as strong as possible through the use of evidence. Facts and opinions from respected sources will make your challenge believable at the outset, leaving your opponents without a good comeback.

3. Challenge your opponents' choice of priorities. This is a way of dealing with opponents' arguments for which you don't have a strong rebuttal; it's a matter of making their arguments seem less important than yours. If you're fighting for a bill to control air pollution and your opponents claim it would work a hardship on the big auto companies, you might accuse them of being more concerned about General Motors' profits than about the health of the millions of people harmed every year by air pollution. Or, to strike a more positive note, you could stress throughout your campaign, "People before profits!"

4. Challenge the argument head-on. Especially useful in answering ethical arguments, which are not based on a showing of evidence, this response usually consists of strongly asserting a rival argument. For instance, in the controversy over abortion, the anti-abortion groups' ethical argument summed up by the slogan "Right to Life" has been challenged by those who advocate legal abortion with the argument that women have a "Right to Choose."

Arguments of this kind are largely appeals to emotion, but they can be made stronger or weaker through the use of respectability tactics, as described in Chapter 11 under the heading "Make It Respectable." Both sides in the abortion controversy have tried to outdo the other in respectability by having distinguished clergy, prominent physicians, and leading women associate themselves with their arguments.

5. Look for inconsistencies in your opponents' arguments. Citizens fighting against electric power projects many times gained ground by pointing out that at the same time the power companies were arguing that they needed more power plants and dams, the same companies were spending millions to drum up new customers in the form of "all-electric homes" and energy-using industries; apparently the new power projects were not as necessary as had been claimed. (Only in the mid-1970s, when the energy shortage became a national concern, did the power companies stop this kind of advertising.)

6. Challenge your opponents' interests or motives. You may be able to undermine some of your opponents' arguments by showing that your opponents have an unworthy reason for their position, a reason that is not stated in their public arguments. For instance, in fights over proposed freeways it was discovered that many of the influential proponents had quietly bought land along the projected route, expecting to sell it to the highway department for a large profit. Exposure of such motives has helped to stop many highway and dam projects.

However, don't challenge your opponents' interests or motives unless you have good evidence for the charge. Unfounded accusations will damage your credibility, detract from the respectability of your cause, and could even be libelous.

Developing New Arguments

New arguments may be easier to find than you think. Most legislative issues are argued primarily on the national level, without getting down to how they affect your state, your congressional district, or your community. Every argument you develop that tells how the issue affects the people at home is in effect a new argument, and because it is about your legislators' constituents it may have more impact than national arguments.

Be on the lookout for arguments that will appeal to local people. You may discover sensitivity to an aspect of the issue that you had previously considered insignificant. This is what brought new support for proposed wilderness areas in Colorado. Wilderness advocates had not seriously considered cattle ranchers to be potential supporters of wilderness; ranchers had usually opposed wilderness, even though cattle grazing is permitted in wilderness areas. But in 1974, through good local contacts, Colorado conservationists learned that the ranchers were more sympathetic to wilderness. Lacking roads, the ranchers said, wilderness areas were good protection against cattle rustlers, who nowadays need large trucks to haul off the booty. In addition, because wilderness is closed to motor vehicles, the cattle are not harassed by motorbikes and other off-road vehicles. Using these arguments, wilderness proponents won the support of key ranchers and thus gained some hard-to-get influence with Colorado congressmen.

An argument need not be based on a certainty. A mere possibility can be enough to gain support. Suppose you are working for legislation to increase federal funding of mental-health research. If a local university or college has done research in this field, you may argue that this institution could get more research funds as a result of this legislation. This could add the local slant that will get your congressman interested. If you can involve the relevant scientists at the university, they may be able to get the university president to visit or phone the congressman in support of the bill.

Sometimes an argument may be hard to prove because there is little evidence on the topic or because the evidence does not have much stature. In this case, if you're convinced the argument is right, you may have to resort to the method laughingly referred to by scientists as "proof by vigorous assertion." That is, if you keep saying it often, and with conviction, it will begin to be accepted as valid. You hope that later your research teams will come up with better evidence, but meanwhile you've at least been able to keep the argument alive. An inadequately supported argument is highly vulnerable to challenge by your opponents, but as long as you don't rely on it too much and as long as your opponents can't use it to make you look foolish, it doesn't do any harm to use it.

This is what happened with the economic argument against the SST subsidy. For the first four months of the 1970 campaign, opponents of the supersonic transport harped on the notion that the project was a waste of money, but without very convincing evidence to refute the claims by proponents that the project would benefit the U.S. economy. Then in September 1970, Senator J. William Fulbright (Democrat of Arkansas) released statements he had solicited, at the suggestion of citizen groups, from sixteen of the country's top economists, all but one opposing the SST on economic grounds. This added strong evidence to what had previously been a vigorous assertion.

Review again your checklist of arguments to see if you've missed any based on the four categories of social good, economics, ethics, and science and technology. For instance, can you develop a new argument based on ethics? In an education issue, you might argue that it's immoral to handicap future generations by providing inadequate education. In a nuclear power issue, you might argue that it's wrong to hand an unsolved nuclear-waste problem on to future generations.

Can you develop a new economic argument? Your opponents will probably claim that economics is on their side, but don't let them get away with it. Consider all the benefits and costs—who pays, and who benefits? Will jobs be lost or created?

The initial cost of a project you oppose may be dwarfed by long-term costs. See if you can make a reliable projection of the total cost over the life of the project. For example, in opposing the B-1 bomber project, the Federation of American Scientists observed that the U.S. Air Force proposal to build 244 B-1 bombers at a cost of $40 billion was less than half the total cost. Over twenty years, the real cost of building and maintaining 244 B-1 bombers would be close to $90 billion, according to the Federation.

Talk your issue over with experts in many relevant fields, because they may see vulnerable arguments that you wouldn't have noticed.

Getting the Evidence

The best arguments always are based on good, hard evidence—facts and opinions that show your argument to be valid. If you're working for an increase in Social Security benefits and you argue that the increase is needed because recipients can't live on the present benefits, you'll have to offer some evidence to back up your claim. In this case the evidence might include the personal experiences of local people who receive Social Security benefits. It might also include a local economist's analysis showing that the benefits have not kept pace with inflation. It might include an informal poll of local Social Security recipients on the question of whether the benefits are enough to live on.

In developing and presenting the evidence for your arguments, always strive for *stature*. In a legislative fight, facts don't speak for themselves; they depend on the stature of their source. A fact is only as good as the person or institution it comes from, because every fact is likely to be challenged by your opponents. (The only exceptions are absolutely uncontestable facts such as that the sky is blue and that the Mississippi River flows into the sea.) Opinions, of course, depend completely on the stature of their source.

From Institutions

The best sources of evidence are experts and institutions active in your subject area but not directly associated with your cause. A university, a research center, or a government agency could fill the bill if you can find the right sympathetic person in that institution. On nationwide issues, national citizen groups usually provide this kind of high-statured information, but to make it more effective in your local campaign you will want to find respected local institutions to vouch for the facts. If you live in Utah, your congressman may have more respect for a professor at Utah State University than for one at Harvard.

Suppose you're working for a law to cut back on the use of cancer-causing substances. You would be able to get from national groups pertinent remarks by national cancer experts on the dangers of these substances. To add an effective local touch, approach the most respected medical people in your community and ask them to offer their views in support of your objective. Give them copies of the national information and the best background data you have, and they should be able to make some cogent remarks on the subject, which you can then use both in your contacts with your senators and congressman and in your campaign for local support.

Some of the best evidence in legislative campaigns has come from short-term studies undertaken by scientists, social scientists, and economists at local colleges and universities. Their stature, expertise, and "ivory tower" position gives them an impact on legislators far greater than the equivalent nonacademician's. So when you see the need for better evidence—either facts or opinions—to support one of your arguments, the first thing to do is sit down with a sympathetic local college professor and talk it over.

The results of such studies have been important in many campaigns. In Wisconsin, for instance, Senator Gaylord Nelson (Democrat) had refused to oppose the LaFarge Dam project on the Kickapoo River until a University of Wisconsin study showed that the reservoir would cause an oxygen deficiency in the river, lowering its water quality and fishing potential.

Another study, done by economists at Portland State University in 1970 at the suggestion of Oregon citizen groups opposed to the supersonic transport subsidy, showed that, contrary to claims by SST proponents that Oregon would gain $3.4 million in contracts through the project, the state would actually suffer a net loss of $8.3 million through taxes spent on it.

It's not enough to get studies done by university faculty. You want your study to reach news media, your legislators, and friendly local politicians. It's best to have the researcher release the report, preferably hand-delivering it to your congressman and senators and mailing it to a list of others which you've drawn up. Then, prompt local news reporters to ask for the congressman's reaction to the report—a move that ensures that he'll notice it.

Many universities have specialized institutes affiliated with them which share the university's faculty and may use advanced students as researchers under faculty direction. If the faculty of one of these institutes shares your viewpoint, it could be a good source of evidence. Georgetown University's Center for Strategic and International Studies, for instance, issued reports that were used effectively by groups opposing a U.S. pullout from the Panama Canal. The Natural Resources Law Institute, associated with the Northwestern School of Law in Portland, Oregon, has done studies on environmental questions that have been used by environmental groups in legislative campaigns.

These research institutes often rely on grants from state agencies, rich people, and corporations. An institute can't take a stand on legislation, but it can study the issues and reach conclusions on what the facts are and what may happen. The institute may benefit from the use of its studies by your legislators or by local officials, because its contributors may be impressed to see that the institute's work is being considered in government decision making. You can help by asking friendly officials to write thank-you letters to the authors of your study.

By Yourself

Inevitably, much of the evidence for your arguments will have to be gathered by you and your co-workers. There isn't always a university or research institute on hand when you need evidence fast. Yet, if you—the issue advocate—say that something is a fact, you won't necessarily be believed, because the congressman will tend to think that you're just getting carried away with your cause.

When you know you've got a fact, don't relax until you've found a way to turn it into believable evidence. Suppose you're working for a bill that would provide federal aid to expand hospitals, and you know for a fact that all the hospitals in town have been turning people away for lack of beds. You have a fact, but how do you make it convincing evidence to the public and to your legislators? **Several ways suggest themselves:**

- Get the hospital directors to cosign **a round-robin letter** to your congressional delegation attesting to this fact, and have them release it to news media so the public will know.

- Have a friendly city council member **call a hearing** on the subject and invite hospital directors, staff physicians, and patients to speak on the lack of space. Make sure news media cover the hearing.

• Get a friendly legislator or local politician to **visit the hospitals** when they are full to capacity, with reporters and photographers on hand to record the event.

• Get a few local physicians who use the hospitals to **write up the situation** and release it as a report to your congressional delegation by, say, the Elmsford Physicians' Study Committee.

These are just a few of the ways in which this particular fact could be established as believable, without going into further research on the point. Of course, if it were necessary, you could deepen your facts by having someone look into the square footage available per patient and how that compares with national standards, and you could look for data on how many patients are being turned away and on how many days of the year the hospitals are full. These kinds of information, if brought out by respected sources, could make the argument even more persuasive.

You never have time to research everything that will help. You have to decide which topics are most vital. In the hospital example above, it would probably be unproductive to devote long hours to deepening your facts for the argument that the hospitals need more space, because that will be quite believable. More crucial and harder to prove will be the fact that the hospitals have no source of funds other than the federal government to finance the needed expansion. Always focus your evidence-finding on what you think will be the most effective arguments and the most crucial facts.

Through Intern Programs

Knowing that you can convert bare facts into believable evidence enables you to use nonexperts to dig for the facts. You can do the digging yourself, you can get reliable volunteers to do it, or you can seek help through college intern programs. Many colleges and universities give undergraduates the chance to spend a semester working on social issues with a citizen action group. The students work full-time on your research tasks, and they receive college credit for it under an internship or independent study course. This is usually arranged through a professor in a relevant field of study. Intern programs usually want you to pay the students a subsistence salary, but they're used to cooperating with citizen groups that can't afford it. **The four essentials in using interns are:**

• **Get students who share your viewpoint** and thus will be strongly motivated to do the job well.

• **Plan the interns' research tasks** so they can be done in the time available and with the interns' level of skills.

• **Be prepared to spend some time** supervising the students as they get started on the project and periodically during their months with you.

• **Keep them involved** in your overall effort. Don't expect them to spend all their time in research, because that can be deadly, but let them do more satisfying things from time to time, so they won't lose interest.

Interns can be among your best workers if you give them good supervision and keep them happy.

Unskilled Researchers

Some fact finding can be done by parties of volunteers without special skills. In Cayuga County, New York, citizens working for a ban on throwaway bottles and cans did a series of litter surveys which showed that 66 percent of the volume of litter collected along roads in the county consists of beverage bottles and cans. Picking up roadside litter isn't anyone's idea of a fun outing, but a get-together afterwards with refreshments and a rock band made it satisfying for the volunteers.

Facts can come from within your opponents' ranks—perhaps a government agency or a corporation—if you've found friendly souls there. You can't cite the source because he might lose his job, but you can get local politicians or newspaper reporters to confront your opponents with the fact and ask them to confirm or deny it. You can also devise other ways to get at the same fact through your research effort, once you know what you're looking for.

Sometimes your fact finding will be slowed by uncooperative people. It can be nothing more than bureaucratic buck passing, or it can be purposeful foot dragging. To avoid this, use any stature you can get to make your request seem more respectable. When you're doing research by mail, you may get a better and faster response by having a college professor, lawyer, doctor, or librarian send your query on his or her letterhead. When you're trying to get an appointment to interview somebody and you're getting the runaround, try having a local politician or VIP call and ask the person to see you, hinting that a refusal smacks of secrecy.

Using Case Histories

Real-life examples are essential to most legislative campaigns. In their daily routine, senators and congressmen constantly have to make decisions based on vague generalities and on nationwide data that are too vast to be readily understood. You can break through this routine and catch legislators' interest by telling how your issue has affected people. Good case histories can persuade a legislator to support your side. They can fortify a legislator who already supports you. And if you have a congressman who is a committed opponent, case histories can bring him down from his cloud of generalities and force him to grapple with the realities you see in the issue.

A case history is simply the story of something that happened that is related to your issue. It could be as local and specific as, in a fight for a consumer protection bill, reporting that Mrs. Nussbaum on the corner had a flooded basement because fly-by-night plumbers installed faulty new plumbing and couldn't be located to fix it. Or it could be as earth-shaking as, in a campaign against a treaty with the Soviet Union, reporting the Soviet Union's past violations of treaties it had signed.

Senators and congressmen, as a rule, will be more influenced by case histories from their own state or congressional district because that is where their attention is focused, it is an area they know personally, and it is where their constituents live. Things that have happened elsewhere can be easily ignored, but things that have happened in one's own state or district must be heeded.

To take advantage of legislators' sensitivity to what goes on back home, build a collection of case histories on how the issue affects local people. Look for the most outrageous and unfair situations, which cry out for solution by the method you advocate.

There's always a temptation to work up case histories superficially, aiming for a long list of sketchy examples. This approach leaves you open to easy challenge by the congressman and by your opponents, because you can't answer questions about the details. Legislators have little patience with case histories that are merely a paraphrase of a brief newspaper story, so don't expect to get by with newspaper clippings. To avoid superficiality, take one or two of the best examples and develop them in depth.

The story of Mrs. Nussbaum's flooded basement, for example, could be expanded by obtaining copies of a receipt, sales slip, or contract given her by the fraudulent plumbers, a bill from the plumber who eventually stemmed the flood and identified the problem in the faulty installation, and a letter or approved claim from Mrs. Nussbaum's insurance company indicating the extent of damage from the flood. Get the dates and times of day; these are convincing details.

The documentation and blow-by-blow story need not be used every time you cite the case history, but you want your legislators to know you have the whole story. An informal report on a case history, with pertinent documents attached, could be turned over to your congresswoman when you have met with her, it could be mailed to her, or it could be submitted for inclusion in the record of a hearing on the subject.

When you use local case histories in your public arguments—in the newspapers, on television, or in your printed material—you'll stimulate other people to write to your congresswoman about their experiences with the issue. For instance, in a fight for stronger work-place health laws, if people see on television that Henry Tillman was unable to get a disability pension after his lungs were ruined by work in the cotton mills, others who have had similar work-place disabilities without adequate attention or compensation will get the idea of writing to their congressman about their own complaints. These can be the most powerful case histories of all because they arrive in the form of letters from people who have probably never written to a congressman before, telling about what has happened to them. These letters won't show great political sophistication and won't press for a commitment, but you can make up for that through other tactics. What these letters do is vital to your campaign—show the congressman that there *is* a problem affecting his constituents, and that they aren't going to forget about it.

Research on People

In the political arena, many decisions are strongly affected by personal factors. Knowing whom a senator listens to and trusts may be more important to your cause than having a carefully documented factual case. A well-organized legislative campaign moves forward on both tracks. At the same time that you're preparing your arguments on the merits of the issue, consider also the people and organizations involved.

Nominees for Government Positions

When your campaign is for or against a nominee to a government position, obviously your research will focus primarily on that person and his or her record. Among the presidential appointments that must be confirmed by the Senate are Supreme Court justices, judges of U.S. District Courts and Courts of Appeals, Cabinet secretaries and assistant secretaries, some agency heads, and members of regulatory commissions. **In each case, your research must concern the nominee's fitness for the job. The crucial questions include:**

- Does the nominee know anything about the subject he will be handling?
- Does the nominee have any conflict of interest, such as financial interests in businesses that would be affected by his decisions?
- Are the nominee's personal convictions consistent with the mission he will have to carry out?

Few legislative battles can equal the drama of that over Richard M. Nixon's nomination to the Supreme Court of G. Harrold

Carswell, which is well chronicled in Richard Harris's book *Decision* (E. P. Dutton, 1971). In the end, Carswell's own deeds—chiefly his decisions and conduct as a judge, showing his hostility toward racial equality—brought about his rejection by the Senate. Good research by citizen groups and the news media made this possible.

A more recent example was the Senate's refusal in 1976 to confirm James Hooper to a position on the board of directors of the Tennessee Valley Authority (TVA). Hooper had been nominated by President Gerald R. Ford as a person who could bring business experience to the TVA board. However, research by citizen groups showed that Hooper had had several bankruptcies in his business history, including the default of a dog food cannery which he had owned. These findings, well documented, shot holes in the President's argument.

Research on nominees has much in common with the personal research you may need to do in an issue campaign. Instead of looking at a nominee's record, you will be looking into the background of the people you want to influence—your senators and congressman—and the people and organizations that oppose your cause. In all personal research, if you plan to use the information publicly you must document your findings thoroughly. Keep Xerox copies of the crucial items, because you will be asked to prove your allegations.

Research into your opponents' backgrounds can be worthwhile if it reveals something the public will frown on and thus makes your opponents less respectable. Imagine that you're working against a new military weapon system (call it the Z-2 missile), and your local opponents have formed a Committee for National Security to push for the Z-2 project. If you can prove that the leaders of this committee have been doing business with the company that would build the Z-2, it will become clear that it's not national security they're worried about, but the size of their bank accounts.

The first thing to do in investigating people is to consult the following reference works, available at public libraries:

• *The Foundation Directory* lists foundations and their officers and directors, with an index of names.

• *Martindale and Hubbell's Law Directory* lists law firms, lawyers in each firm, and the firm's corporate clients, with an index of names.

• *Poor's Registry of Executives and Directors* covers executives and directors of large corporations, cross-referencing each person's board positions with other corporations.

• *Who's Who*, in ten different regional and specialized editions, gives basic biographical data supplied by the subjects themselves.

The techniques of investigating people and organizations in detail are beyond the scope of this book, but they are covered in sources cited in the bibliography at the end of this chapter, chiefly the *NACLA Research Guide* and *The Investigative Journalist.*

Legislators and Their Staffs

You should also take the time to learn about your congressman and senators and their staffs. This will tell you a lot about their stances on other subjects, and from what background they view your issue. When you know the issues your congressman most strongly supports, you may think of a way to tie your cause to one of them. For instance, if you're campaigning for an increase in funds for family-planning programs and you discover that your congressman has been outraged at the high cost of the welfare program, you may decide to stress the argument that increased family planning will greatly reduce the welfare costs resulting from too many unwanted children.

To find out about your legislators' past record in Congress, use these sources:

• *The Almanac of American Politics* contains an overview of each legislator's record, a table of his votes on key issues, and a summary of how he was rated by specialized citizen groups.

• Specialized voting records and ratings are available from groups listed in the Bibliography at the end of this chapter.

• *Congressional Quarterly Almanac,* issued annually, contains an analysis and voting record for each major issue Congress acted on during the year.

• Your local newspaper's clipping file will cover your legislators' public pronouncements and involvement in local affairs over a span of many years.

Senators' and congressmen's biographies (the way *they* want them to appear) are printed in the *Congressional Directory*. To get a more critical view of your congressman, consider interviewing the candidate who ran against him in the last election. You may get a lot of vindictive remarks, but also a few good leads that can be very helpful. This way you may learn that the congressman has a close relationship with an industry that is among your opponents, or that he's friendly with some of your VIP supporters. Check out these leads carefully before you act on them.

Political reporters for local newspapers or television often have a buddy relationship with your congressman and senators, but they will sometimes tell you much about party factions that may be influencing a legislator's actions. If, for instance, your congressman is under the gun from a conservative faction in the party and knows he will be challenged by a conservative candidate in the next primary election, he may be taking more conservative positions this year in order to head off a split in the party. Learning this background, you would be able to plan your campaign accordingly— perhaps by framing your cause in more conservative terms or by getting local conservative VIPs to help.

Senators' and congressmen's campaign finances are open to public scrutiny through the Federal Election Commission, which will send you the reports you want upon payment of a copying fee. Further details on how to obtain these reports appear in Chapter 15, "Getting Influence from Elections."

The Senate and House of Representatives require their members to file financial statements annually. Some congressmen and congresswomen make it easier to see their statements by depositing copies in their field offices and by releasing their statements to local news media. With less cooperative congressmen, your only local source may be newspaper stories, which are likely to appear shortly after May 1, the deadline each year for members of Congress to submit their financial statements.

Be cautious in researching legislators' finances and personal backgrounds. They may hear about your inquiries from congressional employees eager to curry favor. This is even more likely if you are looking into their landholdings or court records at the county courthouse, because old courthouse employees have solid political ties. If you don't want legislators to know that your group is looking into their background, get someone to do this research who is not yet publicly associated with your group.

Presenting Your Arguments

You'll need to use two different approaches in presenting your arguments because you have two quite different audiences—on the one hand, your senators and congressman, on the other, your public supporters and those you hope to enlist in the campaign.

Your popular supporters will respond best to an argument presented dramatically, stressing the rightness and fairness of your proposal, as constrasted with the wrongness and unfairness of the opposite position. Evidence that symbolizes the issue can be important. In the fight to save the redwoods, contrasting pictures of intact redwood trees and pictures of logged-off redwood forests became the public image of the issue. In a fight for hospital construction funds, pictures of overcrowded hospital wards and admitting rooms might serve the same purpose. However, this symbolic evidence is only part of your presentation. You have to get the complete arguments out to your supporters, with enough background facts to make them usable.

Legislators like to think they consider the facts dispassionately and reach decisions on the facts alone. Actually, they are usually influenced more strongly by political pressure of the kind you can generate than they are by the arguments. But because legislators have this notion of calm, unbiased decision making, it's important to cater to it, primarily through your group's direct contacts with legislators—visits, letters, telephone calls—as opposed to contacts by individual citizens. Flatter the congressman by giving him a fact sheet on the issue that presents the arguments, with good evidence to back them up. The fact sheet should not be cast in terms of right or wrong or be emotional; your strong commitment and feelings will be clear from what you tell him in person. By leaving your passion out of the fact sheet, you will make it easier for the congressman and his staff to read your arguments without having to mentally edit out your value judgments. You want him to see that he can rationally justify his vote to himself and his constituents if he's ever challenged on it.

Every citizen group has a right to express its feelings on an issue. Citizens have emotions about issues, and these emotions are a tremendous political force because they are what motivate people to take action on legislative issues. Legislators also have emotions about issues. Indeed, you want your senators and congressman to share your emotional commitment to your issue, so they won't jump ship when your opponents put on the heat. But when you are in the touchy situation of asking a legislator to support your cause and he has not yet agreed to do so, just set your emotions aside for a few minutes—long enough to show him that your arguments can stand on their own, without emotion to prop them up.

Bibliography

Books on Research Methods:

NACLA Research Methodology Guide, 72 pages. Available from the North American Congress on Latin America, P.O. Box 57, Cathedral Park Station, New York, NY 10025. Price $1.75 postpaid.

The Investigative Journalist, by James H. Dygert. Englewood Cliffs, NJ, Prentice Hall, 1976. Price $8.95.

Where's What: Sources of Information for Federal Investigators, by Harry J. Murphy. New York: Warner Books, 1976. Price $3.95. A handbook written by a staffer of the Central Intelligence Agency.

Reference Books on Congress:

The Almanac of American Politics, by Michael Barone, Grant Ujifusa, and Douglas Matthews. New York, E. P. Dutton, 1978; reissued in a new edition every two years. Price: hardcover $16.95; softcover $7.95.

Congressional Directory. Available from Superintendent of Documents, Washington, D.C. 20402. Issued every other year, supplement in years between. Price: hardcover $8.50; softcover $6.50; supplement $2.00.

Congressional Staff Directory, by Charles B. Brownson. Available from Congressional Staff Directory, P.O. Box 62, Mount Vernon, VA 22121. Issued annually. Price $22.00 postpaid.

Congressional Quarterly Almanac. Available from Congressional Quarterly, 1414 22nd Street, N.W., Washington, D.C. 20037. Issued annually. Price $70.00.

Sources of Specialized Voting Records:

Americans for Constitutional Action, 955 L'Enfant Plaza North, S.W., Washington, D.C. 20024. Favors constitutional-conservative viewpoint.

Americans for Democratic Action, 1411 K Street, N.W., Washington, D.C. 20005. Favors liberal viewpoint.

AFL–CIO Committee on Political Education (COPE), 815 16th Street, N.W., Washington, D.C. 20006. Labor union viewpoint.

Consumer Federation of America, 1012 14th Street, N.W., Washington, D.C. 20005. Consumer viewpoint.

League of Conservation Voters, 317 Pennsylvania Avenue, S.E., Washington, D.C. 20003. Environmental viewpoint.

National Associated Businessmen, 1000 Connecticut Avenue, N.W., Washington, D.C. 20036. Favors reduction in government spending, except defense and industry subsidies.

National Farmers Union, 1012 14th Street, N.W., Washington, D.C. 20005. Viewpoint of small to middle-size farmers.

National Security Index of the American Security Council, 1101 17th Street, N.W., Washington, D.C. 20036. Favors strong military programs and anti-Communist viewpoint.

National Taxpayers Union, 153 E Street, S.E., Washington, D.C. 20003. Favors reduction in government spending.

Public Citizen (Congress Watch), 133 C Street, S.E., Washington, D.C. 20003. Founded by Ralph Nader, takes a proconsumer viewpoint.

Ripon Society, 800 18th Street, N.W., Washington, D.C. 20006. Liberal Republican viewpoint.

13

Cooperating with the Congressional Staff

The men and women who make up the staff of the United States Congress do not vote on legislation or participate in floor debate, but they do almost everything else. Some of them almost vote; you'd have to say this of a staffer whose boss always votes just as his legislative assistant recommended.

At the opposite pole is the staffer whose boss makes up his own mind (usually on scanty or inaccurate information because he hasn't used his staff to research the topic) or just follows the crowd. This staffer has none of the decision-making duties, but has the chore of justifying the boss's vote to people back home through letters and speeches he drafts for the boss.

The Staff's Influence

The staff has more influence on the legislator than you do because staffers are hired for their loyalty, their expertise, and their judgment. Even more important than these qualities they brought with them is the personal relationship that grows between a legislator and his or her professional staff. It's not simply a matter of working together. It's closer, involving mutual respect, mutual dependence, and a history of collaboration over a span of months or years. The administrative assistant is often the staffer closest to the legislator, having been a key figure in the election campaign or a close associate even before that. The legislative assistant is usually newer, but personal ties grow fast when you're working together daily on issues that could spell defeat or victory in the next election.

This close tie is reinforced by frequent contact between the legislator and his Washington staff. In research for their book *Congressional Staffs* (Free Press, 1977), Harrison W. Fox, Jr., and Susan Webb Hammond found that nearly half of a senator's professional staff actually see the senator, on the average, once or more every hour. The comparable figure for the House would probably show even more frequent contact between staff and legislator.

One result of this relationship is that whatever the staff presents—facts, analysis, recommendations, opinions—is seen by the legislator as coming from a good and trustworthy source.

Part of the staff member's influence comes from the way he presents the facts. When a staffer prepares a memo about a new bill that you've called to his attention, he's likely to explain the principal arguments and facts on both sides of the issue, but he can make your side look more persuasive than your opponents' if he believes your side has the better case. This might be as simple as knowing what the boss is most interested in and slanting the memo to stress your bill's connection with that interest. For instance, if the issue concerned cancellation of a military weapons system and your senator's deepest concern was to cut down on wasteful federal expenditures, a staffer who was sympathetic to cancellation might stress the savings that would result.

When reporting orally to the legislator about a meeting with a constituent or a lobbyist, the staffer can't help letting his own views and perceptions creep in. If the staffer doesn't think the issue is important, he won't stress it and he may not really try to get the legislator interested. If the staffer distrusts the lobbyist's facts, his tone of voice may show it when he reports to the boss.

In many respects the staff controls the legislator's exposure to the facts, and necessarily so, since there's no way a senator could even read all the information that is sent to his office. By showing him letters, articles, and news clippings that favor a particular viewpoint, the staff influences his perception of the issues.

While the staff's choice of facts is influential on every issue, their choice of information sources may be even more important in the long run. By citing repeatedly information from, say, the American Petroleum Institute (an arm of the oil industry), a staffer subtly influences the legislator to regard the American Petroleum Institute as a trustworthy organization on oil matters. Another staffer who uses data from Ralph Nader's Congress Watch may create a similar identification with that organization. In either case, the legislator who uses and trusts an organization's facts gradually comes to identify with that organization and to trust its opinions and recommendations, as well as its facts. Of course, if a group's information turns out to be flagrantly wrong or misleading, that may destroy the relationship; more often the bond has already been molded, and the legislator trusts the misinformation, too.

Facts and opinions usually go together in staff work. When a staff member has worked up facts on an issue, these are usually presented, along with opinions, in the form of recommendations. For instance, when constituents have been writing in about a new bill, a legislative assistant (LA) may look into the matter, write a memo summing up the arguments and facts pro and con, and recommend a position for the boss to take. Along with the memo, the LA may give the boss a draft speech or a draft letter to be used in answering constituents' letters on the topic.

Similarly, when a staffer briefs a congressman orally on a last-minute amendment, he is likely to suggest a position, such as to say, "A yes vote would be consistent with our position on the Anderson bill last month."

These opinions will be taken seriously, because the legislative assistant is an insider, loyal to the legislator's interests and having a track record of good advice on other issues. A staffer won't tell a legislator what to do, and won't press too hard with his opinions. The legislator, after all, has to bear the consequences if too many voters, or too many big campaign contributors, don't like what he has been doing in Congress.

Within these bounds, a staff member can argue strongly for a given position. Good argument in a congressional office can be very productive. If the staff were only yes-men and yes-women, they would only be supporting the boss in his snap judgments. By arguing, they can help a legislator be self-critical, they can raise questions about the wisdom of a position the legislator wants to take, they can warn of political problems one of his positions is getting him into, and they can suggest ways of extricating himself from that position.

A legislative assistant can also be influential by struggling for some of the legislator's time. Time struggles go on constantly in many offices. A legislator never has enough time to do everything his staff wants him to do, and the time he spends, say, testifying at a hearing on a proposed dam might have been spent buttonholing other legislators to support a new mental-health program, or meeting with a group of constituents to curry their favor for the next election. An LA who is enthusiastic about an issue will win more of the boss's time than if he is only half-convinced. An LA who can persuade the boss that there is political mileage in your cause will get more time than one who just vaguely thinks it's the right stand to take. Of course, every time a legislator does something on an issue, he becomes more committed to that issue.

The staff's follow-up work on a bill also influences the legislator. Once the boss has decided what position to take, the staff may forget about it and merely perform the caretaker duty of cranking out replies to constituents' letters. Or staffers may keep taking the initiative, suggesting and drafting speeches and letters to the editor, or cooperating with other offices in a coalition effort on the bill. Continued activity keeps the legislator involved with the issue and strengthens his identification with it.

A legislative assistant can also push his boss in a particular direction by getting him to meet with the right people at the right time. If the LA wants to impress the boss with the expertise of nuclear power advocates, he might ask a power company to have its top engineers come in for a meeting with the legislator on a day when the schedule won't be too frantic. The staffer's personal relationship with the boss gives him insight from day to day as to when the time is right. He can drop a hint to an association that it should invite the boss to speak at a convention, or he can arrange for the boss to meet regularly with a group's leaders.

One Western congressman, for example, attained a leadership role in environmental legislation partly as a result of this kind of staff influence. Often when the congressman went back to his district, his LA had arranged for a brief meeting with local environmentalists. This regular contact encouraged the legislator's early efforts, gave him plenty of ideas about environmental legislation, and in the end fostered the congressman's strong identification with environmental issues.

When the legislator is invited to speak at a meeting of your organization, the LA may draft a speech that moves the legislator toward your position, knowing that he'll get lots of applause for it. This reinforces the legislator's uncertain move in the right direction, arousing his further interest in the issue both as an issue and as a political factor that can win support for him at election time.

You and the Staff

Your cooperation with a congressman's staff can be rewarding both for your cause and for the staff. A staff member may feel overworked and unappreciated by his boss; the friendliness, respect, and appreciation that you have to offer can be very satisfying to this staffer. And the information and opinions you provide can make the staffer's job easier. If you can be a sounding board for an LA's reactions, ideas, and questions about your issue, you're helping him get ready to be grilled by the boss.

Your rewards from cooperating with the staff include the personal satisfaction that comes from dealing with bright, competent people. Having met a staffer in person makes your future contacts more enjoyable and less impersonal. Even a good chat on the phone can help to build a good relationship. And, most important, you're influencing a person who is in an excellent position to influence the congressman or congresswoman.

Staff members don't always respond positively to an approach by citizens, especially when the citizens are urging a position with which the legislator or staff disagree. When your campaign is putting heat on a congressman, some staffers may get upset. They may feel you're embarrassing the congressman, or they may resent the extra work you're causing them. A highly professional LA will take this sort of thing in stride, recognizing that it's your right and responsibility to bring pressure on the congressman for a cause you believe in. But some inexperienced staffers, and some ossified old ones, take these things personally. When you run into this reaction, do your best to avoid returning the hostility, and strive to maintain mutual respect. After the big vote, make peace so you'll be on good terms the next time your issue comes up.

At your first meeting with a staff person, stress the friendly approach, outline your arguments and facts logically, and be responsive to the staffer's comments and questions. Don't be surprised if the staffer seems to be asking the wrong kind of questions. It's common for an LA to play devil's advocate because he has to anticipate the questions the legislator may ask when he briefs him. An LA has to know the answers. Staff people enjoy this kind of conversation about the arguments, and if you're well prepared, you'll enjoy it too.

You may find that the staff knows nothing about your issue. This is understandable, because in a congressional office there is little time for long-range advance study of legislation. Staffers work on the principle that the squeaking wheel gets the grease. They concentrate on bills that are going to be voted on in the next few days. The only advance study happens when the congressman gets letters from constituents asking him to take a stand; the need to come up with an answer will put an LA into action on the topic. Your visit to the office may have a similar effect, especially if others are visiting, writing, and phoning about the same bill.

The staff usually won't know as much about your issue as you do. Only when it's one of the "biggies" (energy, taxes), or one the legislator specializes in, can you expect the staff to be thoroughly familiar with the issue. On most issues, staffers need good, hard information and analysis, particularly as to how the issue affects your state or congressional district. When you can provide some of this information, the staff will welcome you with open arms.

You can't press a staff member for a commitment as you can a legislator. The staffer doesn't have authority to commit his boss, and he doesn't have to live with the consequences of a controversial vote as his boss does. You can be forthright in expressing your views, but you have to pull your punches. Legislators are used to being confronted verbally; staffers aren't, and they don't have to put up with it. If you can't maintain a friendly relationship with the staff, at least try to keep a bantering, joking relationship, so you can still talk to them when you want to get through to the boss with a phone call, a visit, or a letter.

A staffer who is friendly can be a source of advice to you as well as to the legislator. Being around the boss a lot, an LA can read his moods, and if necessary can warn you, "This isn't the time to see him." This kind of advice can make the difference between a favorable reaction and a turndown by the legislator. A staffer can also tell you how the mail is running on your issue, and what questions particularly concern the boss.

To foster a comfortable relationship, invite a staff member to lunch. Keep it casual, and eat at a cafeteria or sandwich shop near the legislator's office. (During your Washington visit, cafeterias in the House and Senate office buildings are just right for this purpose.) The staffer will pay for his own lunch. The more relaxed mood at lunch, compared to that of the office, and the break from talking nonstop about your issue will help you get to know each other. You'll learn things from the staffer if you keep the lunch on a low key. For instance, ask what's happening with your bill, what the procedure is, what happens next. Ask about the other legislators involved—committee members, opposing legislators, and so forth. Give the staffer a chance to show off his expertise about Congress.

Another chance to get better acquainted comes when you've had a few visits or phone conversations with an LA, and you invite him or her to come on an inspection trip or field trip to take a look at the visible impact of your issue. For example, proponents of national parks and wilderness have taken congressional staff on backpacking trips in affected areas. The informality of the trip and the direct exposure to the land in question have done much to arouse staffers' enthusiasm.

A few times during the year you may show your goodwill by giving your staff contacts something that will interest them and remind them of your issue in a pleasant or witty way. A newspaper cartoon that relates to your issue might get a laugh. An attractive poster or calendar might be enjoyed for months. Most congressional staff have unattractive work space, and they are always on the lookout for something to brighten the scene. Many of the wilderness posters distributed to members of Congress ten years ago by the Sierra Club and Friends of the Earth are still hanging in the offices, decorating staff rooms, reception areas, and legislators' offices.

If you've got a staffer who is sympathetic to your cause, consider giving him or her a book that you've found particularly eloquent on the issue. Books, posters, calendars—all these are ways of recognizing a staffer's competent work on your issue, at only nominal expense. Don't give anything of value, because that approaches the realm of bribery and could be resented by the recipient even if you didn't intend it that way.

In general, building a relationship with staff people has much in common with building a relationship with legislators. The biggest difference is that staffers are more accessible, and you have to be careful not to take unfair advantage of that. A legislative assistant has a phone that rings all day, and a stack of work that is impossible to complete. So don't call an LA just to shoot the breeze or to pass on a tidbit of information that you could have sent by letter. Call when you need to, and make the conversation enjoyable, with a little wit or with a little sympathy for the LA's burden.

While one staff member has the responsibility for your issue, keep the other staffers in mind, too. Contact with staff in the state or district office is very important, because that's where the political antennae are. Use the district office to set up your appointments with the congressman. And drop in three or four times a year on some pretext or other; word will get to the congressman that you're a very interested citizen, and that means that you're somebody whose views should be considered.

Be friendly to the receptionist and secretaries and caseworkers, too. Their impression of you can help or hinder your efforts later on. Many of these staffers are accustomed to being treated as nonpeople by callers who are trying to influence the boss. Go out of your way to recognize them as individuals with names, responsibilities, and personal attributes of their own, and you'll be remembered favorably. This will help when you call to ask for an appointment with the congressman or to leave a message for the LA. Besides, you'll get more enjoyment from your contacts with the office if you know the people who work there.

14

Your Role in Congressional Hearings

Ten Ways to Participate in a Congressional Hearing

The public hearings held by the committees of Congress are the only *official* opportunity for citizens to participate in the law-making process. They are one of the best ways to present your views on current legislation.

1. Even if you've never spoken at a congressional hearing before, **it's nothing to be afraid of.** The tough questioning is reserved for the main speakers who represent organizations, and for those who pick a fight with the committee. It won't be like the Watergate hearings.

2. You'll be more influential if you can **speak for others besides yourself.** If you don't have a civic group or garden club to represent, circulate a petition among your friends and hand it in, with a flourish, when you get up to speak. Ask friends to write letters for you to hand in at the hearing.

3. In writing your statement for a hearing, just be yourself and **draw on your own experience,** your own knowledge, and your own feelings about the issue. Cover the important points at the beginning, so you can stop easily if the chairman imposes a time limit on the witnesses.

4. State your position clearly at the start, so nobody will have any doubt as to where you stand: "I favor S. 1541" or "We oppose H.R. 2114 unless it is strengthened as suggested by the Citizen Action Council."

5. If you or an organization you represent have firsthand experience with the subject of the hearing, be sure to say so. In presenting your arguments, **use real-life evidence**—anecdotes and case histories drawn from your experience and from things that have happened in your community. Rely on information you can substantiate.

6. Send advance copies of your statement to reporters who will be covering the hearing for your local papers and radio and television stations. Send copies also to the editorial page editors.

7. Dress up a little for the hearing, to flatter the committee. Arrive at least a half-hour early to get a seat.

8. When it's your turn to speak, **be brief.** Even if there's no time limit, keep yourself down to five minutes, so you won't bore the committee. You can show by the way you speak how strongly you feel about the issue; there's no reason to hide your feelings.

9. If the legislators question you, **don't get upset.** Answer their questions calmly and factually. Be friendly, even if you're sure they're trying to get your goat.

10. After the hearing, **send copies of your statement** to your own congressman and senators, with a cover letter telling about the hearing and asking them to support your cause.

Most of this book is devoted to the ways you can get your congressman's ear and make him hear what you have to say, when he doesn't really seem to be interested. Congressional hearings, on the other hand, are that rare opportunity in which Congress is interested in an issue and is seeking the views and the information that people have to offer on the subject. In hearings, Congress opens the door to public participation in the legislative process. Indeed, hearings are the only *official* opportunity for citizens to participate in lawmaking by Congress.

Hearings are held by committees of Congress both in Washington, D.C., and in other locations throughout the country. The Washington hearings are usually intended primarily to obtain the views of members of Congress, the executive branch, industrial and citizens' organizations, and experts. Hearings outside of Washington, called "field hearings," are primarily to get the views of regional and local institutions, organizations, and individual citizens. Both kinds of hearings are usually conducted by specialized subcommittees, rather than by the full committee.

Congressional committees gain a lot by listening to individual citizens and spokesmen for small, local citizen groups. These are people who are speaking at a hearing because they care about an issue, not because they're paid to advocate a particular point of view. To legislators the contrast is very clear between the citizen witnesses and the paid Washington lobbyists. To be sure, some legislators are more impressed by the paid lobbyists, but thoughtful lawmakers realize that it's the unpaid citizen witnesses who know most intimately how the issues affect people in their own communities across the land. When citizens speak at hearings, legislators are getting the story straight from the horse's mouth.

To you, as an issue advocate, a congressional hearing is a chance to advance your cause on its merits by good arguments and evidence, and an opportunity to influence Congress by showing public support for your cause. You can influence your own senators and congressman by demonstrating that you and other voters are concerned enough to testify at a congressional hearing, that your side had more support than your opponents did, and that your facts and arguments stood up under scrutiny by a committee of Congress. If one of your legislators is a member of the committee and was on hand for the hearing, he'll get the influence directly. You can influence legislators who weren't there indirectly, through what you and your co-workers send them after the hearing.

Quite aside from your own congressman or senators, you also influence the committee members by speaking at a hearing. Those from other congressional districts and states aren't as susceptible to your influence as your own legislators are, because they don't want anything from you. They don't need what your own congressman needs—your vote, your help in the campaign, your favorable mention of the congressman in conversation with friends. These other legislators are going to be making decisions on bills that concern you, and their attitude toward these bills—their personal convictions, as opposed to their political assessment—will be influenced by what they hear people saying at hearings on the subject. Many other factors will also influence them, but a hearing is a rare opportunity to awaken the sympathetic interest of senators and congressmen who will make most of the decisions on the legislation. The committee staff will also be influenced by what you say, and will take note of the arguments you use and the facts and anecdotes you mention, because the staff has the job of knowing all the arguments and keeping track of all relevant information that could be important when the bill is marked up by the committee.

Even if you have no new arguments or new facts to present, your voice speaking in support of a bill, added to dozens of other voices, is part of the record of support for that bill. This support will be mentioned by advocates of the bill during markup, during full committee action, and during floor debate. It will be mentioned to reporters writing about the bill. It will be mentioned in newsletters of citizen groups, trying to arouse others who didn't attend the hearings to write their own legislators. A bill that has this record of support is hard to stop; one that lacks it can easily be killed because its proponents in Congress can't show their colleagues any tangible evidence that people want this bill and have put themselves on the line at congressional hearings to say so.

To a member of Congress, hearings are among the best opportunities to show Congress—and himself—at work and in touch with the public. Legislators like to have field hearings in their districts so they can show off their position of influence on issues important to the voters. Beyond the reelection motive, legislators view hearings as one of the most positive features Congress can show to the nation, a way of counteracting the low opinion of Congress that people repeatedly express in public opinion polls. So, besides the issue agenda that brings about a particular hearing, there is an unwritten agenda of demonstrating that Congress, as represented by the committee, is a responsible, thoughtful, considerate, and friendly institution with the interests of the public at heart.

For these reasons, people who speak at field hearings are usually well received by the committee. Tough questioning is reserved for the main speakers who represent organizations, or for people who attack the committee's motives or its conduct of the hearing. Even if you have never spoken at a congressional hearing before, it's nothing to be afraid of. One Oregon woman who spoke at her first hearing at age sixty-three says, "The congressmen have looked upon me benignly, and I have felt encouraged to speak my piece, which is as it should be. After one good experience, one is never afraid, or awed, again."

Hearings are not as awesome as you might think. For one thing, the terminology makes a hearing seem more formidable than it really is. At a hearing you're a "witness" and you "testify." But actually it's only you speaking your mind, giving Congress your views. When you think of congressional hearings, the image that springs to mind may be something you saw on television—hearings in a packed room, with reporters and photographers all over, and a dozen senators grilling an unhappy Administration spokesman. It won't be like that when you speak at a field hearing. It's more likely to be after the handful of reporters have left to file their stories, and with only two congressmen who listen but ask no questions. The important thing is to state your views and make a good impression on the legislators, the staff, and any reporters who stuck around.

Congressional hearings don't have the rigid formality of a courtroom. You won't be asked to swear on a Bible. There is no rule against hearsay, and there are no elaborate rules of evidence. A committee wants your reaction to the bills that are being considered and any information you can give them about how the bills would affect you, your community, and the nation at large.

A hearing, either in Washington or in your region, can help your local campaign in several ways:

1. It's an opportunity to **show that you've got solid public support** on your side. If your opponents are generally thought to outnumber you, a hearing is your chance to show it isn't so. This can influence your own legislators, news media, and local politicians.

2. It's a **focal point for your organizing effort,** giving people deadlines to work toward (the date of the hearing and the date the hearing record closes), and giving people specific tasks to carry out (testify at the hearing or write a letter for the hearing record, get friends to testify or write, and get organizations to testify or write).

3. It's an **official forum seeking facts and opinions,** and this can help you nudge recalcitrant local government officials and citizen groups into taking a stand. Once they've expressed themselves in a letter for the hearing record, you can mention their support in other ways.

4. It's a chance to **get the attention of news media.** If the hearing is in your community it will be a newsworthy event. If it's somewhere else in your part of the country, or in Washington, your local news media may be interested in the fact that local people are making the trip to testify, and they may want to send a reporter to cover it, or use wire service stories with local information added to tell about your testimony. A Washington hearing may also be covered by a Washington bureau or stringer for your local paper. All told, the hearing elevates the issue in the eyes of local reporters, editors, and editorial writers—if you let them know about it, and show that local people are involved.

From the standpoint of a congressional committee, a hearing is primarily a fact-finding forum in which the committee inquires into the merits and demerits of a bill. That's the theory. **In reality, there are many different and often unrevealed reasons for holding congressional hearings. Some of these are:**

- To find out what the arguments are for and against a bill
- To get the facts on which these arguments rest
- To find out whether there is much support for a bill, or opposition to it, among the public, among officials of federal, state, and local governments, and among industries
- To find out how the bill would affect individual citizens
- To give a particular legislator a chance to show off his involvement in an issue that's popular with his constituents, his campaign contributors, or with a national constituency he's trying to build (such as for a presidential race)
- To give opponents of a bill their last chance to sound off before the committee approves the bill, so they can't say they didn't have their "day in court"
- To educate the public or particular factions of the public that oppose a bill, by letting opponents voice their arguments and

then rebutting them through careful questioning by committee members

• To show strong public support for a bill by holding the hearings in a city where supporters are strongest

• To show strong public opposition to a bill by holding the hearings where opponents are strongest

• To investigate or expose a problem, whether or not any legislation is being considered on the subject

Hearings are handled differently by the various committees of Congress. A few committees choose witnesses specifically to present diverse viewpoints and contribute expert testimony, and invite only these to appear. More often the committees announce hearings and extend a general invitation to all who are interested in the issue. Anybody who calls or writes the committee saying he wants to testify is placed on the witness list. The committee tries to hear them all, frequently imposing a time limit of a few minutes per witness to give everyone a chance to be heard. When a committee is investigating a problem—as in one hearing that concerned the closure of Crater Lake National Park because of a failure in the water supply system—rather than seeking views on legislation, they will want to spend most of their time questioning those responsible for the problem. But in most hearings, the views of citizens and the information they can provide are completely appropriate.

If the committee staff won't put you on the witness list—possibly because you were too late in calling or because they don't want to hear individuals—attend the hearing anyway and turn in a written statement or letter beginning clearly with a request like this one: "Please include this letter in the hearing record." Or get a friendly legislator or somebody who *is* on the witness list to hand your statement in and make a brief announcement, such as: "Mr. Chairman, I am handing in a statement by Joseph Berman, who is in the room but was told by committee staff he could not testify. Mr. Berman is from Blacksville, California, and he favors H.R. 651. Will you please include his statement in the record?"

Citizens usually do a lot of waiting at a congressional hearing. **The witness list usually begins with bigwigs who are not subjected to time limits, as in this typical arrangement:**

1. Members of Congress
2. Governors
3. Federal agencies (these seldom testify at field hearings)
4. Local elected officials
5. State and local government agencies
6. Private organizations—citizen groups, corporations, industrial associations, and so forth
7. Individuals

At field hearings, the first couple of hours are often taken up by governors, mayors, and state agencies and then the rest of the day goes to organizations and individuals. But it's worth the wait, because the committee members and staff will get their basic firsthand impressions of the issue by hearing you speak. They'll be favorably impressed, or put off, by the quality of your testimony, by the seriousness and conviction you show, and by the way you respond to questions.

After the hearing, the committee staff will analyze the testimony to see what arguments and facts were presented on either side, to tally the number of witnesses who supported each position, and to list the organizations that supported each position. The staff will also tidy up the hearing transcript, made at the hearing by an official reporter, and have it printed as a hearing record. Copies are usually available from your congressman or senators, or from the committee's documents clerk.

So You Want to Testify

Suppose a field hearing has been announced on an issue that concerns you, and it's to be in a city near you. You've decided to go and give the committee your views.

The first thing to do is phone the committee and ask them to add your name to the witness list. The phone number is usually given in the hearing announcement; if not, use the main U.S. Capitol number, (202) 224-3121. Timing is important, because witness lists are often based partly on first come, first served. After phoning the committee staff, follow up with a letter to confirm your request, and keep a copy. Later, if you find that you've been left off the list by mistake, you'll have proof that you asked to be heard.

Next, decide for whom you're going to speak: just for yourself, for yourself and your family or your neighbors, or for an organization. You'll be more influential if you can speak for others besides yourself. If a group you belong to has taken a good stand on the issue, or can do so in time for the hearing, you'll be doing them a favor by volunteering to speak for them at the hearing. Consider every kind of group, not just those normally associated with the issue, including some of the following:

Activist groups	Neighborhood or block association
Apartment tenants' council	Garden club
Athletic club	Labor union
Fan club	Museum association
Business association	Hobby club
Retirement club	Travel club
Women's club	Service club
Church or church group	Professional society

If possible, get an official resolution or at least a firm decision from the group's board of directors or executive committee. Sometimes hostile legislators ask witnesses how their organization reached its decision on the issue; citing a resolution is a good answer to this question.

Sometimes it takes days to get action out of a group, but don't let this delay you in calling to get your name on the witness list. If you're still trying to make arrangements with the organization, just tell the committee you'll be speaking as an individual. You can add the name of the organization later, but don't wait for the day of the hearing because you may get an earlier spot on the witness list as a spokesperson for an organization.

When testifying as an individual, you can multiply your impact by getting friends and neighbors to write letters for you to hand in with a flourish when you testify: "Madam Chairman, I am submitting for the record the letters and statements of sixteen other residents of Silver City who were unable to come to this hearing but strongly favor H.R. 5512." These letters not only add to the numbers supporting your cause, they make you look more respectable in that people have turned to you to present their letters at a hearing. You may have to draft letters for some of your people, but it's worthwhile because it adds their weight to your own presentation. Make copies of your friends' letters and ask your friends to send them to their own congressman and senators.

Another way to increase your impact is to circulate a petition in your neighborhood or work place, to pick up the nominal support of people who wouldn't testify or write letters but who share your concern about the issue. An individual effort like this can be effective even if you only get twenty or thirty signatures. When you hand in the petition at the hearing, it adds to your influence. And don't neglect to have somebody send a copy to your legislators, too; you might draft a cover letter for one of the signers.

Writing Your Statement

There are no special tricks to writing the statement you'll give at a hearing. Just be yourself and tell the committee what you think about the bill they're considering. Draw on your own experience, your own knowledge, and your own feelings to get your point across. You may want to refer to published sources (scientific reports, magazine articles, newspaper stories, etc.) to back up what you say, but go as far as you can on your own experience and beliefs. Don't try to pose as an expert if you aren't one; the committee doesn't expect every citizen witness to be an expert. The committee does expect you to give a sincere statement of your own concerns about the bill.

To make it easy to meet a time limit the chairman may impose (sometimes five minutes per person, occasionally as little as one minute), organize your statement so you cover the important points briefly at the start and then give the supporting facts later.

Stick to the announced topic of the hearing. Committee members will quickly lose patience if you get off the subject and start airing your views on everything that's wrong with the federal government.

Your statement need not follow any set format, but the following suggestions describe a basic outline that has proved effective for many citizen witnesses:

1. The heading can start off something like this:

Statement of Susan Hoffman

Representing St. John's Church, Midvale, Pennsylvania

Before the House Committee on Education and Labor, Philadelphia, Pennsylvania, February 15, 1978.

2. Begin by stating your name and address. If you're speaking for an organization, say so and give the organization's address instead of your own. Include the street address so that supporters of your position will be able to locate you later by checking the hearing record. Your address also tells the committee whose congressional district you live in. If you wish, thank the committee for holding the hearing.

3. State your position clearly on the subject of the hearing, such as: "I favor S. 1541" or "We oppose H.R. 2114 unless it is strengthened as suggested by the Illinois Energy Consumers Council." This sort of explicit statement is important, because it's the basis for the tallies of witnesses' positions that will be made by news media, by the committee staff, and by citizen leaders on your issue. If you leave any doubt about your position, you'll show up in the tally as "noncommittal" or "position unclear."

4. If you or an organization you represent have experience with the subject of the hearing, say so. This will give your views greater impact. This experience doesn't have to be earth-shaking; it might be that your group has members who have visited a proposed national recreation area, even though you haven't been there yourself.

5. Then present your arguments and evidence, stressing concrete examples—anecdotes and case histories drawn from your experience and from things that have happened in your community.

6. Conclude your statement by thanking the committee for the opportunity to express your views, and again sum up your basic position.

If you're speaking for an organization that has adopted a formal position on the issue, include the group's resolution or mention it to make your authority clear. For instance: "Our board of directors adopted a resolution on October 27, 1978, endorsing the principles of this bill." Indicate how many members the group has if the figure is impressive, and mention any other qualifications that make the group knowledgeable on the subject.

On the other hand, if you're speaking as an individual, don't mention that you're a member of any organizations involved in the issue unless committee members ask. Mentioning your membership in such groups doesn't add to your stature; it detracts from it by suggesting that the groups are getting extra witnesses into the hearing beyond the one spokesperson each is usually allowed. To the uninformed legislator, it also suggests that you're not an independent, free-thinking citizen but merely a dutiful member of an organization. Legislators have an erroneous impression that citizen groups simply tell their members to go and testify at a hearing and the members obey. Actually, few members ever respond to a call for action, and those who do maintain a fierce independence.

Don't attack your opponents' motivations or belittle them. Your opponents are guests of the committee, as you are, and the chairman is likely to reprimand you for spiteful remarks about the opposition. Feel free to attack your opponents in a citizen-group newsletter, but at a hearing, restrict yourself to demolishing their arguments and proving their facts wrong. Testimony that is factual and logical will do more to defeat your opponents than anything you could say about their motives or character.

When you're going to speak at a congressional hearing in another city, send copies of your statement to your local news media before leaving home, and make sure they get it at least one day before the hearing. This gives your local media a chance to supplement a wire story by quoting from your statement to add a hometown angle.

At the Hearing

To senators and congressmen, a hearing is a ceremonial occasion. If you want to influence them, pay a little respect to their viewpoint and put on the dog. Dress up a little more than usual. Clothes too casual for the occasion—old Levi's, T-shirts, tennis shoes, shorts, hard hats, overalls—are seen by legislators as a sign of disrespect for the committee and for the hearing, and these clothes undermine your respectability as a witness. It's regrettable that legislators emphasize appearances so much, but as long as they do, it's best to play along and to reserve your fighting spirit for the real issue that brings you to the hearing.

Plan to arrive at the hearing room thirty minutes to an hour early to get a seat. Your opponents may show up early to pack the room. When you get there, find out from committee staff or from citizen leaders where you are on the witness list and when you're likely to be called to testify. It usually takes longer than they think. One citizen leader experienced with hearings may be serving as an informal floor leader or honcho to coordinate the witnesses on your side. If there is one, seek him or her out and introduce yourself.

While listening to earlier witnesses testify, if the chairman allows applause, give a good hand to witnesses on your side. At some congressional hearings the chairman does not permit it, but when he does, don't let your opponents show you up.

Before you testify, hand copies of your statement to reporters, who usually sit at a press table near the front of the room. Some of them may leave before you speak, but this way they'll know what you're going to say. This is especially important for witnesses who represent organizations, because the news media prefer to quote organization witnesses.

Often the order of witnesses will be changed from that on the witness list, to accommodate people who have to leave early to catch a plane or train. Don't take advantage of this yourself unless it's absolutely necessary; it's better to stick around for the whole thing and thus show your interest in the issue. If the audience gradually dwindles, the committee will think the subject wasn't really that important to you. At a field hearing, be prepared to stay until six or seven P.M.

Be in the room when your name is called. It looks bad for your side if the chairman calls two or three names in a row without getting an answer, and the absentees have to be rescheduled later in the hearing. Let your opponents be the klutzes who make life difficult for the chairman and committee staff.

When your name is called and you take your seat at the witness table, before launching into your statement, hand in any letters and statements you've brought from friends and neighbors. Say something like, "Madam Chairman, I am submitting fourteen letters from other people in Oakville who favor S. 143 but were not able to come to this hearing. Will you please include these in the hearing record?" This request will usually be honored.

Now it's your turn to speak. If you've never spoken at a hearing before and you're nervous about it, it may help you to simply read your prepared statement or a cut-down version of it. As a rule, don't talk longer than five minutes unless you have new information or arguments the committee hasn't heard before.

If you feel more confident, you'll make a greater impact on the committee if you hand in your written statement and, instead of reading from it, look the legislators in the eye and speak from the heart, covering in a few minutes the main points you want them to hear. This will engage their attention better than reading from your statement. Ask the chairman to include your written statement in the record, and don't forget to state exactly what position you favor, so everybody in the room will know it.

Even when there's no restriction on time, be brief. You'll put the committee to sleep if you try to read a whole fifteen-page statement. When you're watching the news on television some evening, notice that one newscaster speaks for only a few minutes, then another person gives the next item. The change of face and voice keeps viewers' interest up. "The cardinal rule is: don't bore the committee," says Maitland S. Sharpe, a frequent spokesman at hearings for the Izaak Walton League of America. "You're far better off if they listen carefully to just one point than if they doze through the most comprehensive possible presentation."

Take advantage of legislators' view of the hearing as a sacred institution and play along with the formalities. Be deferential and courteous to the committee when you can afford to be—dress well, be respectful and friendly, address legislators as Mr. Chairman, Madam Chairman, Congressman, Congresswoman, Senator. But when you get into a discussion of your issue, hold firm to your position and strongly but respectfully insist on your viewpoint.

Don't waste time describing your qualifications or background. One or two sentences should do, and your written statement can give full particulars. The hearing time is precious, and the subject is not you.

Avoid taking a lot of time to repeat points made by earlier witnesses, unless you have your own experiences or new information to add. If you come up late in the hearing and everything has been said already, you'll win goodwill for your cause by saying something like, "I favor S. 393, and I don't have anything to add to what other witnesses have said in favor of it. Will you please include my written statement in the record?" However, when you have personal experiences to relate, it's extremely important to mention them orally, because these are the focus of a field hearing—how people are really affected by the subject at hand.

In addition to your statement, you may submit relevant editorials and newspaper articles that support your arguments, or articles from magazines or from professional or scientific journals, asking the chairman to include them in the hearing record. Some—usually short ones—may be printed in the record with your testimony, and others may be kept in the committee files.

You can also use props to get your message across:

• **Maps, charts, and graphs** should be mounted on stiff backing, so they can be placed on an easel in front of the committee. You may have to provide your own easel or have a friend hold the display while you point to its significant features. If you want one of these displays printed in the hearing record, submit a reduced, camera-ready version, but even so it may not be used.

• **Photographs** should be presented as enlargements, either mounted on stiff backing for display or in a binder to be passed around by committee members.

• **Color slides** may sometimes be shown, if you provide the projector and screen. Keep it down to a dozen or so slides. Color-slide presentations are usually best left to the principal witnesses for your side, except when you have some vital facts that can only be substantiated by showing slides. They won't appear in the hearing record anyway, and you can usually make your point better by using color enlargements that can be passed around by committee members and staff.

When using visual aids of these kinds, describe orally what you're pointing to, so it will be clearly understood in the hearing record. For instance:

"Here, at Graves Meadows, the proposed park boundary swings out to the west."

"In this graph showing incidence of the disease in Marion County from 1967 to 1977, the peaks are 125 cases in 1972 and 140 in 1975."

"This photograph of Tabor House shows the need for historic restoration. The cornices are crumbling, the porch is collapsing, and . . ."

Don't use your time to lecture the committee on topics they're expert in. The Education and Labor Committee won't be interested in hearing you talk for five minutes on the need for public schools. They *will* be interested in your views on what the schools in your community are doing well and what they are doing poorly. The lecture material can be in your written statement, but skip it when you speak.

There are several no-nos that fall under the heading of etiquette at a congressional hearing:

- **Don't challenge the motives of the committee** or claim that they're biased against you. Even if you know different, for purposes of the hearing you have to take the position that the committee is considering the issue in good faith. If you don't, and show it, it will alienate them still further from your viewpoint.

- **Respect the formality of the hearing.** Legislators sometimes address one another by first name in a hearing, but they expect witnesses to address them as Senator Brown, Congresswoman Black, or just Senator, Congresswoman, or Congressman.

- **Don't get into partisan politics,** knocking the Democrats or Republicans. Stick to the issue. Partisanship is resented, because legislators themselves keep partisan differences at a low key, and especially in a hearing try to achieve a nonpartisan spirit. You may need the votes of legislators whose party you're attacking, and you won't get any more votes from the opposite party by doing so, either.

- **Don't indulge in name dropping or self-aggrandizement.** Never mind that you were, say, one of President Carter's classmates at the Naval Academy; mentioning it will be resented and will raise a question about your judgment before you even say anything about your issue.

• **End your oral statement when the chairman indicates the end of your time.** You can't argue with the chairman about the conduct of the hearing, though you certainly can argue with him, respectfully, about your issue.

On Being Questioned

When you've finished your oral statement, the committee members have an opportunity to ask questions. The chairman and ranking minority member go first, followed by the others in order of decreasing seniority, alternating between Democrats and Republicans. In House hearings, each member is entitled to five minutes on the first go-round.

The most detailed questioning is usually directed to the principal witnesses for your cause and to experts. Individual citizens often are not questioned at all. However, you want the committee to question you because it will show that you caught their attention and it may give you another chance to hammer your points home.

A congressman who favors your position may question you to find out more about an experience you mentioned, because this may help him persuade others on the committee. He may want to know more about the organization you represent, or he may want to clarify your position on the bill.

A legislator who hasn't made up his mind on the bill may question you to find out how solid your facts are; he may doubt the accuracy of something you said. He may be trying to learn enough about the subject so he can decide how to vote. Remember, you know more than he does about how the issue affects you and your community.

A congressman who opposes your views may not ask questions at all, so as not to attract attention to your statement. But he may question you to try to discredit your testimony, to mislead you into taking back some of the things you said, or to convince you that your concern is groundless. A favorite tactic of hostile legislators at field hearings is to question a witness something like this (a fictitious example):

> CONGRESSWOMAN: I compliment you on a very thoughtful statement, Mrs. Garcia. You express strong views in favor of this bill.

Were you in the room this morning when others spoke against the bill?

WITNESS: Yes, I was.

CONGRESSWOMAN: They said this bill would wipe out many jobs in our state. Do you recognize that this is a legitimate concern, just as your viewpoint is?

WITNESS: Yes, Congresswoman.

CONGRESSWOMAN: Would you agree that it's our responsibility as members of Congress to take both concerns into account as we consider this bill, and try to resolve the differences?

Here the congresswoman is trying to lead the witness into giving the committee carte blanche to compromise the bill or mangle it beyond recognition. Don't let her get away with this. Strongly assert your basic position. Continuing the dialogue:

WITNESS: Congresswoman, I think it's your responsibility to pass legislation in the public interest, and I feel that this bill is definitely in the public interest as it now stands. It should not be weakened. The concern about jobs has been answered by competent economists who testified earlier.

Be wary of simple, factual questions that call for a yes or no answer. This is the way legislators often begin leading you down the garden path to a conclusion you wouldn't agree with.

A hostile congressman may want to discredit your testimony by showing that you're not an expert. Don't be afraid of this, because in most cases you don't purport to be an expert. Respond something like this: "Congressman, I don't claim to be an expert on the technical details of this program, but I do know how it affects our city, and I'm telling you the results are bad, and it should be changed as proposed in H.R. 5327."

Watch out for "do you know" questions. A hostile legislator will use them to put you on the defensive. For instance, an oil-state senator who opposes a new national park on grounds that oil may be found there may ask a pro-park witness, "Do you know how much of our oil is imported from foreign countries?" He wants to catch the witness on unfamiliar ground and make him answer, "No." That leaves the senator at an advantage, so he can say, "Well, I'll tell you. We import fifty percent of our oil and that supply could be cut off at any time. That's why we have to seek oil in this proposed park area, an action which you apparently oppose."

The best way to avoid giving him the "No" he wants is to come back at him with an argument that shows the irrelevance of the point he's getting at. In the above example, the witness might say, "Senator, I'm concerned about the oil supply, too, but I think that's irrelevant here because even if we developed all our domestic oil sources we would still be importing oil sooner or later, so it's not an either/or situation. This proposed park occupies less than one-tenth of one percent of our total land area, and turning it over to oil production won't save us from importing oil."

Avoid reacting hostilely to hostile questions. They may be only devil's-advocate questions. Your supporters on the committee may want to find out how you'd answer the questions they'll be asked by other, skeptical legislators when they start moving the bill to full committee and to the House or Senate floor. Try to agree with part of the concern implied by a hostile question, then go on to give your real answer. For example, imagine a hearing on legislation to bar mandatory retirement at age sixty-five, and a senator is questioning a witness who favors the bill:

> SENATOR: Isn't there a danger that, by banning mandatory retirement at sixty-five, we'll be keeping millions of older workers on the job and thus preventing young people, who now have a serious unemployment problem, from finding jobs?
>
> WITNESS: I couldn't agree more with your concern—we have to help the young people enter the job market. But this bill won't have any significant effect on that. The U.S. Department of Labor has estimated that only two-tenths of one percent of the nation's workers would take advantage of this law and keep on working.

If a legislator, while questioning you, asserts facts you know aren't correct, simply cite the source of your correct facts. You don't want to make even an opponent lose face in a hearing, but you do want to show that his facts are wrong. Present the correction calmly and forthrightly, setting aside your emotions, as in the following fictitious exchange at a hearing on highways:

> CONGRESSMAN: In your statement against this highway bill you complain that people are being ousted from their homes. You're

on shaky ground there, because the state highway department relocates all those people in other housing.

WITNESS: Congressman, our city's Department of Human Resources found that three hundred and twenty-two families were displaced by the Midtown Freeway project and only seventy-eight of those were relocated by the highway department in other housing. The rest were left on their own. Those figures are in the department's report dated January 26, 1978. If you haven't seen it, I'd be glad to get you a copy.

Always be alert to your own feelings while you're being questioned. If you feel your temper rising, cool it. A legislator may try to get you mad so you'll blow your top and thereby discredit your cause or the organization you represent. Don't let him get your goat. It's all right to show enthusiasm and concern about your cause, but getting mad at a legislator isn't the way to show that, and it isn't the way to win the committee's support. You may be able to calm yourself by waiting a few moments after a legislator asks a question before you begin your answer. Take a deep breath; a slight pause to collect your thoughts isn't frowned upon.

Also be alert to defensiveness, which you may feel if you're being questioned unfairly in an attempt to destroy your credibility. When the going gets rough, keep in mind the justice of your cause and be confident of your position and your right to advocate it. You have as much right to express your views on legislation as anybody else in the room. A legislator who tries to demolish you through unfair questioning will succeed only if you give in to defensive feelings. Maintain a strong stance and you'll look as good as or better than your questioner.

The etiquette of answering questions in a hearing can be summed up as follows:

• **Let the questioner finish his question, and don't interrupt.** In a normal conversation, you may interrupt people's questions, but in the more formal situation of a hearing, it's better to let the legislator talk as long as he wants. Besides, the question may be more of a speech than a question; in that case, you wouldn't want to thwart the legislator's desire to talk.

• **Answer calmly and factually.** Don't be drawn into a shouting match, even if the congressman starts to raise his voice. Your calmness under fire will impress the committee and the audience.

• **Be patient.** When a legislator doesn't seem to understand what you've said and keeps harassing you with questions, just keep explaining again and again, trying to get your point across. Your questioner is probably going to be influenced far less by your answers than the other legislators, reporters, committee staff, and spectators will be. Your explanations will be understood by somebody who has influence.

After the Hearing

If your oral statement departed much from your written statement or if you were questioned, you may want to check the transcript to correct the official reporter's errors, check the spelling of place names and technical terms, and edit your lapses in grammar. Find out from committee staff whether the transcript will be available for correction. The transcripts of Washington, D.C., hearings are usually available for this purpose in the committee office a day or two after the hearing. With many field hearings, this is not possible because the transcript won't be completed until the committee returns to Washington.

To spread the influence of your appearance at the hearing, send copies of your statement to any of your senators and congressman who weren't there, with a cover letter commenting on the hearing. If the witnesses from your state favored your cause by a ratio of, say, twelve to two, mention this. If local newspapers covered the hearing well, enclose clippings.

If the hearing was in Washington, D.C., go and visit all of your legislators in person and discuss it with their staff. Especially important is the visit to a legislator who was on the committee, because he will soon be voting on the subject. In this visit you can find out the legislator's reaction to the hearing, learn whether he has any remaining questions that you may be able to answer (either now or when you get back home), and encourage him gently in the right direction. Before leaving Washington, report the results of these visits to the national leadership of your cause.

15

Getting Influence from Elections

"The groups that win their legislative fights are the ones that get involved in congressional elections," says Brent Blackwelder, chairman of the League of Conservation Voters. "Participating actively in elections is important because it shows that you have clout."

The influence derived from election work has greater impact than almost anything else you can do. The reason is that legislators are highly sensitive to election activities. It's a matter of survival to them. They know that almost anything can tip the balance in a close election or can cause an upset victory by a rival candidate. They know that many issues contribute to victory or defeat and that your issue could be one of them.

This is in the back of a legislator's mind whenever he is handling your issue. However, most legislative issues a congressman or congresswoman deals with are never prominent in the election campaign, and voters who are concerned about these issues seem to shun partisan politics or don't care enough about their issue to get involved in elections. There has for too long been a feeling among issue advocates that election politics is "dirty," and they wouldn't lower themselves to participate in it.

Whether the cause is apathy, naïveté, or misguided idealism, the result is that a legislator never sees these issues as ones that could seriously help or hurt his reelection. In his mind he assigns these issues a lower priority—ones that can safely be neglected.

The contrast is dramatic when an issue is raised in an election.

It hits the legislator smack-dab in the eye, and he has to deal with it or risk losing votes he may need on election day. He can't even duck the issue any more; when there is another candidate to throw the spotlight on him, even the usual evasiveness can cost votes.

Election tactics can be particularly helpful if you're advocating a new issue which isn't identified with "the establishment." You may have had trouble getting your congresswoman to take it seriously because she regards it as too far-out and she probably thinks there are only a handful of her constituents who care about it, a mere extremist fringe element. This is the situation that at first confronted, to cite three examples, citizens who opposed the Vietnam war, those who were concerned about the dangers of nuclear power, and those who favored an antiabortion amendment to the Constitution. In each case, citizen advocates had to convert their issue from a far-out one to an acceptable, reasonable issue. Election tactics played an important part in each of these examples.

When your congresswoman sees that your issue has been much discussed during the election campaign or that it has been influential in her own election race—or in another race in your state—she will see it in a new light. If people who favor your cause have helped her or her opponent with volunteer work or contributions, she will see your issue as one that lies within the political establishment, rather than one that concerns only nonpolitical people. Even if your people were mostly opposing her, she is likely to gain a new respect for your issue and for your political sophistication. This will help you when you go to ask for her support on related legislation.

At election time and for months preceding the election itself, the candidates are asking for people's help. Their ears are open, listening for issues and ideas that will help them gain that support in the form of active volunteer work, contributions, endorsements, and finally in masses of votes. The candidates are simply more sensitive to the voters, and especially to organized causes, at this season. This heightened sensitivity is one of your sources of influence.

You may think that your issue isn't big enough to win or lose an election. That's true of many public interest issues; they usually can't be said to have won the election. You won't see newspaper headlines proclaiming that your issue cost a congressman his seat. Yet every politician knows that beyond the oversimplifications of the headlines lies a heavy truth—that an election victory is built on many issues.

The conventional wisdom of our time has it that elections aren't won or lost by issues at all, but rather by the voters' perceptions of the candidate as a respectable, honest, hard-working, glamorous, friendly, and intelligent person who is close to the people. Even if this is true, it's the issues that give the candidate a loyal following of campaign contributors and volunteers, without whom the candidate would be virtually unable to get word to the voters about his sterling qualities. And it's through his public participation in issues that a candidate shows his seriousness, creates an identification with voters' interests, and, not least important, gets into the news from week to week.

While some politicians try to avoid the issues and run on sheer charisma or on name recognition, the vast majority are supersensitive to issues even while they base their media campaigns on nothing but image. A candidate might prefer to avoid issues, but he knows that the issue he ducks might be the one that costs him the election. A victory margin of a few thousand votes could be the result of taking the wrong stance on two or three issues, displeasing some voters, turning off potential volunteers, and causing contributors to stop giving money.

Even if your organization is small, it can be influential through elections. The amount of energy your small membership channels into an election race, the cooperation you get from other, larger organizations, and the reliability and seriousness you apply to the election can give you influence far out of proportion to your size. When you have used some of your resources in an election, politicians will be quick to realize it and word will get around. They will want to be on your good side, so they will begin to consult you when your issue is coming up in Congress. They may not always follow your recommendations, but you've got one foot in the door where, before, you couldn't get anybody to notice that you were knocking to get in.

You don't even have to win the election to gain influence. If a challenger you helped came close to unseating the incumbent congressman, you're likely to have more influence with that congressman afterwards. For example, after ten years in the House of

Representatives, Congressman Burt L. Talcott (Republican of California) in 1974 barely survived, by a 1 percent margin, a challenge from Julian Camacho (Democrat), who made much of Talcott's poor record on environmental issues. Talcott had received low scores of 31, 0, and 35 in the League of Conservation Voters' ratings for 1972, 1973, and 1974. But after his close call in the 1974 election, Talcott's score shot up to 43 in the following year (still below average), and environmental leaders in his district found Talcott courting their support and actively pushing conservation measures on which he had previously dragged his feet. It was an abrupt transformation, but it wasn't a thoroughgoing one; Talcott still voted against the environmental position on many issues. In the 1976 election a more active environmental candidate, Leon E. Panetta (Democrat), defeated Talcott by a 6 percent margin. The 1974 election had shown Talcott that his constituents were not in agreement with his attitude on the environment, but he didn't change his views fast enough to keep up.

The election activities described in the remainder of this chapter will help you achieve the political influence that is latent in your cause. There are times when some of these activities are out of the question, however. If you're lucky enough to have a senator, say, who fully agrees with you and is working to advance your goals in the Senate, it would be in bad faith to go behind his back and cooperate with his opponent. When a legislator is that good, you want to help him get reelected, using some of the methods described in the section of this chapter on "Supporting a Candidate." (But be sure to meet with the challenger, give him your position papers, and ask for his support of your cause. Keep a line of communication with every challenger, because one of them just might get elected.)

Using the Election

There are ways of using the election to advance your cause without actually supporting or opposing particular candidates. In an election season you have more power than you usually have, simply because legislators then have a heightened sensitivity to the views of the public, and especially to those of organized groups.

You can apply tactics that take advantage of this favorable environment.

If your congressman has failed to support you on several votes since the last election and his record on your issue is generally poor, give him one more chance. This is what we call the Redemption Tactic, and it works best when you have a vote coming up in Congress a few months before the election. You meet with the congressman, explain your concern about his record on the issue, and point out that he has a great opportunity to please your cobelievers by voting your way on the present bill. In essence, he has a chance to redeem his prior record by voting right on this one vote. However, be careful not to make it a direct or implied threat, because threats are always resented.

The Redemption Tactic is worth considering only if these three conditions apply:

1. Your people are a **significant block of voters,** or can influence a significant block of voters through volunteer work, campaign contributions, or endorsements within the time remaining before the election. Having an emotional issue (such as animal protection, or abortion) helps.

2. Your people have **somebody else they might support** as a challenger in the election if the incumbent doesn't do right. You don't mention this to the congressman, but it has to be obvious. If the only challenger in sight is even worse than the incumbent on your issue, the congressman won't have to worry about losing your votes.

3. The legislator **needs your people's votes,** or wants voters in general to think he supports your cause. This may be your greatest leverage. The possibility that you might publicly criticize the congressman's record on a popular issue just before the election is something a congressman will worry about. The possibility that you might praise his vote is a positive incentive to change.

The Redemption Tactic depends on one thing above all: the congressman has to feel some danger in being unrepentant. If your stance is unpopular among the voters, your visit won't cause him any concern. If your issue is truly controversial, with both sides fighting it out, each looking about as popular as the other, again he won't feel compelled to follow your advice, because he might lose as many votes as he would gain. However, if your side is obviously well organized and your opponents are not, the legislator's caution might be swept aside by his desire for campaign support, or by his fear of opposition.

This is probably the factor most responsible for the growth of congressional support for antiabortion laws. A few years ago, Congress was resisting the proposals of Right to Life groups, but in 1977, after a great expansion of Right to Life organizing and participation in elections, the House of Representatives voted solidly and repeatedly in favor of antiabortion measures. The other side was only poorly organized and seemed to lack the religious fervor of the Right to Life adherents.

If local opinion is heavily in your favor, or if you have an apple-pie issue that nobody could be against (such as better schools, health, or a tax cut), a legislator should be able to see that he has a lot more to gain than to lose by coming out on your side during the election campaign. Sometimes it takes a nudge to get a legislator to recognize this, and that's why you go to see the congressman about it.

When your congressman agrees to your suggestion and votes accordingly, reward him with a letter thanking him for his vote and explaining why his decision is in the public interest. Release a copy of the letter, with a news release, to local news media. This doesn't fall into the category of election endorsements, because you aren't making any judgment on the congressman's overall record and you aren't urging people to vote for or against him. Yet it will let people know that he supported your cause.

If the congressman won't do what you ask, the next thing to do is go and see the challengers and ask them to take your position and raise the issue in the campaign. This tactic was used successfully in 1970 during the Senate fight over President Richard M. Nixon's nomination of G. Harrold Carswell to the Supreme Court. Senator Thomas J. Dodd (Democrat of Connecticut) was at first supporting Carswell. But when, as the primary election drew near, a rival candidate, Joseph Duffey, berated Dodd for this in speeches and broadcast appearances, Dodd switched to opposing Carswell.

When you approach the challengers, provide them with documentation of the incumbent's stance (letters, the text of a speech, his voting record on the issue), the basic facts and arguments on the issue, and a few good sentences of campaign rhetoric that you have drafted. If you don't know the challengers, perhaps some of your people who are campaign contributors can introduce you.

You don't want the incumbent to react the wrong way and merely harden his position, so whenever possible the challenger should be encouraged to needle him, calling attention to his failure to adopt your stance, rather than launching a head-on attack. The challenger can ask questions, such as: "Why hasn't Senator O'Brien come out in favor of the No-Fault Insurance Bill? Is he representing the people, or just the trial lawyers who are getting rich from insurance lawsuits?"

If your issue has strong popular appeal, a challenger can both win votes and help your cause by taking further action. He might testify at a congressional hearing on the subject, stressing how the issue affects your state. He might visit relevant Administration officials to call for action. He might meet with the governor about it. Anything of this kind is an opportunity for news coverage, with television and still photography. The challenger need not refer to the incumbent's name or mention his position on the issue.

These overt moves to seize the issue will be immediately recognized as such by your target legislator, and he'll have to decide how to react. His main options are the following:

• He can take the same stance and do something equally active or more so.

• He can ignore it, if he thinks the issue won't affect votes he needs.

• He can take the opposite stance and accuse the challenger of being wrong.

When a legislator fears election challenge in the primaries, even an undeclared candidate can get results by raising your issue in this fashion. What you need is someone who is a popular, local public figure who plausibly might run for Congress. You might help create this perception by starting a rumor that will reach the ears of the incumbent's staff from a source they trust, to the effect that Joe Smith is thinking of running. This will heighten the incumbent's attention to what Smith says in public about any issue—until the primary-filing deadline is past.

A friendly challenger can help you even when the incumbent has done something right, but not enough. Suppose your congressman has cosponsored your bill, but declined to testify on it or write to committee members or do anything else to push the bill. The challenger can say, "This is typical of Brown. He's a do-nothing congressman."

If the congressman's neglect is coupled with a concentration on some far-removed subject, such as international relations, the challenger might say, "Brown's inaction on this bill shows once more that he is too far removed from the people who put him in office. He's spending all his time on foreign affairs, and ignoring the problems that trouble the people of our state." Many elections have been won by challengers basing their campaigns on the charge that the incumbent has grown isolated from his constituents. It's one of the most potent challenges there is, and the incumbents know it.

If your plan to "up the ante" is more than a one-shot move, you'll want to avoid publicity, unlike the examples mentioned above. Once a candidate (especially an incumbent) has taken a public stance, he won't want to change it; doing so involves a loss of face and gives the appearance of indecisiveness. Candidates who flip-flop on the issues get a bad public image. So if you can afford to wait, keep the situation fluid until the pressure is greatest, just before the election. A public commitment any earlier than this would only blow your chance of winning more gains later.

On the other hand, you may not be able to wait so long, possibly because your big vote is long before the election, or because your opponents are getting organized and you want to get a commitment before they put the pressure on. However, when you have the time, use it to wring first one concession and then another from your legislator. The key factor here is the pressure you can bring to bear, and you apply it to all the players. This pressure stems from the candidates' desire to please both the voters and those who might help in the campaign. By using this pressure thoughtfully, you can effect great changes in the positions taken by the candidates.

Several tactics are designed chiefly to expose your issue during election year. A challenger can raise your issue during a debate with the incumbent, if you have provided him with enough facts beforehand. However, this is a blunderbuss approach, and you never know whether it will drive the legislator to adopt your stance or will just reaffirm his old position.

Since candidates get a good deal of attention from news media, a challenger may be able to raise the issue through some novel event, or he may protest the unfairness of your opponents' tactics or the inaccuracy of their facts. A friendly candidate can release some of your best facts and case histories for you. You'll have to do the homework, in collaboration with the challenger's campaign manager. Be careful that you're not linking your cause exclusively with one candidate; your objective is to get others to follow suit.

If none of the candidates in a congressional race will pick up your issue, take it to candidates for state and local offices. By raising the subject in their election campaigns, they show that you have an issue with popular appeal—even though the issue has nothing to do with the offices they're running for.

In the 1977 race for lieutenant governor of Virginia, one of the candidates, State Senator Joseph Canada (Republican), took a strong stand against the Panama Canal treaties, which were then under consideration by the U.S. Senate. He mentioned the issue in speeches, and he testified at a U.S. Senate hearing, receiving substantial news coverage for himself and the issue. Canada was capitalizing on the well-known conservative bent of Virginia voters, and he tried to link the issue to local concern by charging that the treaties "could have a disastrous effect on the economy of Virginia" by jeopardizing jobs and profits in Virginia ports and in the railroad and coal-mining industries. His opponent, Charles S. Robb (Democrat), who eventually won the election, reacted by insisting that the treaties should not be an issue in the race, because "the lieutenant governor has no role to play in treaty ratification."

Issues irrelevant to the office in contention are raised all the time in elections by candidates trying to capitalize on a popular cause. Apple pie and motherhood have figured in elections from time immemorial. For instance, Congressman Nick Joe Rahall II (Democrat of West Virginia) headlined newspaper advertisements in his 1976 election, "Honor thy father and thy mother," although no issues concerning honor of fathers and mothers were being considered by Congress. He was trying to tap the father-and-mother vote. Look at elections in your state and you'll see plenty of this kind of thing. It's simply using an issue that strikes a responsive note with voters, even though that issue is irrelevant to the office in question.

Your objective is to have a friendly candidate raise your issue in this way, and thus show your legislator that at least one local politician thinks the issue has popular appeal. Not every issue is suited to this tactic, and not every politician can do the job for you. The tactic could backfire if the legislator you're trying to influence regards your local politician as a nut, or sees the issue as lacking seriousness. To avoid this pitfall, use a responsible politician as your spokesman, and do your best, in drafting remarks for him, to tie the issue to concerns that are relevant and popular in your state.

There is another way to raise your issue in the legislator's consciousness without speeches or publicity. When leaders of other organizations, slightly out of your field, are interviewing candidates for possible endorsement, ask them to raise questions about your issue, linking it with their issues. For instance, an environmental group might ask a better-schools group to quiz candidates about their stand on expanding the Environmental Education Act. A labor union might ask the Lung Association to raise questions about strengthening the Occupational Safety and Health Act.

This sort of questioning shows the legislator that your issue concerns far more than your group. The unexpectedness of this interest will have a direct impact on candidates and move them in your direction. When they find themselves being asked about your issue by a wide spectrum of citizen groups, they will realize that the whole community is interested in your cause.

The organizations most open to this kind of cooperation are those you've worked with over the past year or two—those that participated in a coalition with you and those you helped on their issues. You may be able to exchange questions, so you ask a couple of their questions when you interview candidates. (The interview process is described in the next section of this chapter.)

In some congressional districts the election is a mere formality because the incumbent is so well entrenched as to be opposed only by a token candidate, or no candidate at all. These legislators are not going to be as sensitive to constituents' opinions as those who have to campaign hard for reelection. But you may still use the election to get their attention. A few years ago in Oregon, for instance, Congressman Al Ullman (Democrat) was dragging his feet in getting action on a bill he had introduced to protect part of the Minam River valley as wilderness. His constituents who favored the bill were trying to get him to push the bill through, using the substantial power he had as second-ranking Democrat on the Ways and Means Committee. Ullman was unopposed in the general election, so the conservationists couldn't use the normal election tactics. Instead, they used the write-in line on the ballot, urging voters to show their concern by writing in "S. T. Minam," short for the motto "Save the Minam." Hundreds of write-in votes for the nonexistent S. T. Minam made the point, and Ullman responded in the next Congress by moving the bill through to enactment.

Supporting a Candidate

Members of Congress represent all of their constituents. But some constituents get more representation than others. Those who helped a legislator get elected are always among the favored ones. It's a fact of life, even though a legislator may mean to be even-handed in his treatment of constituents. More access, more serious consideration, more frequent consultation—these are some of the advantages of being a campaign supporter.

There are plenty of ways a citizen group can help a candidate. Before trying any of the methods described in this section, find out what the law is. Write to the Federal Election Commission (FEC—1325 K Street, N.W., Washington, D.C. 20463) and ask for a copy of the FEC regulations. The FEC also has a toll-free number (800-424-9530) from which you can obtain informal advice on the legality of actions you're contemplating. Also find out what the state law says by inquiring through your secretary of state's office.

If your organization is tax exempt, you'll need to check the tax laws, too. Some of the FEC regulations may seem like unnecessary red tape. Be patient; these regulations were set up to end the domination of Congress by monied interests that previously backed the candidates secretly. Now there are limits on the amounts people and organizations can contribute, and there is mandatory reporting of contributions over a certain figure.

If you want to support a candidate, the first, most important rule is this: place your efforts under the supervision of the campaign manager and his or her staff. The manager is supposed to be an expert in campaign operations, and you should recognize that this is a very different field of endeavor from the legislative work you're more accustomed to. The campaign manager knows where the swing votes are and how best to win them. He has a systematic plan to get the greatest results from the limited resources the campaign has at its disposal. If you go off on a tangent, however well meaning, without the okay of the campaign manager, you could unwittingly do the candidate great harm.

This may seem like a minor point, but it's not. "It's important," says Kathryn Fahnestock, an experienced campaign staffer based in Washington. "The candidate and the campaign manager know best how to use your help. Don't plan your own tactics for the candidate. Put your volunteers into his campaign organization." The campaign work your people are assigned to will probably have nothing to do with your issue. Don't let this bother you. Doorbell ringing, telephoning, and envelope stuffing are crucial to every campaign. If your people do the work reliably and well, your organization and your issue will receive the attention you really want—that of a legislator who owes you some of the credit for his election.

Consider establishing a political action committee (PAC). A PAC (pronounced "pack" by campaign professionals) can do things that most nonprofit, issue-oriented groups are prohibited from doing—basically any action that advocates the election of a particular candidate. Further information on how to organize a PAC appears later, in the last section of this chapter.

A candidate's most urgent need is for money. Old, well-established legislators with power in Congress get plenty of contributions from national industry executives and others who hope for their favor on legislative issues. Younger legislators and especially challengers can't depend on these national sources. They need the help of interested citizens and organizations in their congressional district and state. Campaign contributions early in the year are the most valued of all because they can be used more effectively than last-minute money. The early contributions pay for advance organizing work that can make all the difference, for the candidate's travel on campaign trips, and for early booking of broadcast advertising time and preparation of the ads. "Ten dollars in March is worth fifty in September," is the rule of thumb. This is most crucial for challengers, who need months of campaigning to build good name-recognition among voters.

You may think that you can't possibly add more than a drop in the bucket. This might be true in some high-budget Senate races, but in many elections every $100 counts. Reports filed with the Federal Election Commission show that in the 1976 elections, most Senate candidates' expenditures were between $200,000 and $900,000. In the House, the Democratic candidates averaged $80,965 and the Republicans $77,440; FEC calculated that 47 percent of the money came from individuals' contributions of less than $500.

A survey done for the FEC by pollster Peter D. Hart showed that, when primary-election candidates are included, 43 percent of the 1976 House candidates polled spent less than $15,000, and only one in four employed a salaried campaign manager. "Most congressional campaigns in 1976," summarized *Congressional Quarterly,* "were 'mom and pop' operations, low on both money and professionalism."

A campaign budget of $20,000 may still look like big money to a citizen group whose annual budget is only $5,000. But think of this: if you and your co-workers help a candidate raise $2,000 of that, you'll find your efforts highly appreciated and most certainly remembered by the candidate.

Since you don't have that kind of money yourself (and you couldn't contribute more than $1,000 per election anyhow, under federal law), you need to look to others who have money. Consider some of the wealthy people who share your views and would be sympathetic to your candidate. Ask them to send the candidate a contribution with a letter clearly linking it with your cause. For instance:

> Dear Congresswoman:
> I was so pleased by your support of the Labor Law Reform Bill, S. 1883, that I am moved to make the enclosed contribution to your campaign fund. . . .

The letter is important. Otherwise, the contribution doesn't do your cause any good because the candidate will never know what she did to deserve it.

FEC regulations are exacting on the routes followed by campaign contributions, in order to prevent people from exceeding their lawful contribution through sleight-of-hand. This is partly a response to the old practice, revealed during the Watergate scandal, of "laundering" money. If you yourself get involved as a conduit between the donor and the campaign fund, you may have to report it to the FEC, and it could count against your own contribution limit. You can avoid this by having the donor send the money directly to the campaign committee, with a cover letter associating it with your cause.

If your issue is a popular one in your community, you may be able to raise a few thousand dollars by having a fund-raising event to which your cobelievers are invited, paying $15 to $100 a head. Receptions, dinners, barbecues, picnics, and clambakes are all possible fund-raising events. If you can induce prominent entertainers or a national leader on your issue to attend, you'll attract a larger crowd. These fund-raisers are best organized under auspices of a PAC, because they require central processing of contributions and expenses. If you don't have a PAC specific to your issue, the candidate's campaign manager or treasurer will help you figure out how to handle the financial end. Sometimes a candidate will want to set up an affiliated committee to identify him with your issue, such as a "Consumers for Morrelli," but fund-raising events are more often handled by the candidate's principal campaign committee. Your people will have to do the work in either case.

Some of the organizations that have cooperated in your legislative fight may have PACs of their own, either at the state or national level. Common in the labor, education, environmental, agriculture, and industry fields, these multicandidate political committees regularly contribute to candidates who are good on their issues. The national PACs rely heavily on grass-roots groups' advice on congressional candidates, particularly when a right-thinking challenger is running to unseat a bad incumbent. So ask your local cooperating groups to approach their national PACs for contributions to your candidate.

The national leaders will want hard data on the candidate's record. Challengers who have never held any major elective office are notoriously hard to evaluate, so put together everything you've got that shows your candidate as a person who shares your views and has been effective in carrying them out. Candidates who take the right positions are a dime a dozen; candidates who have really done something effective and who are electable are few and far between.

The greatest contribution most citizen groups can make to a political campaign is volunteer workers. All but the most deeply entrenched legislators depend on volunteers to carry much of the load. Volunteer work makes the campaign dollar go farther, and it provides the person-to-person contact that is missing from radio and television advertising. The FEC regulations don't limit volunteer work or require it to be reported. And since volunteers are doing the work as individuals, your organization need not get involved if it's barred from doing so by its tax-exempt status.

Deliver your volunteers *physically* the first time you participate in each campaign. This shows the campaign manager and the candidate that you can deliver on your promises. When the campaign staff sees you walk in with the twenty-five people they asked for, to help in one evening's canvasing, they will recognize your cause as one that is actively and visibly involved in the campaign. If instead you had merely asked your people to show up at campaign headquarters, the campaign manager would never identify any of them as being connected with your issue.

Here's how to do it. Let the campaign manager know you're ready to provide, say, twenty volunteers. A few days later the campaign staff calls to ask for your twenty volunteers at seven P.M. next Tuesday at the East County campaign office. You get busy and call enough of your people (members, supporters, friends) to cover the twenty, plus extras to make up for no-shows. A rule of thumb among campaign staffers is that for every volunteer who shows up at the appointed time, you need four people who said they'd come. To get those four, you need to call sixteen people.

When you're calling for volunteers, you don't tell them to go to the East County campaign office. That would be throwing away your influence. Instead, have them meet at your group's headquarters or at some central location. Then you escort them en masse, by car pool or public transportation, to the East County campaign office. Tell the campaign manager these are the volunteers from your organization.

Of course, if you promise to deliver twenty bodies and you fail to do so, you'll be written off as ineffectual and your group will lose influence with the candidate. On the other hand, if you're reliable in delivering the promised volunteers, you will be asked to do more. This builds your influence during the months of the campaign, and the growth continues on to the candidate's entry into office. You'll be consulted then, too, because you and your people have become part of the legislator's circle of supporters to whom he owes a lot of the credit for his election.

You can also help a candidate by letting him use your mailing list for a fund-raising mailing (unless your group has tax-exempt "501(c)(3)" status). The Federal Election Commission does not consider the sale of a mailing list to be a campaign contribution unless it is sold at less than the usual price. If your group doesn't normally sell its list, you can sell it to the candidate at the cost of reproduction without its becoming a contribution. However, be cautious about handing over your mailing list. Get the campaign manager's assurance that it will be used only for the specific purpose you've agreed on. Your list is valuable as a source of active volunteers and of money for your organization. Don't undermine your own future use of the list by turning it over unconditionally to a politician, because he or she may turn into a formidable competitor for the same resources.

The candidate may be better off by using your list in activities planned jointly with you and openly featuring involvement by your leaders, perhaps as official hosts listed on the invitation to a fund-raising barbecue, or as cosigners of a fund-raising letter. Your people will respond best to an appeal that comes from their regular leaders.

Your candidate may want to be endorsed by your organization. Tax-exempt organizations are barred from endorsing candidates, but nonexempt groups and PACs are free to make endorsements. Endorsements give a candidate credibility with your people, whether they are members of your organization or cobelievers among the general public. Frequently a candidate has done excellent work on an issue but has never received much news coverage for it. You can help this candidate by acknowledging what he did, publicizing it as part of your endorsement statement.

If you don't have an organization that is qualified to make endorsements, your leaders can act as individuals, such as by signing a round-robin letter of endorsement, or by making a public appearance together to announce their support for the candidate. Your leaders may also volunteer to serve on an issue-oriented campaign committee if your candidate uses them—something like "Educators to Reelect Goodman."

Sometimes an endorsement is impossible because more than one good candidate is running for the same office. This happens often in the primaries, when several local politicians who favor your cause are contending for the nomination. You can't afford to endorse only one of them and antagonize the others. The losers will be back in the city council or state legislature next year, and you need their help there. In this situation, *some* of your leaders should help the best candidate by writing to their personal mailing lists, visiting newspaper editors to tell about the candidate's good record, and pursuing other low-key tactics. Meanwhile, keep some of your leaders out of the campaign, so they can rebuild your alliance with the rival candidates when the election is over.

If you plan to endorse a candidate, invite each of the candidates to an "endorsement conference," to determine whether you should endorse any of them. This procedure is valuable whether you're operating as an organization or as an informal group of individuals. An endorsement conference is an interview. A small group of your leaders, possibly two or three, sit down with a candidate for an hour or so, explaining your position on the issues that concern you, and asking what the candidate's position is on them.

These interviews can be educational both for the incumbent and for the challengers. In the legislative rough-and-tumble, politicians often miss some of the essential logic of your position and fail to grasp the basic facts. But now they're listening carefully because they want your help. Your chances of getting through to them were never better.

Endorsement conferences also give challengers some ideas as to issues they can raise during the campaign. Perhaps equally important, the conferences give you a hedge against an uninformed candidate being talked by your opponents into coming out against your cause, before he has got your side of the story.

At the very least, a candidate learns what issues you're interested in. This may seem unnecessary, but remember that news coverage of citizen groups' activities is spotty, and people may not realize how broad your group's concerns are. For example, many congressional challengers interviewed by the League of Conservation Voters, an environmental PAC, showed surprise when they were told that environmental groups were concerned about the population problem. In their endorsement conferences with the League, they seemed to be learning for the first time that there was a connection between overpopulation and the scarcity of resources and that environmentalists were active on population issues. Politicians can be more naive than you think.

After you've completed the endorsement conferences, let the candidates sweat for a few weeks, wondering what you decided. Then announce your endorsement, with appropriate publicity, and privately meet with each candidate to explain why he did or didn't get your endorsement. In planning your announcement, be guided by the candidate's wishes. One candidate may want you to shout it from the rooftops, while another may want you only to spread the word among your cobelievers. It's a matter of reaching those voters the campaign manager thinks will be favorably influenced by your endorsement, and avoiding those he thinks will react negatively. For instance, in a community populated by labor union members, an endorsement by union-busting "right to work" groups would probably hurt the candidate, yet in a nearby community where industry executives live, it would help.

Don't let candidates use your endorsement conference or any other meeting for campaign purposes unless you intend that. In his reelection year of 1972, Senator Mark O. Hatfield (Republican of Oregon) was in the doghouse with many of his environmentalist constituents, who felt he had been consistently unresponsive to their concerns. During a meeting between Hatfield and two environmental spokesmen to discuss current legislation, Hatfield unexpectedly ushered in a photographer, who proceeded to take pictures of the meeting. To the two visitors, the purpose seemed obvious—an attempt to get pictures that could be used in Hatfield's campaign to associate him with the environmental cause. They put a stop to that simply by refusing to sign releases for the pictures.

You can both help the candidate and gain influence by drafting position papers on your issue. Follow through by cooperating with the candidate and campaign staff to hammer out a final draft which the candidate will release publicly. (You can also draft position papers for the opponents, to make sure they don't go wrong.) This effort helps you in the following ways:

• It confirms the candidate's position in writing, which will make your task easier when he is elected and you're trying to influence him on a particular piece of legislation. Your people can always point to the position paper as evidence of what he said in the campaign, and try to hold him to it.

• It raises the candidate's consciousness of your issue, and makes him look into it far enough to decide whether to adopt your draft position.

• It shows the candidate what topics really matter to your people. In a draft position paper, you stress the points that are crucial and omit or deemphasize those that are not.

The position paper can help the candidate, too:

• It helps convince your wealthy cobelievers that the candidate is really on your side, and thus helps shake loose campaign contributions.

• It shows your activists that the candidate is on your side, and thus helps to recruit volunteer campaign workers.

• It helps the candidate clear up his thinking on the subject, so he'll be ready to respond cogently when he is asked about it by voters or newspeople.

Consider having informal meetings to discuss your issues with each of the candidates, if you aren't having endorsement conferences. Spending an evening together, with refreshments, can be mutually beneficial, and it poses no problem for tax-exempt organizations. The place to have it is at somebody's house, preferably that of a person who is well known to the candidate so he will feel at home there. The best time for this is early in the election year, say January or February. Include three or four of your people who know your issues thoroughly and know what's happening with them in Congress and the executive branch. If possible, include a couple of people from the candidate's political party who have money; this helps get the candidate's attention, because at this time of year he's already seriously looking for campaign money. Have a prepping session with your people ahead of time, so you can reach agreement on the agenda and on your issue priorities.

You can help a candidate unofficially by giving his activities good coverage in your newsletter. When he does something good, run his picture, or a picture of the candidate conferring with your leaders. By the same token, cover the bad deeds of the rival candidate. Good newsletter coverage is especially appreciated by candidates from large metropolitan areas which lack small local newspapers; House candidates rarely get much attention from newspapers whose territory covers several congressional districts. However, if your organization is tax exempt, this coverage has to be justifiable as legitimate news. The IRS is particularly restrictive on "501(c)(3)" organizations in this regard.

If your organization can legally endorse candidates, you may also send your members handbills or leaflets advocating election of those you endorsed. The candidates must report the expenses for such material to the FEC if the sum exceeds $2,000 per election.

If your group's tax-exempt status bars endorsements, you have two options. One is to have a "separate segregated fund" do the endorsing (for details, see the last section of this chapter, concerning political committees). The other is to work individually as citizens. You are known as leaders in your field, and you have influence with your members and co-workers. You can send a campaign flyer to your personal mailing list or Christmas card list. With this in mind, it's worthwhile to build your personal list during the year by noting names and addresses that are published in newsletters. Some organizations list new members' names and addresses in their newsletters, and some send all members a complete membership list once a year. Keep your personal list separate from your organization list. Unless you've organized a separate segregated fund, it would be unlawful to use the organization's mailing labels, Xerox label matrix, or address cards for partisan political purposes.

Your organization can invite the favored candidate to speak at a meeting, giving him a platform from which to speak about your issue and showing that he's associated with your cause. If the opposing candidate asks for time to present his views, you can add him, too.

An alternative long used by tax-exempt organizations is the "candidates' night" or "candidates' forum." You invite all the candidates for a given office to attend a meeting of your membership or a public meeting. You ask them to present their views on your issue (in, say, ten minutes each) and then to answer questions from the floor. You can invite news media, and thus get some of the results out to a wider audience. However, the IRS has barred tax-exempt "501(c)(3)" organizations from holding such meetings.

Opposing a Candidate

Negative campaigning has one strike against it from the start. People would rather hear praise than criticism. Yet negative campaigning can be highly effective if the issues it's based on are vital ones to your audience. Remember the Nixon-McGovern race in 1972? The biggest point in the Nixon campaign was the assertion that Senator McGovern's election as president would be bad for the country. This argument gave Nixon a victory by landslide.

In some congressional races, you may not have much good to say about your good candidate but you've got plenty to say about the bad opponent. If your case against a bad candidate is well founded and will hit home with many people strongly enough to affect their votes, you might be wise to plan a negative campaign.

Don't do anything without first consulting the campaign manager of the candidate you favor. A negative campaign has a high risk of backfiring, and you wouldn't want to be responsible for defeating your own candidate. Let the campaign manager decide. This consultation will mean that your campaign expenditures of over $100 will have to be reported as in-kind contributions to your candidate's campaign, but even without consultation you'd have to report them yourself as "independent expenditures."

Your presentation to the public must be calm and dignified. In print media, such as newspapers, posters, and leaflets, your message must avoid superlatives and extremes, because these strike people as marks of a rabid, extremist group. On radio and television, which carry more emotional content than print media, you can be more outspoken. But always be *calmly* negative. Anything that comes across as carping will only win sympathy for your opponent.

A negative campaign must be based on the candidate's bad record. Before you come out against the candidate, marshal the facts carefully, in detail and in writing, so you can show the news media your evidence when they ask for it. For a candidate's bad votes on legislation, have ready the dates, names, and numbers of the bills involved and an explanation of each vote. For positions a candidate took on nonlegislative matters, have exact quotes from speeches, letters, or news interviews. In your campaign you may prefer to raise some of these topics as questions, rather than as accusations, so as to seem less malicious: "Why did Matthews vote against the School Aid Bill?" "Why did Klein support the General Motors subsidy?"

Another part of a negative campaign may be to show the candidate's financial ties to special interests. This requires research. If the candidate has previously run for local or state office, a record of contributions to his campaign may be available at the local board of elections or at the secretary of state's office. Contributions of twenty-five dollars or more usually must be reported.

In congressional races, the candidates must report contributions of $100 or more to the Federal Election Commission, which has all reports since 1972 on file. These reports may be inspected at the FEC office in Washington, or you can order copies. The reports are also supposed to be filed with your secretary of state, but they are not always kept up to date or made easily available to public inspection. For the names and addresses of contributors, what you need is the "contributor pages" of the candidate's quarterly reports.

To order reports, write to the FEC's Public Records Office, 1325 K Street, N.W., Washington, D.C. 20463, and ask for the reports on, say, Congressman Dutton, Massachusetts, Fourth District, and specify which reports you want—quarterly, final, or all reports—and the dates, such as "quarterly reports for 1976 and 1977" or "all reports for 1978." The FEC will reply, telling how many pages are involved, itemized so you can decide which reports you want badly enough to pay the copying charge of ten cents a page. You can order just the contributor pages, if you wish. If the FEC needs more than a half-hour to process your request, they will charge you $2.50 per half-hour as a research fee. They can usually handle 100 pages in a half-hour. At peak season during election years, FEC's turnaround time on mail requests is about two weeks.

When you have a list of contributors in hand, go through it and check on the big donors. Watch for several donors with the same last name; this could be a rich family's way of skirting the limit on an individual's contributions, but it's legal if each person used his or her own money. In congressional elections, one person may give up to $1,000 per election. (The primary election, general election, runoff election, and nominating caucus or convention are each considered a separate election in the FEC regulations.) **If some of the big donors are not known to you, look them up in sources such as the following:**

- Your city directory, which lists people's occupations
- *Who's Who*, published in regional and subject-area editions
- *Poor's Registry of Executives and Directors*, which covers people active in big business
- *Martindale & Hubbell's Law Directory*, which covers lawyers
- Your local newspaper's clipping files

Organizing a Political Action Committee (PAC)

Citizen activists in many fields have realized that for effective, sustained participation in election politics, it's worthwhile to establish a political action committee, or PAC. This organization provides a central vehicle and public identity for work by members of many small citizen groups in your state that are active on your issue.

Each PAC has the ability and the legal authority to endorse candidates, to rate and publish candidates' voting records, and to raise funds and contribute those to candidates or spend them in activities that support candidates. The legal requirements can be handled in a few hours per month by a competent lawyer and an accountant, who may contribute their time or work for fees lower than the going rate.

Several types of PACs are allowed by the FEC regulations. Some are used chiefly by candidates themselves. The two most useful to citizen action groups are the multicandidate political committee and the separate segregated fund.

A *multicandidate political committee* is an independent organization that is free to raise campaign funds from the public and to spend the money in advocating the election or defeat of candidates for federal office. Upon registration with the FEC, a political committee is free to spend up to $1,000 per candidate per election. After having been registered for six months, if the committee has qualified as a multicandidate political committee by having at least fifty contributors and having made contributions to at least five federal candidates, the spending limit goes up to $5,000 per candidate per election.

The multicandidate committee is the format best suited to the coalition approach, providing a vehicle for the participation of leaders and members from many citizen groups in your state active on your issue.

A *separate segregated fund* is a political arm of a membership organization or a corporation. The parent organization may be a tax-exempt "501(c)(4)" organization or a nonexempt organization. It may be an issue-oriented group formed to work for legislation, or it may be a professional association, a business corporation, or a labor union. The biggest drawback is that a separate segregated fund established by a membership organization may solicit contributions only from members of its parent organization, and not from the general public. On the other hand, this type of fund has a significant advantage: the costs of establishing and administering the fund and of soliciting contributions to it may be paid by the parent organization, so long as this does not conflict with applicable tax laws. A separate segregated fund may contribute or spend up to $1,000 per candidate per election, and if the fund also meets the criteria for a qualified multicandidate committee, this limit goes up to $5,000 per candidate per election.

The separate segregated fund is a format primarily useful for citizen groups that have large memberships and budgets capable of covering administrative and fund-raising expenses for the political activity.

If you decide to organize a multicandidate committee in your state, the first thing to do is find a lawyer who knows about the applicable federal and state election laws. Then find a person who will do the organizing and run the PAC. It's a time-consuming job, requiring at least three hours a day on the average. That's one volunteer spending every evening on it. You can't do this in a casual way, because the legal requirements are strict, and all the work must be done carefully if you're to achieve the credibility and respect of politicians in your state. There is less room for error in election work than in your normal legislative efforts. Everything you say about a candidate has to be supportable with documentation or authoritative opinions. If you can't produce either, your opponent will charge that your committee is just a tool of his opponent or of the opponent's party, and you won't have a good answer for the charge.

If your PAC is to involve people from many groups, have a small first meeting to raise the idea and talk it over. Invite a few people from different parts of the state who reflect different elements of your cause (particular issues or particular philosophies). Talk about the PAC idea and find out whether the others favor it seriously and are willing to commit some time and money to getting it off the ground. If the response is good, then go right ahead and set up your PAC. You can get further detailed advice from a national PAC in your field, or from a reasonably sympathetic state PAC in a related field.

A good first project for a political action committee is to compile and publish a voting chart on your state legislature. This task will show you whether you have competent people who are willing to work, and it will show what the issues are in your state—sometimes quite different from those involved in your national legislative efforts. If the chart and its ratings are accurate, they will establish you as credible in the eyes of politicians and news media. No doubt there will be howls of dismay by legislators who have gotten by for years on talk, rather than action. If you're prepared for that, you can handle it. Your newly established credibility will be the basis for your next move—to endorse and support candidates, which has already been discussed earlier in this chapter.

Three basic rules should be your guide in everything you do in your PAC:

• **Be absolutely accurate in any statement you release.** Triple-check your voting charts for typographical errors. To a candidate whose election hangs in the balance, the difference between 65 and 75 in your ratings can be cause for apoplexy. If you show a legislator as voting "yes" when he was really absent, you'll get an angry phone call about it. Such errors, even if they are few, can badly hurt your credibility at the outset.

• **Don't bite off a bigger piece of the action than you can chew.** Don't get into too many races at first. Start small, in races where your chances of winning are good. You can't afford to be a big loser the first time around. Success in a modest effort will give you real influence.

• **Be bipartisan.** If you look hard enough you can find a candidate from that other party, even if it's in a race for sewer commissioner. It may be difficult, but it's vital. Without a bipartisan slate, you will be tagged by politicians and news media as a bipartisan tool, and your independent judgment will be called in question from then on. Also include both men and women, ethnic minority and majority candidates in your slate, and avoid being identified as an elitist group.

A political action committee need not be a large organization with hundreds of members. In fact, it will gain more cooperation from leaders of existing citizen groups if it is discussed from the start as a small nucleus that will help all the groups to marshal volunteer help and funds in election campaigns, and thereby increase all the groups' influence on future legislation.

16

Building Long-Term Influence

When you've got a Senate vote coming up in two weeks and your senators are on the fence, all your energies naturally go into action that will get quick results. There will always be lots of this hasty, eleventh-hour work to do on your issue. However, there are ways to build relationships with your legislators in Congress that will bring you better results in the long run. By working at these influence-building tactics over many months, you will make your future efforts much more productive. Someday you'll be able to deliver those Senate votes with half the effort it now takes you.

If you keep tending your relationship with a legislator month after month, you'll find that you can influence him with less effort and faster. This is true of you as an individual and it's true of a citizen organization. If you and your co-workers keep doing things that sustain the relationship and create durable ties with the legislator, someday you'll notice that you've crossed the threshold between the "outs" and the "ins" and now you can easily get to see the legislator or reach him on the phone and persuade him of your views.

This transformation doesn't happen overnight, and it won't happen unless you work at it. All over the country there are people and groups that have taken one step toward this goal—such as by making a campaign contribution every two years or by inviting a congressman to speak at a meeting—and have never gone further. They end up with no more influence than the man or woman on the street. Others have devoted energetic efforts to influencing their legislators' votes year after year on, say, the education appropriations bill, but the rest of the time have been so consumed by the latest hot issue that they didn't have time to slow down and work on the relationships with those legislators.

We don't advocate relationships based on compromise by your side. No indeed! A good relationship makes it easier for you to sustain your position against compromise, because the legislator realizes that your cause is a valid one, based on real human needs and advocated by responsible people, and he realizes that he could hurt his chance of reelection if he doesn't do what you ask. You don't achieve that kind of relationship if you let a legislator compromise your position every time. If you compromise easily, it indicates that you aren't really people of principle. Hang tough, and you show that you have principles that concern you deeply and that you're willing to fight for.

A legislator has a lot to learn about your cause. A continuing relationship gives him opportunities to do that learning. He has to learn that your cause is not a fad that will have been forgotten by the next election. He has to learn that your organizations are composed of reasonable people—his constituents—who strongly believe in their cause and that your organizations are part of the decision-making process—not outsiders or spoilers, as he might think at first. He has to recognize that your position is based on deeply felt principles that you won't give up. To a legislator, all of this indicates that if he has to choose between your side and your opponents' on a big vote, he can't expect you to excuse him for voting against you. He has to learn that you aren't politicians, who compromise all the time, but citizens working for something you believe in.

You don't want to be the legislator's buddy, to the point of losing either your right to criticize him or your willingness to do so. A responsible congressman will respect your criticism and your right to influence him through public pressure. For example, one Midwestern congressman who had had a close relationship with environmentalists in his state for more than fifteen years found himself at cross purposes with his old allies over a shipping canal project. He was willing to acquiesce quietly in the canal proponents' views and let the project go ahead. After considerable soul-searching, the environmentalists used the news media to draw attention to what the congressman was doing. This so embarrassed him that he fell into line and wrote to a leading environmentalist, "Okay, you win!" After that, the relationship was as solid as ever.

"You can't rely on friendship," says Stewart M. Brandborg, a twenty-year veteran of wildlife and wilderness issues in Washington. "Legislators all suffer from the attitudes and temperaments of the moment. All are overcommitted. A legislator may disappoint you by being indifferent to a bill that threatens to undo a program he himself spent years getting established. Often he's simply preoccupied by other interests just when you need him the most."

So while the relationship has elements of friendship, it's tougher than friendship. You're always entitled to go behind the legislator's back and bring pressure on him if you need to, and he'll expect it of you.

Identification with Your Issue

You want your legislators to identify with your issue—not just to passively agree with your position, but actively feel that what you stand for is right and that the issue is worth fighting for. This goal may seem impossibly remote if you're still struggling just to get your congressman to vote with you for the first time. Some legislators will never have much interest in your issue because their interests lie elsewhere. But if you do things which, bit by bit, involve the congressman in your issue in ways that are satisfying to him, you'll have the best chance of making him into a real advocate of your cause.

Once the congressman has voted with you for the first time, make him feel appreciated. It doesn't matter whether he did so willingly or had to be pressured into it by weeks of your effort. Whatever the reason, you want him to see that he's onto an issue that can help him. So use the thank-you techniques described in Chapter 11, "Tactics for a Legislative Campaign," but don't stop there.

Have the congressman address meetings of your organizations to talk about the issue on which he voted right. The applause and friendly reception he'll get will help keep him on your side in the future. Try to arrange these meetings soon after the big vote, while the topic is still in the congressman's mind.

Open your newsletter to the congressman, too. Perhaps he'd like to provide a brief article on the same topic to appear under his by-line. (You might offer to draft one for him or adapt something he said in a House speech.) This offer will be particularly attractive to a legislator who gets little attention in your public news media. If your own organization has only a small membership, get one of your larger cooperating groups to give the congressman some space.

Another possibility is to get the legislator on radio or television, talking about your issue. Local interview and talk shows offer good opportunities. It's your job to get the station interested, if the legislator tells you he's willing. If a talk show uses multiple guests, the legislator might be accompanied by one of your most articulate leaders to furnish local anecdotes and facts that the legislator may not remember. This broadcast exposure can mean a lot to a little-recognized congressman or congresswoman.

When you've got your congressman started voting for your cause and you've given him some positive reinforcement, the next step is to give him more work to do on the issue. Make it easy for him, but keep at it. Your aim in doing this is to keep building his identification with the issue and his investment in it, so that when the next big crisis comes, he'll be more strongly committed and willing to do more for you.

Some of a legislator's influence in Congress requires more gumption than merely voting or cosponsoring a bill. For instance, when you ask a congresswoman to testify at a hearing, to write to a committee chairman, or to buttonhole committee members, you're asking her to use some of her time and her influence. Many members of Congress won't do any of these unless you've gotten them involved long before you ask for this kind of help.

The following activities can help keep a legislator involved in your issue during the months when nothing much is happening on it:

• Arrange to have the legislator praised in local, state, or national publications concerning your issue (if he deserves it), and send him copies.

• Have people attend his campaign fund-raising events and mention the issue.

- Have different groups ask him about the issue when they interview him for possible endorsement.

- Invite the legislator on an inspection trip to see how your issue affects local people, and have news media there to cover the event. Senator William Proxmire (Democrat of Wisconsin) has made a practice of spending a day working at a constituent's job— in a factory, on a farm. Something like this might work on your issue.

- Visit the legislator every couple of months to keep him informed and ask his advice on what your organizations should be doing. Legislators like to be flattered by being asked for advice, and they usually have a lot to give (but don't let it influence you if you think it's wrong).

- If he's getting mail from your opponents, help him work up a standard letter or fact sheet to be used in reply.

- Get friendly reporters from newspapers and magazines to interview him on the subject, if you're sure the interview will give him satisfaction. No hostile interviewers, please!

If your legislator doesn't deserve some of this attention, then scale back your tactics accordingly. Use your imagination to extend the list, using varied activities that give the legislator something small to do about your issue, from which he'll get a good feeling, or from which he'll get public approval.

Some activities may also stir a legislator's outrage at your opponents' stance or tactics. For instance, if you were working for legislation to require decent wages and working conditions for agricultural workers, you might take your congressman to see how workers now live. During your inspection trip you might drop in on a wealthy farm owner who uses such workers, choosing an owner with a short temper whom you can count on to explode at the congressman's questions.

Praise and recognition from outside your congressional district or state can be very influential. Congressmen and congresswomen are so often anonymous outside their own district, in contrast to senators, who are often nationally known, that they swell up with pride to find that their efforts are being noticed elsewhere. This can be especially important to a House member who wants to run for a statewide office such as senator or governor. In the Senate, praise from out of state can similarly encourage a senator's dream of running for President.

In general, aspirations for higher office are not the greatest factor. Legislators simply like to be noticed and praised, and they enjoy having a regional or national reputation for good work on an issue. If your legislators deserve praise, think about getting them some from outside their district or state. By the same token, you can give credit to legislators from other states who have taken the lead on your issue; mention them in your newsletter, and send them copies.

You can also give your good legislators continued reinforcement by mentioning them favorably in your publications even when nothing new has happened. When writing about the issue in your newsletter, for instance, work in a reference to your congressman's support on that vote back in April. When you put out a news release, mention the legislators who voted with you. And send copies to the legislators you've plugged.

Put legislators on the mailing list for your newsletter, so they and their staff will see some of your news every month. If you've got a good legislator, get him a subscription to a national publication representing your cause, too. A conscientious legislator who is just getting involved in your cause will read this and learn from it. (Some national organizations routinely keep members of Congress on their free subscription list.)

If you have developed new and newsworthy information supporting your position, consider letting the congressman release it. He can probably get better news coverage than you can, and it gives him a chance to shine in the context of your issue. You may either have him credit your group with the research, or let him take the credit.

You may provide a legislator with attractive photographs or paintings pertinent to your issue, with which to decorate his office. This requires professional-quality work. If the issue isn't especially photogenic, perhaps a good photographer can capture the human element of the issue in candid photography, such as with school or labor issues. Industrial lobbies have done this kind of thing for years, providing large photographs of ships, factories, and sawmills. Then environmentalists came along with pictures of wildlife and untouched forests. Consider what your issue has to offer visually.

Many members of Congress, especially in the House, distribute a weekly or monthly column to newspapers in their districts, or tape a weekly report that is broadcast in the district on radio or television. Most publish a newsletter several times a year. If you have a skilled writer in your group, offer to draft something about your issue for use in one of these media. The offer will be appreciated, but don't push it if you find it's not welcomed. The legislator's staff may regard this as their bailiwick and resent amateur interference. If you get the go-ahead, study examples of the legislator's prior columns, broadcasts, or newsletters to see how he likes it done.

When you feel strongly supportive of a legislator who has done well on your issue, suggest that he mail to a list of your members and supporters in his district a form letter reporting on his accomplishments in your field and asking for people's reactions and ideas. Draft the letter yourself, or help his staff do so. Then make sure your people respond enthusiastically to the letter. This exercise can be particularly encouraging to a freshman legislator who has just completed his first year in Congress, as well as to a legislator who has only become involved in your issue during the past year or two.

Identification with Your People

Some of the ways to build long-term influence concern the legislator's relationship with your people and your organizations more than with your issue. Instead of leading a congresswoman to identify with your cause, these methods lead her to feel close to your cobelievers in her district. It's a different emphasis, not a substitute for building a cause-oriented relationship. **Depending on the circumstances, you could end up with any of three relationships with a congresswoman who votes with you often:**

• She supports your cause and fully believes in it, but she is not comfortable with your people, possibly because they're from a different ethnic or social background or because they simply think differently than she does. This personal unease makes your communication job more difficult, and it stands in the way of realizing her full potential as an active legislator on the issue.

• She goes along with your cause because she has come to know, trust, and feel close to your people. She has been supported in elections and been constantly encouraged by them. Here, the lack of focus on the issue may result in the congresswoman's never taking the time to really learn the facts well enough to hold her own against more committed opponents.

• She identifies fully both with your cause and with your people. If she's unsure about a particular amendment that you've urged her to support, her identification with your people helps her decide to vote with you. And if she has had a falling-out with some of your more short-tempered people, her basic belief in the cause helps to prevent her reacting vindictively in the next vote.

Build ties on both personal and issue identification, and you'll have one to fall back on when something goes wrong with the other. Moreover, the combination is more than the sum of its parts. Each enhances the other, giving you a more committed, more willing legislator.

Personal identification may begin with existing friends of the legislator. If you've got his campaign manager and his best friend in your town talking with him about your issue, that's a good start. But as soon as possible, broaden the scope of your personal contact with the legislator so he'll get the impression that large numbers of people are involved and so he'll find that you are reasonable, likable, and supportive people. A few of the ways to do this follow.

Support in elections can have a strong element of personal identification, as well as issue identification, particularly if some of your people advance to positions of responsibility in the campaign or put on campaign functions at which the candidate meets your people in numbers.

Whether or not you support your congressman for reelection, you should attend his fund-raising events. This may stick in your craw, because you're a man or woman of principle. But just think of the admission price as a necessary expense to achieving your cause objectives. At many events the tariff is less than fifty dollars. Ask the congressman's staff to put you on the mailing list for his fund-raisers. Attend them, preferably with enough cohorts (say, three or four) to have an impact, and make your presence known.

If the congressman doesn't recognize you, go over and introduce yourself: "I'm Jim Jones, of the Allentown Consumers Committee. We surely appreciate your fine work on consumer issues." Then he knows you're there, and why. If the setting is informal, rather than a receiving line, raise some new aspect of the issue with the congressman—not something you're trying to influence him on, but a point of interest that will intrigue or encourage him. Use any chance you have to engage him in friendly conversation, listening to what he has to say as much as telling him what's on your mind.

Informal social events arranged by your organization can also provide superb opportunities for growth of personal relationships. The best are events that have an issue focus, such as the wilderness trips used by environmentalists to show legislators the areas proposed as parks, wilderness, and wild rivers. The purpose is serious—to inspect an area involved in legislation—but the trip is enjoyable and inspirational, and there is so much informal personal interaction during a few days in the wilderness that, if the people were chosen well, the legislator becomes closer to the people as well as to the cause.

It's hard to get a legislator away from his fragmented daily schedule long enough to provide a situation conducive to personal interchange. Only on issues of great interest to the congressman can you get a half-day with him, away from the crowds. A small seminar with enjoyable experts, in somebody's vacation house, sometimes works. You have to make it worthwhile on the issue level, so a legislator can justify the time to himself and his top staff, when in the same time he could have gone to half a dozen public events and shown his face to thousands.

Any time you have a chance for a few minutes with a legislator over drinks, don't miss it. To citizen activists these opportunities don't come often, but sometimes around six o'clock, if a legislator doesn't have early evening commitments, he or she might accept an invitation to hoist a beer with two or three of your people. Make it an impromptu thing.

News stories and Washington novels have described the big-time industrial lobbies' use of sex as a way of influencing Congress. Industry lobbyists, they say, supply legislators with willing sex partners and expect legislative results in return. Whether it's true of industrial lobbyists or not, this is not an approach used by citizen groups, and we don't recommend it. It's not only wrong, it's probably ineffective. This sort of thing has little in common with the kind of personal identification we have recommended above.

Another form of influence used by industrial organizations is the lecture fee. It was common for trade associations to invite their best friends in Congress to come and speak briefly at conventions. They would be paid exorbitant lecture fees—a thinly veiled way of bribing legislators for past and future favors. New congressional rules limit lecture fees to $1,000 for each appearance.

Citizen action groups have often had legislators speak at major meetings and conventions, not as means of bribing them—because that's both wrong and beyond the means of such groups—but as a chance to reinforce legislators' interest in the issue by having them address a friendly audience. If you would like to do this, but your budget can't cover a normal speaker's fee, consider arranging for a nearby university lecture series to invite the legislator and pay the fee and travel expenses out of university or student-body funds. A legislator might welcome the free trip, especially if his state is far from Washington, D.C., and the lecture is in his home district. Congressional travel allowances only cover a limited number of trips to the district every year.

Your organization may want to show its high regard for your congressman by making him an honorary vice president or honorary member of the group. Special awards should also be considered, if you're sure the legislator deserves one. The following example is a text which might be used by a labor group, presented to the legislator as an engraved plaque or framed certificate:

A CITATION
in recognition of
Congressman John A. Bernard
for his significant and sustained
achievements in behalf of working people
June 10, 1978
Millville Central Labor Council

Such awards can be given and cosponsored by any organization, even those that are barred by tax laws from significant legislative activity. If you can get all your cooperating groups to cosponsor the award, you'll have an impressive list at the bottom of the plaque. Sound out the legislator's staff to see if he'd welcome an award before you start organizing one. He may want to take advantage of the award ceremony and the award itself in his reelection campaign, which is all the better for you.

Your personal ties with the legislator can also be strengthened by helping him find experts who can advise him on important issues outside your group's area of concern. Suppose your issue is education and you have active members on a college faculty; these faculty members may be able to identify people in the biology and chemistry departments who can advise the congressman on air pollution matters. By helping a legislator recruit experts, you form a network of people you know whose views the congressman respects. Then when your issue comes to a crisis, they can help you by using their relationship with the legislator to further *your* issue.

If your organization sponsors events that involve a printed souvenir program, invite the congressman to use a space in it as he chooses. These include high school yearbooks, college dance programs, annual banquets, and charities' fund-raising dinners. By offering the legislator free space, you're reversing the usual setup in which the sponsors ask him to buy an ad in the program. In an election year, you might extend the same opportunity to the other candidates.

If your organization displays the American flag at its meetings, one of your legislators can obtain for you, at cost, a flag that has flown over the Capitol in Washington (however briefly). You might invite the legislator to present the flag to the group at its annual banquet and be photographed for coverage in your next newsletter.

Consider whether you can help a legislator's son or daughter find a summer job in your cause. Having congressional offspring work in your organization, either as staff or as volunteers, has drawbacks, among them the possibility that the new recruit may get involved in the intramural dissension that many organizations constantly suffer, and carry bad reports back home. We recommend that you take on a congressional son or daughter as a volunteer, to work on current issues under good supervision, only after careful scrutiny of his or her real interests and potential for commitment to the cause.

Another possibility is to help find the son or daughter a job in a state, local, or federal agency that's active on your issue. You should have good contacts with relevant agencies, and by using these connections you could do the legislator a favor and at the same time involve the legislator's offspring in your cause.

Getting into Party Politics

You can gain long-range political influence, going even beyond your present legislators, by getting involved in local party politics. Doing responsible volunteer work for a political party gives you a status in the party that will help you influence your legislators of the same party, and it puts you on good terms with local politicians who have even more influence with those legislators. Party work makes you an insider, a known quantity, to your congressman; this helps when you ask him to do something on your issue.

It doesn't hurt with legislators of the opposite party, either. It shows them that you're part of the political system and, while you probably wouldn't vote for them, you're clearly in a position to hurt them through vigorous party work. If you're leading an organization, you can try to get some of your people to become active in each party, so you'll have the best of both parties.

Party politics used to be dominated by a small clique in each state and county, but it's not like that any more. In most places in the country, party leaders are looking for willing hands to help with party work. To get started, call the local party office and express interest in helping. Ask when the next party meeting will be. Then attend it, and get into conversation with some of the active people. You usually won't have to volunteer; you'll be asked to do something—perhaps to be on the membership committee, or to be a poll watcher in your precinct at the next election. By making yourself useful from time to time (but without being deflected from your cause), you'll become known over a year or two as a responsible and active party worker.

The parties' work is primarily in three areas: nomination of candidates, getting out the vote for these nominees in the general election, and fund raising. As a citizen activist without ties to big money, your main role will be in the nomination process and in getting out the vote.

Nominations are the business of party conventions. Depending on the system used in your state and county, the nomination process for state and local offices may include a state convention, county conventions, congressional-district conventions, and local party meetings (sometimes called mass meetings). For the conventions, delegates must be selected by the local party. If you've been active in the party, you might become a delegate. Get a friend to nominate you when delegates are being selected. As a delegate, you would have influence and your support would be courted by candidates for various nominations. Your stature as a delegate carries over into your issue work, and when you need to round up the support of local politicians for your cause, you should find a willing reception among those who plan to seek the party's nomination next time around.

Coping with a Grudge

The path to influence isn't necessarily a smooth one. Legislators who have been in Congress for ten or twenty years may react badly to your pressure because it upsets their old way of making decisions. Such a legislator may take the whole thing personally and develop a grudge against you. This has happened quite often with new, activist citizen groups, despite the groups' best efforts to be reasonable and straightforward with their legislators.

If you have a falling-out with your congressman, don't despair. Your cause will survive it. Simply push other citizen advocates into the limelight, while you wait in the wings until the congressman has forgotten what he was mad about. This is one of the advantages of having an organization or coalition with new leaders always being trained; you're ready to replace anybody who is taken out of the front lines by a legislator's grudge, or by illness, family obligations, or job commitments. If the grudge is against a whole organization, then have a different organization in your coalition step forward and pick up contact with the congressman.

Midway in the campaign for preservation of Hells Canyon, on the Oregon-Idaho state line, Congressman Al Ullman (Democrat of

Oregon), in whose district the Oregon side of the canyon lay, seemed to be pursuing his own course of action. He even introduced a Hells Canyon protection bill of his own, without consulting the Oregon citizen groups that were leading the campaign. These groups had tried to develop cooperation with Ullman, and now they tried again, sending Larry Williams, executive director of the Oregon Environmental Council, to visit Ullman in another attempt to seek better communication. The congressman's response to Williams's request for better consultation was blunt. He got mad and stomped out, Williams recalled later.

After that meeting, Williams stayed out of sight for a while and let other people go to see Ullman on behalf of the Hells Canyon coalition, particularly Marilyn Cripe, a vice president of the Oregon Environmental Council who lived in Ullman's district. The setback was only temporary, and Ullman became the best advocate in the House for the citizens' goals, using his power as chairman of the Ways and Means Committee to marshal the support of other legislators. After the bill was enacted into law, Larry Williams had the pleasure of hosting Ullman at the Oregon Environmental Council's annual banquet in 1975, celebrating Ullman's good work in the Hells Canyon fight.

Grudges generally fall into three categories. The first is a grudge that a legislator gets against a person or group that he feels distorted his record during an election campaign. This is one good reason to be supercareful in compiling voting records, and to avoid basing endorsements on vague impressions that can't easily be explained. An election grudge can happen even when you've done your homework well. Some old legislators think they've been doing good work for your cause for the past fifteen years, but now you come along and say it wasn't good enough. This kind of legislator has been fooling the public, and possibly fooling himself, because there was no active citizen group to analyze his performance on the crucial votes. He'll trot out a voting record showing that he voted for every important bill in your field. However, these votes were on final passage, not on the floor amendments that weakened the bill or strengthened it.

There's not much you can do to avoid an election grudge except be accurate in all your election work and keep the focus on the issues. Resist the temptation to get nasty and say what you really think of the legislator; that's asking for a grudge. If you end up with a grudge against you, simply keep quiet for a few months and let others who stayed out of the election battle, or who supported the legislator, carry on for you.

The second type of grudge is reserved for "outsiders" who a legislator feels are invading his congressional district or state and trying to tell him what to do. The invasion is often imagined and the objects of the grudge are actually his constituents, but he thinks they're outsiders. He may have got this impression because people failed to stress their residence in his district, because their group is a chapter of a nationwide organization, or because their opponents started a rumor that the group's efforts were inspired by outside agitators.

In Utah in the 1960s, for instance, the local Sierra Club chapter was widely regarded as a bunch of "outsiders from California." As soon as this chapter began to be influential, some Utah legislators formed grudges against it. Other legislators, however—notably Senator Frank E. Moss and Congressman Wayne Owens (both Democrats)—cultivated the Sierra Club group and gained election support from its members.

Al Ullman's grudge, mentioned above, was an outsider grudge. The object of the grudge, Larry Williams, was not from Ullman's district, although his organization had many members in the district. But as Williams learned later, Ullman was not even sure that he was from Oregon.

To avoid outsider grudges, always stress that you and your organization are from the appropriate state or congressional district. A legislator can't so easily get mad at you if he knows you're his constituents.

The third type of grudge is the frustration grudge, which a legislator holds against a citizen group that has applied so much pressure that he's caught between what you want him to do and what he wants to do. This usually happens when a citizen group is new on the scene and is interfering with something the legislator has always favored or something he has always done at the behest of your opponents.

For instance, since President Theodore Roosevelt's time legislators have always advocated federally funded dams in their districts, and everybody thought dams were a good thing. Dam building got a new boost from the New Deal. Every congressman and senator was out to get as many dams built as he possibly could, and he took his lead from the local flood-control district, irrigation district, and the local office of the Corps of Engineers or Bureau of Reclamation.

Since the 1950s, when dams began being questioned on grounds of cost-effectiveness and environmental impact, legislators have had great difficulty adjusting to the new mood. Many old congressmen, as a result, have formed grudges against dam opponents in their districts. On one hand, the congressman believes deeply in building more dams and he gets pressure on this side from local construction companies, business groups, and land speculators. On the other hand, he gets strong pressure against dams from environmentalists, farmers, historic-preservationists, and a broad segment of the public who have been alerted by these groups.

Most legislators know how to handle pressure, and it's nothing new to them. They usually respond well to it. But some legislators "freak out" when they find themselves caught in a bind created, in their view, by pressure you stimulated, and hold it against you. There is really nothing you can do to head off this kind of grudge. If one happens, by all means keep up the pressure and try to find some old VIPs—perhaps retired politicians—who can make the legislator realize it's an issue that won't go away. Have another, more establishment-oriented organization assume more prominence in the fight. Keep emphasizing that it's local people who are doing the fighting, so the legislator can't write you off as outsiders.

Appendix A:
Your Visit to Capitol Hill

Whenever you go to Washington, D.C., you have an opportunity to build your influence with your own legislators in Congress. It doesn't matter what brought you to Washington. If you live far away, it's likely to be a vacation or a business trip, rather than a trip specifically planned to influence legislative issues. To legislators and their staff, the mere fact that you are in Washington, expressing your views on legislation, carries weight that few letters or phone calls ever did. A brief visit to the nation's capital can make a big difference if you use your time well.

One of your objectives is simply to demonstrate your concern about an issue. Your presence in a legislator's office, and your brief conversation with the legislator or with his or her legislative assistant, does the job. When you and others who share your concern do this, it leads the legislator, consciously or unconsciously, to see your issue as a real concern of his constituents. On the other hand, if nobody ever stops in at the office to talk about it, he'll think nobody cares.

We have known people who went to Washington to see their congressman, then went home again without going to see their two senators. They were throwing away their influence and wasting part of the time and money they spent in getting to Washington. Even if your issue isn't coming up right away in the Senate, don't miss the chance to call at your senators' offices. See the senators or see their staff, but see somebody just to make your presence felt.

There are six people you should try to see during your Washington visit, at the very minimum. They are your two senators, your congressman or congresswoman, and the staff member who handles your issue in each of their offices. Get appointments by calling their nearest field offices in your state or congressional district. For the best chance of seeing your legislators in person, plan to spend several days in Washington. Advance appointments may make this unnecessary, but legislators often have to postpone meetings because of unexpected changes in their legislative schedule, so you'd be smart to allow time for postponements.

When you're setting up appointments, consider whether you want a photograph of yourself with your legislator for use in an organization's newsletter. The legislator's office can arrange for a congressional photographer to show up during your appointment and take a couple of quick shots. The cost is covered by Democratic or Republican party campaign funds or by the legislator himself, not by the taxpayers. Printing a photograph in your newsletter will give the legislator credit for his cooperation and identify him with your cause and your organization.

Plan to have a place in Washington where people can leave messages for you. Legislators may need to reach you to confirm or change your appointments, and when you're running around town you have to rely on messages to keep in touch with people you want to see. If you stay in a hotel, the switchboard can handle simple messages. If you stay with friends or anyplace where there is not a regularly attended phone, you may be able to use the phone number of a national group that is active on your issue. Visiting environmentalists, for instance, sometimes get their messages at the offices of Friends of the Earth or the Sierra Club. Ask the group with which you cooperate whether they'll take messages for you.

Another alternative, if you've got the money, is to hire an answering service. For example, forty-five dollars will buy you a month's service, twenty-four hours a day, with up to seventy-five messages. If you want the phone answered in your group's name, it will cost you ten dollars more. The firm offering these services is Sincerely Yours; for current information write them at 325 Pennsylvania Avenue, S.E., Washington, D.C. 20003. Other such firms are listed in the Yellow Pages under "Telephone Answering Service."

Before you get to Washington, prepare the written information you will leave with your legislators and their staff. Leaving something tangible, with your name and address on it, makes your visit more memorable to the people you're trying to influence, and it adds something to the legislator's file on the topic as evidence that you came in. This is important whether you're speaking for yourself or for an organization. A fact sheet or letter you've written specifically for this purpose, a one-pager summarizing the current status of the issue, a digest of the arguments, a relevant map or diagram, a reprint or Xerox copy of a pertinent news story or magazine article—anything of this sort will do, as long as you add your name and address. Bring at least six copies—one for each legislator and one for the staff member who handles the issue in each of their offices.

Plan to visit the Washington office of organizations that provide the national leadership on your issue. They may have new information that will help you when you go to see your legislators. Your presence will be a source of encouragement to their efforts, and if you have information on how the issue affects your community, they may be able to use it, too. After seeing your legislators, give them a report on the reactions you got, because this will help them in their continuing work on the subject. Don't make demands on the time of citizen-group staffers. Even more than congressional staff, these people are struggling to keep up with an always impossible load of legislative work. There is never enough time in the day to do everything that needs to be done. So resist your tendency to spend an hour chatting with the staff of your national citizen group. On the other hand, if they ask you to stick around for lunch, you'll know that they value your efforts and want to help you do more.

If you represent an organization, either large or small, there are several other visits to make during your Washington stay. These will be covered later in this appendix in the section "For Organization Representatives."

When you arrive, any legislator's office can give you gallery passes admitting you to see the House and Senate in session. However, far more interesting and representative of Congress in action would be a visit to a congressional committee hearing or markup session. To see what meetings are scheduled, consult the listing in each morning's *Washington Post*. They are open to the public unless listed as "closed," but seating is limited and you may have to get there half an hour early to get a seat.

Finding Your Way

Getting to Capitol Hill is easy, except by car. If you drive to Washington, leave your car somewhere and take public transportation—subway, bus, or taxi—to Capitol Hill. There is no visitors' parking area, and the on-street parking is limited to two hours.

When you enter the Capitol or the House and Senate office buildings, your parcels, briefcase, or handbag will be inspected by Capitol police. The search is aimed at bombs and weapons, a result of infrequent bomb incidents and threats aimed at legislators in the past. Plan ahead so your belongings can be easily inspected.

If this is your first visit to Capitol Hill, a basic orientation tour will help you get your bearings. Consider taking the well-conceived tour hosted by Ralph Nader's Public Citizen Visitor Center. Led by college interns, the tour includes visits to a congressional hearing, to the House or Senate chamber, and to your own congressman's office, if you wish, where the staff will answer your questions about your legislator's work load, constituent mail, and anything else you're curious about. Limited to eight people per group, the tour begins at ten A.M. in the lobby of the United Methodist Building at First and Maryland Avenue, N.E., opposite the Supreme Court, and ends three hours later. Reservations are necessary a day in advance; make one by calling (202) 659-9053 or by writing to the Visitor Center at 1200 15th Street, N.W., Washington, D.C. 20005. Special tours for the handicapped are also available. The Center also publishes a self-guided tour booklet entitled, *Guide to the U.S. Capitol*, available for a dollar from the same address, and a tape cassette for the blind, priced at two dollars.

The standard tourist sights in the Capitol building are shown on thirty-five-minute tours led by Capitol guides. These tours, free of charge, form in the Capitol Rotunda every fifteen minutes from nine A.M. to 3:45 P.M.

You may encounter a problem in seeing the House or Senate in session. During the heavy tourist season, from March through September, so many visitors want to see the House and Senate that doorkeepers must rotate spectators, allowing each person only a few minutes in the visitors' gallery. If a bill of great interest to you is being debated on the House floor and you want to see the whole debate, your congressman can escort you into a special gallery.

When you get hungry on Capitol Hill around lunchtime, you may have to look hard for a place to eat. The House cafeterias are reserved between 11:30 and 1:30 for legislators, staff, and witnesses testifying at hearings. You can eat before or after those hours (between eight A.M. and three P.M.) in cafeterias in the basements of the Longworth and Rayburn House office buildings. Both serve good, economical food, with an emphasis on Southern home-style cooking. Carry-out shops in the basements of the Cannon, Longworth, and Rayburn buildings are always open to visitors; the Cannon and Rayburn carry-outs have stand-up counters to eat from. In good weather, you can always grab something at a carry-out and go outdoors to eat on the lawn of the Capitol grounds.

The Senate has a visitors' cafeteria in the basement of the Dirksen Senate Office Building (the South Cafeteria), but in spring and summer it's usually crowded, and from June to September the Senate staff and witnesses testifying at hearings get priority between noon and 1:30. Witnesses are also welcome to eat in the staff cafeteria (the North Cafeteria), reached through a passageway from the South Cafeteria. The Senate has no carry-out shops that are open to visitors.

Outside of the House and Senate buildings there are two cafeterias on Capitol Hill. The more posh of the two is the Supreme Court cafeteria, open from eleven to two (except for fifteen minutes at noon and one o'clock, when court employees get their chance). To get there, enter the ground-level door at First and Maryland Avenue, N.E., and ask the guard for directions. The more mundane is the Library of Congress cafeteria, open from seven A.M. to 3:30 P.M. It's in the cellar of the library's main building, and you get there by entering the rear doors of the library, on Second Street, going down a flight of stairs, and following the "cafeteria" signs. Another cafeteria will be opened in the library's new Madison building across Pennsylvania Avenue.

In case you're not in the mood for cafeteria fare, there are clusters of good and reasonably priced restaurants within six blocks of the Capitol in these locations:

• Near the House office buildings, on Pennsylvania Avenue, S.E., between Second and Seventh Streets. Most noted for their food are Taverna the Greek Islands, Toscanini Ristorante, The Delly, the Hawk and Dove, Jenkins Hill, and Mike Palm's. There is also a McDonald's at 625 Pennsylvania Avenue and a Roy Rogers at 317 Pennsylvania.

• Near the Senate office buildings, on Second between D and F Streets, N.E., you'll find a soup-and-sandwich place, the Third Party; a California-style restaurant, the Gandy Dancer; and at Second and D, the Club II. The Man in the Green Hat is at Third Street and Massachusetts Avenue, N.E., and the fancy (and expensive) Monocle, frequented by high-priced lobbyists, is at 107 D Street.

• Also near the Senate buildings, at New Jersey Avenue and D Street, N.W., are three restaurants in the Hyatt Regency Hotel and another across the street in the Quality Inn.

At Your Legislator's Office

Senators, congressmen, and congresswomen are usually tied up in committee meetings between ten A.M. and noon, so you're most likely to get an appointment in the afternoon. The afternoons are supposed to be devoted to meetings of the whole House and Senate, but since the floor debate on most bills involves only a small proportion of the legislators— those most interested in an issue or most knowledgeable on it—the others use the time to work in their offices, walking over to the floor when the bells signal a vote or quorum call. (Some committee meetings also continue into the afternoon.)

As a result, your afternoon meeting with a legislator may be interrupted at any moment by his having to go and vote. If this happens, and if you're a fast walker, ask if you can walk over with him. You'll be able to continue your conversation on the way over and back. You won't be able to go with him into the House or Senate chamber, but you can wait outside the door. Don't get down to the heart of your subject while walking; this is a more informal time, good for discussion of anecdotes and case histories, and a good time to ask for his views on the procedure your bill will follow.

Then when you get back to his office, get down to what he is going to do about the issue. If he tries to bid you goodbye before this happens, say something like this: "Senator, we haven't talked about how you plan to vote on this bill. This is important to me (and to members of our Citizens' Council). Could we talk about that before I leave?" If he slips away from you without discussing this basic point, there's nothing to do except go home and bring pressure to bear on him. If he was in favor of your position, he would have said so.

Sometimes you may be in Washington on short notice, perhaps during an unexpected business trip, without having had a chance to arrange for an appointment ahead of time. Don't leave town without trying to see your legislators. First, try to get an appointment, even with this short notice. Let's suppose your congresswoman's appointments secretary says she doesn't have a spare moment all week. Don't give up yet! You may not get a chance for a real conversation with the congresswoman, but you may still be able to get her attention long enough to shake hands and tell her what's on your mind.

Here's how to do it: Ask the appointments secretary or receptionist whether the congresswoman is going to be in a committee meeting the next morning, because you'd like to see her in action, and find out where and when the committee meets. Then show up at the committee meeting, see if your congresswoman is indeed there, and hand a committee staff person a note you've written to the congresswoman, giving your name and hometown and asking if she has a moment to meet you. During a lull in the meeting, she'll probably come out and have a chat with you in the corridor.

Another possibility is most useful in the afternoon. Ask the receptionist whether the congresswoman is on the House floor. If so, walk over to the second floor of the Capitol, go to the appropriate door of the House chamber (east door for Democrats, west for Republicans), and hand the doorman a card giving your name and hometown, and ask the doorman to find out if your congresswoman can come out and see you. If she's there, and not in the midst of a vital debate, she'll probably visit with you for a few minutes in the corridor or in a nearby reception room.

It's always more difficult to see your senators, unless you're from one of the least-populated states. While your chances of success are less than in the House, the ways to see your senators when you can't get an appointment are about the same. They can be seen at committee meetings as was described above. To see a senator who is on the Senate floor, the procedure is a little different. In this case, go to the second floor of the Capitol's Senate wing and ask guards to direct you to the Senate reception room. Fill out a card at the attendant's desk. One of the reception room attendants will go into the Senate chamber and hand it to your senator, who may be able to join you in a few minutes for a brief conversation. (The Senate reception room is well worth a visit in any event, as it is one of the most beautiful rooms in the Capitol.)

None of these impromptu meeting places—noisy corridors and reception rooms—is as relaxed and conducive to serious discussion as a visit in a legislator's office, but at least you'll be able to make your presence known and your views felt, and that is important and worth every minute you put into it.

Chapter 6, "Face to Face with a Congressman," went into detail on how to make the most of your visit with a legislator when you're trying to win his or her vote on current legislation. Sometimes when visiting Washington you'll be in a slightly different situation. When a vacation trip, say, takes you to Washington, there may be no immediate action scheduled on your issue, and yet you don't want to waste your presence in the nation's capital. There's no reason to waste it, either. Go and see your legislators anyhow, and you'll be showing your concern about your issue, and demonstrating that your interest goes deeper than just writing a letter now and then. Your visit will have impact even when no vote on the subject is coming up.

What do you talk about at a time like this? Tell your legislators or their staff about the latest facts you and your cobelievers have unearthed, and ask their reactions to these facts. Mention a recent anecdote or case history that supports your position. Ask whether any new questions have come up and whether your opponents are being heard from. Ask your congressman how he thinks the House will react to the issue. Your basic goal is to say something in favor of your position and get the legislator or staff interested, at least for a few moments.

The other major item on your Washington agenda is to meet the staff member who handles your issue for each of your legislators. This staffer may be located either in the legislator's own office suite or in a committee staff room. In either case, drop in at the legislator's main office first to make your presence known and sign the guest book. Whenever you can, go and have a chat with the staff person the day before you're to meet with his or her boss. If you ask the right questions, a sympathetic staffer will tell you what's troubling the legislator about your issue—how he's leaning, what arguments are influencing him, and so forth. Armed with this knowledge, you'll be able to plan your presentation to allay the legislator's doubts and build upon his points of agreement.

Give the staffer the same written material you give the legislator. A congressman may take his copy home to read at night or he may misplace it. The staff member may misplace his copy, too, but by giving both of them copies, you've doubled the odds that it will be read and acted on.

In your rush to get everything done during a short stay in Washington, don't neglect the "instant replay." After each meeting, stop and assess what happened, and take a few notes. Spend a few moments over a cup of tea or coffee in the cafeteria or find a quiet spot in the corridor where you can think it over. What did the congressman really say? Was it a promise or was it a vague remark that your own wishful thinking turned into a statement of support? What arguments did the congressman react best to? What opposition arguments did he bring up? This assessment process will tell you what kind of work you need to do when you get back home.

For Organization Representatives

If you're in Washington as a spokesperson for an organization in your community, find out what key person is handling your issue in the relevant government agency, and go to see him. On most bills that involve primarily one program and one agency, there is a civil service employee (bureaucrat, if you will) who looks after that bill and gives Congress his agency's viewpoint on it. This person can be quite influential, but like many bureau people he may be isolated from the public and may tend to lose his interest in the matter. If he's on your side, your visit can encourage him by letting him know how people in your community are affected by the bill. If he's opposed to your position, draw him out on the subject so you can see what arguments he uses. Your legislators have probably heard the same arguments, either from this person or from other representatives of the same agency.

Also go to see the Administration official who has authority over the agency. Now you're getting to the policy-making level, and it's these officials who send the order down through channels to your key bureaucrat as to what the agency's position will be. The Administration people you want to see are presidential appointees, and they usually have titles such as assistant secretary or deputy assistant secretary. This visit is important to strengthen the stance of an official who favors your position, and to sow doubts in the mind of an official who opposes your position. You can't get anywhere by arguing with a bureaucrat, because he doesn't make policy, but you may get somewhere by arguing constructively with an Administration official, because that's where the power is. Your visit, together with visits by others and pressure from national organizations, may lead this official to take a less aggressive opposition stance, which would greatly help your cause on Capitol Hill.

You should also visit the people who cover Washington for your local news media. Before leaving home, check with your newspapers to find out whether they have a Washington bureau, a Washington correspondent, or a stringer (a free-lance journalist who writes for them on assignment), or whether they belong to a newspaper chain that has its own bureau, such as the Newhouse News Service or the Copley News Service.

Many papers have no Washington coverage except the wire services, Associated Press (AP) and United Press International (UPI). These services are so understaffed on Capitol Hill that they rarely can get down to the details of how your congressman is going to vote. When a legislator wants to get coverage of some momentous action he is about to undertake, he'll usually work directly with newspapers back home, instead of trying to go through this bottleneck, in competition with 534 other members of Congress struggling for the attention of the news media. Your most effective contact with wire-service reporters is to drop by the AP and UPI desks in the House and Senate press galleries, on the third floor of the Capitol, and leave them copies of your current information, with a note as to where you can be reached and how long you'll be in town. This should at least pique their interest in the issue.

If your newspaper has a genuine Washington correspondent, do all you can to awaken his interest and sympathy. Try to get an appointment to see this correspondent, perhaps over lunch in a congressional cafeteria. You can tell him how your issue affects people in your community, and sketch in for him some of the political factors—who's for your cause, who's against it, and what the main arguments are. What he's going to be most interested in is how your legislators are lining up on the issue and what's influencing them behind the scenes. He'll want to have some good questions to ask the legislators. If you meet with him after you've seen your legislators, you'll have more to give him as the basis for a story.

Check with news directors at your local television stations and principal radio stations to find out whether they have their own Washington coverage, aside from the major network news. Some stations have joined with others in the same region to maintain a Washington news bureau, but most rely on network news and therefore carry next to nothing about Washington events affecting the local scene. If one of your stations has a Washington newsperson, approach him just as we suggested above for newspaper correspondents. With television, a good visual angle can make a big difference, so if you have petitions to present, or thick reports, or maps and charts, mention them or show them.

If you represent a statewide citizen group and want to foster cooperation among several members of your state's congressional delegation, you may want to go beyond your individual meetings with legislators and try to get the legislators or their key staff people together. This is most practical at the staff level; legislators' schedules are so different that it's almost impossible to get a half-dozen of them together in the same room.

For an ordinary meeting to discuss the issue or plan legislative tactics, a congressman's office can get you free use of a committee room somewhere in the House office buildings. If your organization wants to spend some money, you could put on a meal or reception in one of the rooms used for such purposes, mostly in the Rayburn Building, Dirksen Building, and Capitol. Your congressman can put you in touch with the House Catering Service, which handles such events competently every day. The 1978 prices started at $2.85 per person for breakfast, $4.50 for lunch, $10.00 for dinner, or $7.50 for buffet service. The most popular offering was a cold plate, at $2.89. Bear in mind that legislators and staff attend dozens of these affairs every year. You won't impress them by putting one on, and it might lead them to think your group has money behind it, instead of being a struggling citizens' group. But it's still a good way to get people together, and you'll get better attendance by having it in the Capitol complex than anywhere else in town.

Information Sources

General information for visitors to Washington, D.C., is easy to find. Free information may be obtained by writing the Washington Area Convention and Visitors' Bureau, 1129 20th Street, N.W., Washington, D.C. 20036.

The city is covered in such regional guidebooks as the *Mobil Travel Guide* (Middle Atlantic states) and *Exxon Travel Club Vacation Travel Guide* (Southeast), both of which are revised annually and provide ample information on accommodations, restaurants, and things to see.

Guidebooks about Washington include two highly useful ones, both available in paperback: *Washington, D.C., on $10 and $15 a Day*, published by Arthur Frommer, Inc., $3.95; and *The Washington Post Guide to Washington*, published by McGraw-Hill, $4.95.

Two guidebooks published by *Washingtonian* magazine are available by mail from Washingtonian Books, 1828 L Street, N.W., Washington, D.C. 20036 (include 50 cents postage per order). *The Best of Washington* ($2.50) is a general guide that lets you in on some of the best (and least-known) sights, shops, entertainment, and eating places in town. *The Black Guide to Washington* ($2.00) covers features of particular interest to black people.

We also recommend starting your Washington stay with a stop at the National Visitor Center, which occupies the old Union Station, next to the new railroad station, four blocks from the Capitol. (It's on the Metro subway Red Line.) You'll find plenty of tourist information there, a film introduction to Washington, and a bookstore and gift shop under the auspices of the National Park Service.

Appendix B:
Getting in Touch

How to Find Organizations Active on Your Issue

If you're concerned about something Congress is about to act on, but don't know what citizen groups are leading the fight, this appendix is for you.

When you're just starting to work on an issue, it's important to get in touch with organizations that will tell you what's happening to the issue in Congress and what you can do to help. A good citizen group will give you cues—when to ask your congressman to cosponsor a new bill, when to write a letter for the hearing record, when to put the heat on the congressman just before a floor vote, and so forth.

Link your efforts with at least two groups. One should be a national organization that does Washington lobbying on your issue. This group will give you the Washington news directly and provide you with the arguments and facts used at the national level. This information usually is distributed through a magazine, newspaper, or newsletter sent to members of the organization or to a list of grass-roots leaders like you, who volunteered to help. Join this national organization; your dues help pay for the national leadership effort, without which your local efforts would be futile.

The other organization should be a local group that is leading the fight on your issue in your community. (On some issues there may not be an active group in your neighborhood or city, but there may be one in a larger city that provides statewide leadership on the issue.) A good local or statewide organization will keep you informed of your own congressman's and senators' latest actions on your issue, will give you the arguments and facts on how the issue relates to your state, and will devise tactics specifically to influence your legislators. These groups usually do a better job than the newspapers at telling why your congressman voted one way or the other.

Even if you know of several groups that are concerned with your issue—either nationally or locally—it's not always easy to know which groups are really effective. There are plenty of citizen groups that do a lot of talking, publish elegant newsletters, and have prominent leaders, but aren't seriously active on legislative issues. Many groups spend all their time raising money and spending it on noncontroversial projects, and they avoid getting into legislative battles. **To identify groups that are active, and are probably effective, on legislation, look for these clues in the groups' newsletters and magazines:**

- Articles that **ask you to write your congressman** or your senators.
- Articles that **tell how your legislators voted.** If they voted against your position, the article should explain what excuses the legislators gave and what your opponents did to pressure them.
- Articles telling **what the organization has been doing** to influence legislators—meeting with them, corresponding with them, testifying at hearings, issuing statements that praise or criticize their votes.
- Articles that **present the arguments in favor** of your position and refute your opponents' arguments, with plenty of facts included. Such articles are evidence that the organization is taking a leadership role on the issue by giving its members enough facts to start their own legislative efforts close to home. The same kind of information may also be published in leaflets or booklets.

These four clues concern the kind of information a group publishes, rather than the group's choice of words. An organization's rhetoric in newsletters and public statements doesn't necessarily show whether it's an active group or a do-nothing group. An effective group will suit its words to the occasion, knowing that there's a time to be friendly and conciliatory toward a congressman, just as there's a time to be blunt. In April they may accuse him of a "sellout" on a crucial amendment in committee, and in May they may praise him for his "courageous vote for the public interest" on the House floor. Don't be afraid of an organization that states its views forthrightly. Most of the time, that's the best way to get the point across to legislators.

How to Find National Organizations

The following methods will help you find national organizations that are active on the issue that concerns you: First, ask pertinent citizen groups in your state what national organizations they recommend. Every grass-roots group has its sources of Washington information, and would be glad to tell you which ones work on your issue.

Second, look for the names of national groups in recent books about your issue and in current newspapers and magazines. If necessary, consult back issues of magazines at the public library, using the *Reader's Guide to Periodical Literature* to help you find pertinent articles. Once you've found an organization's name, look up its address in one of these sources, available in libraries:

> The Washington, D.C., telephone directory
> The *Encyclopedia of Associations*
> The *Washington Information Directory*

Or get the organization's phone number from Washington directory assistance (area code 202-555-1212) and call to ask for the address.

Third, write your congressman or one of your senators and ask what national associations do the lobbying for your viewpoint. If the legislator is sympathetic to your position, he will be glad to refer you to the right organization. However, an unsympathetic legislator may refer you to a weak or ineffective group simply because he prefers it to the more active groups, which may have made his life uncomfortable at times.

If your own legislators are not sympathetic, write to a legislator from a nearby state who is well known as an advocate of your viewpoint. Such leaders in Congress usually answer letters from cobelievers, even those who aren't their constituents. To keep your letter from being shunted off to your own legislator, phrase it something like this:

> Dear Congressman:
>
> I'm writing to you instead of my own congressman because I know you're a leader in support of the No-Fault Insurance Bill. I need to know what national organization to contact that is working for passage of the No-Fault Bill. Since my congressman opposes the bill (and I'm trying to influence him to support it), he isn't the person to ask.
>
> Can you help me by providing the names and addresses of the main citizen organizations that are working in Washington to get the No-Fault Bill enacted?

Then add a note of congratulations on the legislator's good work for your cause. Don't count on getting a reply if you write to one of the most famous members of the Senate, but your chances are good with the lesser lights in Congress.

How to Find Local Organizations

Citizen groups in your community can be hard to find. They are often not listed in the phone book because they have no telephone or office. They usually are run entirely by volunteers, who devote their evenings, weekends, and odd hours to the cause. The headquarters is most likely somebody's basement or garage.

If you start asking around in the right places, you'll find somebody who knows how to reach the group you want. Try these:

- **Ask friends who have been interested in the issue.**
- **Ask the leaders of related civic groups and businesses.** If you were trying to find a historic preservation group in your city, for example, you might ask neighborhood associations or architectural firms.
- **Ask librarians at your public library.** A librarian who covers your subject area is likely to know about local organizations active in that field. If not, the librarian can refer you to local directories and other published sources that will help you in your search.
- **Ask relevant city or county agencies.** An active citizen group is likely to have cooperated with these agencies or influenced them. In your search for a historic preservation group, likely agencies would include the city planning agency, housing agency, and historic preservation commission.
- **Ask college teachers in related fields.** Faculty members usually keep track of local citizen groups that are interested in their professional field. A professor may have spoken at a meeting of the group, or helped the group prepare its arguments.
- **Check local newspaper stories to see what organizations are active.** Except in the largest cities, the reporters and editors usually know what organizations are doing the work. You can even phone them and ask, if there has been nothing about your issue in the news lately.
- **Ask the staff in your congressman's field office.** Usually these staffers at least keep in touch with the organizations most active on legislation, although the real substantive staff work is done in Washington.

Appendix C:
A Sample Fact Sheet

The fact sheet reproduced here was used by the Sierra Club in 1978 in the campaign against legislation concerning electric power in the Pacific Northwest. It illustrates the principles about fact sheets described in Chapter 9, "Your Publications."

FACT SHEET ON H.R. 13931 (S. 3418)

"PACIFIC NORTHWEST ELECTRIC POWER PLANNING AND CONSERVATION ACT"

There is an effort underway to press through H.R. 13931 (S. 3418), the Pacific Northwest Electric Power Planning and Conservation Act.

This is unwise legislation. Its most objectionable features are <u>not</u> being removed or ameliorated in the present mark-up in the Interior Subcommittee on Water and Power Resources.

The Sierra Club, other national environmental groups, and virtually every conservation group in the Pacific Northwest join in opposing this bill. There is simply not adequate time in this session of Congress to give this newly drafted bill the kind of thorough deliberation required. This bill would re-write the whole structure of the electric power system in the region, setting many significant and undesirable national precedents. Yet it has not been exposed to any field hearings accessible to the people of the region it will impact.

The bill in its present form is opposed by a number of Members of Congress from the Pacific Northwest. It is also opposed by the leading national organizations in the public utility/rural cooperative field: the American Public Power Association and the National Rural Electric Cooperative Association.

Finally, this is <u>not</u> really a "planning and conservation" bill. Such a bill, directing the region's electric energy institutions to make a full commitment to open, public planning procedures and to truly serious energy conservation efforts, would be desirable. But, under a thin veneer of weak conservation language, this bill has just one real purpose: that is to gain open-ended congressional authorization for "guaranteed purchase". This would give the Bonneville Power Administration (a federal agency) authority to sign long-term contracts to guarantee that it will purchase, in advance, 100% of the "output" of privately constructed and owned conventional power plants (coal-fired and nuclear), at whatever cost and -- in the words of the bill -- "whether or not operating or operable."

Such a guarantee amounts to Federal guarantee of privately assumed debt. It is undesirable in its consequences for the region, and a thoroughly bad precedent. This provision is flatly opposed by the Department of Treasury.

"GUARANTEED PURCHASE"

Many citizens, elected officials, environmental and public interest groups and local political party units have opposed granting BPA this new "guaranteed purchase" authority. These are the key arguments --

1. BPA "GUARANTEED PURCHASE" AUTHORITY IS UNNECESSARY.

Public and private utilities have a long history of construction of power plants in the Pacific Northwest (as elsewhere) -- which they have been able to finance without federal involvement of any kind, in the free, private capital market. We believe that the Northwest utilities should be treated the same as utilities around the country: financing of power plants should be a private function and not a federal one.

2. BPA "GUARANTEED PURCHASE" AUTHORITY REMOVES THE RISK OF INVESTMENT FROM INVESTORS.

Private investors who bought bonds or stock that financed power plants, backed up by such "guaranteed purchase" contracts, would have absoulutely no risk that their investment and interest or dividends would not be repaid.

Such risk is a crucial part of our free-enterprise market economy and it serves to insure that the best possible economic decisions are made. Risk and profit go hand in hand.

3. BPA "GUARANTEED PURCHASE" AUTHORITY OBLIGATES THE FEDERAL GOVERNMENT TO PAY.

Contracts signed under a previous, limited and now expired BPA "guaranteed purchase" authority said:

> "The United States of America, Department of the Interior, acting by and through the Bonneville Power Administration, has purchased the entire capability of the project. Bonneville is obligated to pay the total annual costs of the Project, including debt service on the Bonds, whether or not the Project is completed, operable·or operating and not withstanding the suspension, reduction, or curtailment of the Project output."

4. BPA "GUARANTEED PURCHASE" AUTHORITY DENIES LOCAL OPTION TO DECLINE TO PARTICIPATE IN POWER PLANT CONSTRUCTION.

Recently, more than one hundred utilities, both public and private, investigated and carefully weighed, in individual decisions, whether or not they wished to participate in a joint effort to finance and construct two nuclear power plants (without federal involvement). Eventually, 89 utlities agreed to pay the costs, accept the risk, and get the power, when and if produced. In the process, however, many utilities declined to participate, citing many different reasons: no additional power needs, cheaper sources available, costs too high, and conservation as a better option.

343

This legislation would remove such local option decision making from local utilities and the officials responsible.

Once, one person, --the BPA Administrator--, decided to sign such a "guaranteed purchase" contract, all the utilities and their customers would have the higher rates and the risk of investment such plants bring, whether or not they needed the power or the plant, or had chosen to participate.

5. BPA "GUARANTEED PURCHASE" AUTHORITY IS LIKELY TO RESULT IN MORE EXPENSIVE POWER PLANTS.

Recent experience has shown that BPA has exercised little or no oversight over the construction costs of the power plants constructed under its now-expired "guaranteed purchase" contracts. BPA has left such oversight to the utilities constructing the project. Those utilities, of course, have a lessened incentive to keep down costs, because of the previously discussed cost sharing aspects of "guaranteed purchase". As a result, cost overruns have been the name of the game. Congressman Don Bonker, in is recent testimony on H.R. 13931, cited such overruns on the power plants under construction in his district, by the Washington Public Power Supply System. The Plants are only 3% complete, but on only one subcontract the overrun is $51 million, more than doubling that subcontract.

(This lack of effective oversight, on the part of BPA, and the cost increases in the plants covered by the "guaranteed purchase" contracts, is the subject of an audit of the projects by the Director of Audit and Investigation, U.S. Department of the Interior dated September 14, 1977.)

6. BPA "GUARANTEED PURCHASE" AUTHORITY PREEMPTS STATE UTILITY COMMISSION RATE SETTING MECHANISMS.

Under this bill, when the BPA Administrator signs a "guaranteed purchase" contract, he will increase the rates of all the BPA utility customers, inorder to pay off the costs of the power plant whether "operating or operable".

Currently, state utility regulatory bodies, not the federal government's BPA, decide on whether or not a consumer should pay for a new power plant. State regulatory bodies are charged with determining whether a power plant is "used and useful" and thus the consumer should pay for it.

The bill would have the Administrator charge utilities for power plants that might not be "used and useful" and it has no provision for state regulatory agencies to make that determination.

Similarly, many states do not allow utilities to charge consumers for power plants that are under construction, but no such prohibition is put on BPA's proposed "guaranteed purchase" authority.

7. BPA "GUARANTEED PURCHASE" AUTHORITY WOULD INCREASE THE COSTS OF MUNICIPAL BONDS ALL ACROSS THE NATION.

The legislation would have the federal government giving debt guarantees to federal tax-exempt bonds. Billions of dollars of these bonds would be sold. As the Assistant Secretary of the Treasury, Roger C. Altman, put it:

"Federal guarantee of tax-exempt obligations creates a security that is superior to all other tax-exempt securities issued by state and local governments. This adds to the pressures on tax-exempt markets and consequently tends to increase the borrowing cost of schools, roads, hospitals, and other essential public facilities." (emphasis added)

344

Selected Bibliography

We have selected fourteen books now in print that will help you the most to find the information you need about Congress and to gain an insider's viewpoint on the Senate and House of Representatives. These are books of general value to you in planning your efforts to influence legislators. Other books useful in more specific ways are listed in bibliographies following several of the chapters in this book.

Directories

The Almanac of American Politics, by Michael Barone, Grant Uji-fusa, and Douglas Matthews. New York: E. P. Dutton, 1978. Revised every two years. Hardcover $16.95, softcover $7.95. This is the best all-around directory of legislators in Congress. It contains a brief and perceptive analysis of the political situation in each state and congressional district, and also includes voting records, congressional district maps, and committee lists.

Congressional Directory. Published in odd-numbered years; a supplement is published in alternate years. Available from Superintendent of Documents, Washington, D.C. 20402. Hardcover $8.50, softcover $6.50, supplement $2.00. The little-noted but useful contents of this directory include a list of all news media personnel accredited to the House and Senate, and seniority rankings of all members of Congress.

Congressional Staff Directory, by Charles B. Brownson. Published annually. Available for $22.00 postpaid from Congressional Staff Directory, P.O. Box 62, Mount Vernon, VA 22121. Lists all members of a legislator's staff with their titles. Also covers committee staff and contains capsule biographies of many staffers. Because it provides basic data on legislators, too, it can be used as an all-purpose directory when you're dealing with a large number of legislators. However, it's not worth the price if your efforts concern only a handful of legislators.

Legislative Directory. Published annually. Available for $2.25 postpaid from American Gas Association, 1515 Wilson Boulevard, Arlington, VA 22209. The best cheap, pocket-sized directory of Congress, containing the basic data on each legislator, with congressional district maps and the names of the administrative assistant and the legislative assistant who handles energy issues.

"War" Stories

It's hard to imagine what a legislative fight on Capitol Hill is like unless you've been through one yourself. The following books paint an accurate and fascinating picture of legislation in the making. Each tells the story of a legislative battle, including the interaction of legislators with industry lobbies, citizen groups, the executive branch, other legislators, and congressional staff. All three are chiefly about action in the Senate; nothing has come to our attention that describes House action as well. These books have the additional drawback of focusing on powerful, nationally known senators, rather than on the less powerful, less conspicuous legislators who make up the majority of the Senate and House.

The Dance of Legislation, by Eric Redman. New York: Simon & Schuster, 1973. Hardcover $9.95, softcover $3.95. Redman, a former aide to Senator Warren G. Magnuson (Democrat of Washington) tells the story of the drafting and enactment of the National Health Service Corps bill, of which Magnuson was the lead sponsor.

Decision, by Richard Harris. New York: E. P. Dutton, 1971, $6.95. The story of the Senate battle over President Richard M. Nixon's nomination of G. Harrold Carswell to the Supreme Court. Particularly good in showing the role of citizen groups and Senate staff.

The Senate Nobody Knows, by Bernard Asbell. New York: Doubleday & Co., 1978, $10.00. Follows Senator Edmund S. Muskie (Democrat of Maine) through the year, in 1975 and 1976, when Congress enacted amendments to the Clean Air Act. Not a history of the clean-air fight, since the author bases the book on several incidents taken out of context, yet an excellent look at how the Senate works.

Legislators Look at Congress

Many legislators have written books, but most of them either focus primarily on the issues rather than on how Congress works, or present a

Pollyanna view of Congress that cannot be taken seriously. The following books stand out in their field as worthwhile and accurate portrayals of Congress.

The Job of the Congressman, by Donald G. Tacheron and Morris K. Udall. Indianapolis: The Bobbs-Merrill Co., 1970. Second edition. Softcover $7.55. A how-to-do-it book for new members of the House of Representatives. Has become the bible for all newcomers to Capitol Hill, legislators, staffers, and lobbyists alike. Also contains a good bibliography of political science books about Congress.

O Congress, by Donald W. Riegle, Jr., with Trevor Armbrister. New York: Popular Library, 1976. Softcover $1.50. Based on a year of Riegle's diary while he was a congressman from Michigan. (He was elected to the Senate in 1976.) Riegle describes the frustrations of a young congressman, trying to influence legislation in the House, keep his supporters happy back home, and maintain a life of his own.

Political Science

To experienced citizen activists, the writings of political scientists about Congress often seem naive, perhaps because these works fail to take full account of the personal and subjective factors that influence every legislator's votes. People who studied political science in college and then went to work in Washington often complain that their studies were no preparation for political or legislative work; they had to learn everything from scratch when they arrived on Capitol Hill. Even so, political science has much to tell us about Congress purely by describing the institution and how it functions. We recommend the following books, which are strong on description, without dwelling on theory. (For further references, consult the excellent bibliographies in *The Job of the Congressman,* cited above, and *Congressional Staffs.*)

Congressional Staffs, by Harrison W. Fox, Jr., and Susan Webb Hammond. New York: The Free Press, 1977. $12.95.

Congressmen in Committees, by Richard F. Fenno, Jr. Boston: Little, Brown and Company, 1973. Hardcover $7.95, softcover $5.95. The author examines six House committees and, more briefly, their Senate counterparts, drawing conclusions on how the committees make legislative decisions.

Home Style: House Members in Their Districts, by Richard F. Fenno, Jr. Boston: Little, Brown and Company, 1978. Softcover, $5.95. A description of how legislators view their constituents, and what they do during trips home.

The Role of the Congressman, by Roger H. Davidson. Indianapolis: Pegasus, 1969. Softcover, $4.35.

U.S. Senators and Their World, by Donald R. Matthews. New York: W. W. Norton & Co., 1973. New edition. Softcover, $3.95.

Index

About the Authors

GEORGE ALDERSON is currently on the Wilderness and Environmental Areas staff of the Bureau of Land Management. He has worked as a lobbyist for The Wilderness Society and Friends of the Earth, and he is also a professional musician who has played in the Kennedy Center Opera House Orchestra and the Filene Center Orchestra at Wolf Trap Farm Park. His articles have appeared in magazines such as the *Sierra Club Bulletin, Not Man Apart, Environmental Action,* and *The Living Wilderness,* and he has contributed chapters to *The Voter's Guide to Environmental Politics* and *Nixon and the Environment.* In 1968, he won the Special Achievement Award of the Sierra Club.

EVERETT SENTMAN is a professional publishing consultant who has worked in various editorial positions for encyclopedias for over thirty-three years. He has worked for the Chicago *Daily News* and the Chicago *Sun Times* as well as for Field Enterprises Educational Corporation, and United Educators, Inc. and is presently head of Sentman Publishing Enterprises.